THE TOWER
AND THE ABYSS

ERICH KAHLER

The Tower
and the Abyss

AN INQUIRY INTO

THE TRANSFORMATION OF

MAN

New York / THE VIKING PRESS

VIKING COMPASS EDITION issued in 1967 by
The Viking Press, Inc., 625 Madison Avenue, New York, N.Y. 10022.
Second printing May 1969

Distributed in Canada by
The Macmillan Company of Canada Limited.

This edition published by arrangement with George Braziller, Inc.
Printed in U.S.A.

ACKNOWLEDGMENTS

For permission to include selections and quotations in this volume, grateful acknowledgment is made to:
Random House, Inc.: René Char, "Lightning Victory," from *Hypnos Waking*, translated by W.S.Merwin, copyright 1956 by Random House, Inc. W.H. Auden, "Petition," from *The Collected Poetry of W.H.Auden,* copyright 1945 by W. H. Auden.
Estate of Gertrude Stein: Gertrude Stein, *Brewsie and Willie,* copyright 1946 by Random House, Inc.
Alfred A. Knopf, Inc.: Stephen Crane, "The Upturned Face," from *Stephen Crane: An Omnibus,* edited by Robert Wooster Stallman, copyright 1952 by Alfred A. Knopf, Inc.
The Macmillan Company: Marianne Moore, "Those Various Scalpels," from *Collected Poems,* copyright 1951 by Marianne Moore.
Harcourt, Brace & World, Inc.: T.S.Eliot, excerpts from *Four Quartets,* copyright, 1943, by T. S. Eliot. Excerpts from *Collected Poems 1909-1962,* copyright, 1963, by Harcourt, Brace & World, Inc.; copyright © 1963, 1964 by T. S. Eliot. Virginia Woolf, *Orlando.* Adolf A. Berle, *The Twentieth Century Capitalist Revolution.*
New Directions: Dylan Thomas, *The Collected Poems of Dylan Thomas.* Paul Eluard, "Poésie Ininterrompue," from *Selected Writings,* translated by Lloyd Alexander. Ezra Pound, "A Pact," from *Selected Poems of Ezra Pound.* Reprinted by arrangement with New Directions.
Harper & Brothers: Claire Huchet Bishop, *All Things Common.* Gardner Murphy, *Personality.* T.H. and Julian Huxley, *Touchstone for Ethics.*
Yale University Press: David Riesman, *Faces in the Crowd* and *The Lonely Crowd.*
The Westminster Press: Oscar Cullman, *Christ and Time,* copyright 1950 by W.L.Jenkins.
William Morrow & Company, Inc.: Julien Benda, *The Treason of the Intellectuals,* translated by Richard Aldington.
Pantheon Books, Inc.: André Gide, *Anthologie de la Poésie Française. Selected*

iv

Prose of Hugo Von Hofmannsthal, translated by Mary Hottinger and Tania and James Stern, Bollingen Series XXXIII.

Cambridge University Press: William H. Rivers, *Instinct and the Unconscious.*

Rinehart & Company, Inc.: Erich Fromm, *Man for Himself* and *Escape from Freedom.*

W. W. Norton & Company: Rainer Maria Rilke, *Sonnets to Orpheus,* translated by M. D. Herter Norton, copyright 1942 by W. W. Norton & Company, Inc.

Oxford University Press, Inc.: C. Wright Mills, *White Collar. Poems of Gerard Manley Hopkins,* edited by Robert Bridges.

John Wiley & Sons, Inc.: Norbert Wiener, *Cybernetics,* copyright 1948 by The Massachusetts Institute of Technology.

Little, Brown & Company: John P. Marquand, *Point of No Return.*

Schocken Books, Inc.: Martin Buber, *Tales of the Hasidim: The Early Masters* and *The Later Masters,* translated by Olga Marx.

Charles Scribner's Sons: Ernest Hemingway, *The Sun Also Rises, In Our Time,* and *Death in the Afternoon.*

E. E. Cummings: *Poems, 1923-1954,* published by Harcourt, Brace and Company, Inc. Copyright 1954 by E. E. Cummings. Selections reprinted by permission of E. E. Cummings.

"Rien ne s'arrête pour nous. C'est l'état qui nous est naturel, et toutefois le plus contraire à notre inclination; nous brûlons de désir de trouver une assiette ferme, et une dernière base constante pour y édifier une tour qui s'élève à l'infini; mais tout notre fondement craque, et la terre s'ouvre jusqu'aux abîmes."

(Nothing stands still for us. This is the state which is ours by nature, yet to which we least incline: we burn to find solid ground, a final steady base on which to build a tower that rises to Infinity; but the whole foundation cracks beneath us and the earth splits open down to the abyss.)

PASCAL

Comprendre c'est avant tout unifier.

(To understand is first of all to unify.)

CAMUS

CONTENTS

CONTENTS

PREFACE

THE PRESENT study evolved from series of lectures which were given first in 1947 at Black Mountain College, then in 1948 at Cornell University, and finally, in the Spring of 1955, in a new and much amplified version, under the auspices of the Christian Gauss Seminars in Criticism at Princeton University.

In a certain respect, the train of thought here expressed is a sequel to the ideas presented in my book *Man the Measure* (1943; 4th ed. 1956). Basically, both of these books deal with the evolution and transformation of the human form and of human consciousness. The present study follows this process of transformation to our time and in our time. It attempts to derive from the assemblage of manifold evidence a coherent picture of our human condition and to convey a full awareness of the grave perils with which it is fraught.

The completion of the book has been furthered and encouraged by the aid of friends to whom I have every reason to be profoundly grateful.

First among these is Miss Hanna M. Loewy who not only helped me in all the various operations which the finishing of a book involves, such as revising the manuscript, selecting and pondering material of documentation, checking references and so forth, but beyond all these special tasks took the book in her comprehensive care, devoting to it the unusual gifts of her mind. She also contributed some fine translations.

I am greatly indebted to Professors Richard P. Blackmur and E. B. O. Borgerhoff for giving me the opportunity to expound my views in the Christian Gauss Seminars and profit from the discussion with its members. Particularly, I wish to acknowledge valuable suggestions by Professors Ernst H. Kantorowicz and Leo Spitzer. My special thanks go to Mr. J. B. Leishman, St. John's College, Oxford, who was kind enough to revise the poetry translations and translate two poems for this book. Miss Eleanor Wolff, by her good advice, added new to my old, inestimable indebtedness to her.

Finally, I want to express my obligation to my publisher, Mr. George Braziller, and to Mr. George Brantl and Miss Ruth Hein for giving the book their full support.

E.K.

Manchester, England, 1956

INTRODUCTION

TODAY we are witnessing and are deeply involved in a huge process of human transformation, a process which goes on silently, anonymously, in the most varied places and spheres of our world. This transformation seems to tend toward some formation beyond the individual. However, it manifests itself in diverse processes of disruption or invalidation of the individual.

The subject of this book is the situation of the individual in our present world. Its aim is to show the various evolutionary forces which have converged from different directions to effect his disintegration.

The individual as such is no end in himself and is not even an indisputable value. The identification of humanity and individuality is by no means a matter of course. If one believes, for instance, as a powerful group of medieval schoolmen did, in the reality of "universals," of general entities not recognizable by mere sensory perception, then the human qualities would be immediately inherent in the *genus humanum* as such, irrespective and independent of their expression in individuals. The great peoples of the East, to give another example, have undergone a process of individuation similar to that of the Western world and have, at the peak of their civilization, fostered, in their different ways, the same commonly human values, but they never came to set such store by the individual as the West.

Yet, although man and individual are not necessarily identical, man's fate has been closely linked with the fate of the individual. Following the trend of our Western history, the most precious, the essentially human qualities in man—self-determination and self-transcendence—have been represented by the individual. The development of a distinctly human quality in man was linked with growing individuation and the value and dignity of human life has increased in proportion to the appreciation of individuality and personality. Thus, Judaeo-Christian and Western civilization has been inclined to treat human affairs mainly in terms of the individual, has identified man with the individual or with the sum total of all individuals. Not only the doctrine of liberalism, but also Marxist ideology in its original form regarded human welfare as the well-being of the human individual; the former identified it with the well-being of the "greatest number," the latter with the well-being of the entire number of individuals.[1]

In the transformation which is taking place, what seems to me of prime importance and what has prompted the writing of this book is not concern for the individual *per se,* but concern for the human qualities and values as they have evolved with the evolution of the individual from Greek and Jewish antiquity to our time and which have come to be represented by the individual. Among these the crucial value is the unity and integrity of the human form.

The development of the individual in history is not an altogether edifying spectacle. It has been an ambivalent process which has produced both good and bad human properties—good and bad in the sense of being productive or destructive to humankind—but its one indisputable glory is that it brought forth a peculiarly human quality in man, a distinctly human form of existence, a coherent structure of the human mind. All features, good or bad, which have developed with the individual could be called strictly human since they all remained within the confines of the human being, and maintained the human form. Even wicked, evil attitudes can be called human inasmuch as they spring from human motives and serve human ends, inasmuch as they cohere in a human center.

What we are concerned with, however, is precisely *the breakdown of the human form,* dissolution of coherence and structure; not *inhumanity* which has existed all through history and constitutes part of the human form, but *a-humanity,* a phenomenon of rather recent date. Up to now in the Western world the human form has been represented by the individual. Hence the breakdown of the human form becomes apparent in the disintegration of the individual.

Scrutiny of such disintegration will compel us to recognize that the processes leading up to it, besides appearing unpreventable and irresistible, were, like the rise of the individual, of an ambivalent nature; they had both fruitful and perilous effects. Just as the agencies creating the individual were not altogether humanly beneficial, those causing his decline are not plainly detrimental. While jeopardizing the human form, they have vastly extended human reach and vision. Yet it seems to me of vital importance to have a clear record of the implications of this complex happening so that we may try to counteract its evil effects and carry over into a changing order the qualities and values that keep man human.

Some of the observations presented in this book are doubtless common knowledge—although they are by no means commonly acknowledged, which is a different matter. At times even the most familiar phenomena take on a new aspect when seen, not as isolated facts, but in the context of a broader stream of events. My main emphasis will be on the correlations between happenings and processes which at first glance seem far apart and unrelated. For instance, the horrors of the Nazi regime, its use of the most up-to-date techniques for atrocities of the lowest, sub-human, indeed sub-bestial kind, such happenings are in some way related to the subtlest intellectual experiences manifesting themselves in the arts and the sciences. What made its appearance in the fascist states, in fact even in the First World War—the sudden slump of humanity from an overwrought civilization into that strange, systematized bestiality, *ce crime collectif absolument neuf,* as one of its victims, Germaine Tillion, has called it in her report on Ravensbrück—this and the subsequent co-existence and co-development of both tendencies, overcivilization and dehumanization, have, as far as I know, scarcely been studied methodically. Yet they are, so it seems to me, the basic, the most serious events of our age.

THE TOWER

AND THE ABYSS

CHAPTER ONE

The Human Scene:

INDIVIDUAL, COMMUNITY, COLLECTIVE

IN THE COURSE of this study we shall see the evidences of disintegration of the individual in all fields of contemporary experience, from social, political and economic processes to those in learning, art and poetry. They are but different aspects of one vast, comprehensive transformation that has come to affect the very inner structure of man and threatens the human values which were inherent in him as an individual.

Before detailing the various manifestations of this transformation, it will be helpful for us to delineate broadly the scene of human happenings, what we might call a social and psychic topography. This may serve as something of a working model for our investigation and reveal those vulnerable points in the human structure from which disintegration starts.

What, then, are the basic entities, the main human actors and factors involved in the happenings which we are going to contemplate. There is the individual and there are groups. The individual has two dimensions and aspects: his existence in relation to social groups and to that general social environment which we call society; and his existence and structure seen in itself, without regard to group relations, that is, as a person. Among the groups we distinguish two fundamentally different types: the community and the collective. Closer observation will show us the psychic implications of the interrelations between these various entities, the development of different layers of the unconscious and different modes of consciousness.

Man as Individual. The primary characteristic of the human structure as an individual is *indivisibility,* implying coherent unity, wholeness. In daily experience the individual is given as a compact unity. Because the individual unit is the only entity immediately evident to our senses, the positivistic view current in contemporary science regards it as the *one* unquestionably real thing. The individual is therefore the elementary empirical datum on which all general statements are to be based. Groups, in this view, are considered mere assemblages or associations of individuals, an interpretation clearly distinguished from former views which attributed separate reality to "universals," spiritual and transindividual entities.

Our concept of individuality is confirmed by the etymological origin of the word. The word *individuum* was created by Cicero as a translation of the Greek *átomon* when he wanted to expound the atom theory of Democritus.[1] So "individual" and "atom" are actually the same word; the literal meaning of both is "indivisible." (*"Atomon"* means more precisely the "uncuttable," "unsplittable.") The atom, as we all know, is no longer unsplittable; science has succeeded in splitting it. And the same is true of the individual; he is no longer indivisible either. A variety of interconnected developments, in which science also had its part, has effected his split. Both events took place in the same period, in our period.

Thus, when we speak of man as an individual, we are implying that to divide him is to destroy him as a human. As long as he remains human, he must maintain his indivisibility.

Man as Person. Indivisibility, solid unity, is only one of the basic characteristics of the individual. There are others which will come forth clearly when we consider the individual in his internal aspect, irrespective of group relations, that is, as a person. Commonly, "individual" and "person" are seen as identical. However, the term "person," as used throughout the ages, shows a much greater complexity and reveals additional qualities of the individual which are just as essential as indivisibility.

The meaning of the word "person" runs the whole gamut between diametrical opposites, between the most outward and the most inward, the most superficial and the most intrinsic, the most physical and the most spiritual concepts of the individual.[2] Indeed the concept of "person" is capable of transcending that of "individual" in various respects, of assuming an entirely abstract character.[3]

The earliest known significance of the word *persona* was that designating the actor's mask and from this meaning the most diverse concepts of "person" evolved. Even in ancient and medieval Latin and its derivative languages, *persona* indicated, on the one hand, the bodily, outward appearance of a man and, on the other, his psychic, most essential and innermost being (whether his most individual characteristic, his character itself, or the generic human quality as contrasted with the nature of the animal). It is easily seen how both of these diametrically opposite concepts arose from the actor's mask. For the mask signifies the most external nature, the sheer appearance of a person, and at the same time the distinct character of the person represented, his psychic peculiarity.

This fluctuation of meaning has continued to our own time. While personality was seen as inner being by Locke and Kant, Goethe and Coleridge, Nietzsche and Bergson, others have adopted the interpretation of personality as outward appearance.[4] C. G. Jung, for instance, explicitly referring to the actor's mask, regards the *persona* as "a mask of the collective psyche, a mask that feigns individuality, that has others and oneself believe that one is an individual, while in reality it is only a stage part, spoken by the collective psyche. . . . It is a compromise between individual and society, a compromise regarding that 'which one appears to be.' "[5]

One recent example will reveal adequately the attempt to account for the dualities I have mentioned and to stress additional qualities of the individual as they have come to the fore through man's growing awareness of his development as a person. Gordon Allport explains personality in a way which combines most of the modern interpretations: "Personality is the dynamic organization within the individual of those psychophysical systems that determine his unique adjustment to his environment." [6] The essential points to note are "organization *within* the individual" and "unique." "Adjustment to the environment" is a modern biological phrasing of the external interpretation of personality. Clearly, however, what the meaning of personality adds over and above the individual's primary attribute of indivisibility is *selfhood,* or self-realization, and *uniqueness.*

ALTHOUGH the individual, in both aspects, is defined by wholeness and selfhood, he is constantly involved in interchange and interaction with other entities. There is not, therefore, and there never has been an integral individual. In particular, each individual is permanently and intrinsically connected with groups of various kinds, he participates in them and, conversely, the groups participate in the individual, they have a share in the individual. These groups are on their part not mere assemblages of individuals, but separate, distinct entities. Since the appearance of Gustave Le Bon's *Psychologie des foules* (1895) and Georg Simmel's *Soziologie* (1906), psychologists and sociologists have recognized that groups are not at all identical with the sum total of their members, but develop a character and a form of behavior entirely their own. A group as a whole reacts very differently from its single members.[7] So too the behavior and the reactions of a person may vary greatly when he is confronted with a situation as an individual from when he acts as a member of a group.

An individual, accordingly, is not only an individual, he is at the same time more than an individual inasmuch as he participates in groups. And the kind of group which predominates in this participation has a momentous influence on his life and personality. Therefore it is crucial for an understanding of the modern crisis to distinguish the general types of groups in which the individual has a part.

The individual stands, indeed he is a junction, between two essentially different types of groups: community and collective.

The Community. Groups, such as the family, the tribe or the nation, which substantially as well as genealogically or historically precede their individual members and constitute the basic, unconscious layers of the personalities of their individuals, we call communities. These pre-individual or sub-individual groups are primordial, archaic social entities, out of which individuals are born or into which they have slowly and habitually grown. They transmit patterns of form and behavior—countenance, gesture, manners, language, style of life—and archetypes of representations and attitudes, which imperceptibly motivate individuals through generations. Communities form traditions; they are the soil, the constantly, silently shifting ground in which the individual is rooted. Indeed, everyone's psyche reaches down to the very origins of life; it is at any moment as deep as life itself.

As C. G. Jung has shown, our unconscious is populated by archetypes stemming from various mythical group layers. They interact, intertwine, influence and assimilate personal experiences, the acquisitions of individual consciousness. The different layers of archaic group patterns together form what C. G. Jung calls the "collective unconscious"—to be distinguished from Freud's individual unconscious or Jung's "personal unconscious." "Collective unconscious," as used by Jung, seems to me a misleading term. I prefer to call the same psychic zone *"generic unconscious"* because the word "collective" presupposes a number of separate individuals who assemble together. Archaic groups, however, being sub- or pre-individual groups, did not form through collecting or being collected, through assemblage of pre-established individuals, but through spontaneous phylogeneration, as it were. This distinction is all the more important since in recent times, under the impact of modern collectives—political parties, unions, associations of all kinds—there has developed a truly collective unconscious which will have to be clearly set apart and considered in its own specific character.

In genuinely primitive clans or tribes, where the "tribal self" [8] prevails over undeveloped or half-developed individuals, this generic unconscious may be observed in action. Dr. William Halse Rivers, the famous British psychologist and explorer, relates the following incidents: "When studying the warfare of the people of the Western Solomon Islands, I was unable to discover any evidence of definite leadership. When a boat reached the scene of a headhunting foray, there was no regulation as to who should lead the way. It seemed as if the first man who got out of the boat or chose to lead the way was followed without question. Again, in the councils of such people, there is no voting or other means of taking the opinion of the body. Those who have lived among savage or barbarous peoples in several parts of the world have related how they have attended native councils where matters in which they were interested were being discussed. When, after a time, the English observer found that the people were discussing some wholly different topic, and inquired when they were going to decide the question in which he was interested, he was told that it had already been decided and that they had passed on to other business. . . . The members of the council had become aware, at a certain point, that they were in agreement, and it was not necessary to bring the agreement explicitly to notice." [9]

It is very important to realize that all archaic groups act upon the individual *from within,* through unconscious channels; if not in the quite primitive way of immediate action as exemplified above, they influence the individual through archetypes, rituals, traditions, constitutional habits or tastes. In this way archaic groups are embedded, indeed embodied, in the very individuality of the individual.

The influence of archaic groups is most powerful. There were periods in history when they were all-predominant, when they hampered and at times thwarted the individual in his formative period. But never did they disrupt the individual, for they do not shatter the substance of personality. An American, for example, cannot help following certain patterns of feeling and thinking, of living, dressing, eating and loving. His inclinations, predilections and prejudices are to a certain degree generically American and not merely his own as an individual. In no way does this prevent him, however, from being the complete individual he is; indeed it forms part of his very individuality. Being an American, of Irish or Italian stock, belonging to a certain family, being an instance of Homo Sapiens: all this is indissolubly interwoven in the texture of his personality. A person may become gradually aware of his ancestral traits, his national peculiarities and limitations; he may rationalize them, sublimate them. He may even be endowed with a mind strong and broad enough to raise himself beyond these limits and become what we would call a true personality; but he will never rid himself completely of those innate or habitually acquired generic ties.

Such archaic residues may be used and misused by groups of a different character, by political or economic power interests. National or religious or "racial" feelings may be whipped up to frantic emotion and mass hysteria and in this way become extremely dangerous. They may swamp everything that is actually individual in a person, sweep away his conscious ego, his clear thinking. Yet they do not by themselves alone break up the structure of personality. The damage is temporary; it may be repaired and the original condition restored, when emotions have ebbed away.

The Collective. Political parties, work organizations, economic, occupational or technical combines, corporations, cooperatives, unions, form a second type of group which we call collectives. These supra-individual or post-individual groups develop through the joining of pre-established individuals for some specific purpose. Collectives are established by common *ends,* communities derive from common *origins.*

Collectives have become particularly prevalent in more recent times. Their development has been hastened by the progress of industry and technology, the division of labor, the growing influence of scientific mechanization in trades and professions, specialization in the sciences and the extensive mass production and standardization of goods. Modern means of communication, too, have favored their development. Radio, television, movies, omnipresent advertising, mass slogans, the functional lingoes of business and the professions, have all produced and fostered those stereotypes of public opinion upon which a collective thrives. The modern state too, be it democratic or totalitarian, must be regarded as an accomplished collective. Through the vast scope of its tasks it has become overwhelmingly bureaucratic, a monstrous, rationalized and systematized organization of individuals.

Collectives are the only groups which function primarily as groups. To be sure, a family or a nation is a group as well, but its primary function is internal; it acts upon the individual through common feelings, dispositions and habits. Whenever a community acts as a group, this function is derivative; whenever a nation acts as a group, it becomes a state. Conversely, the influence of the collective is an external one; and its internal effects on the individual are derivative. Its standards and stereotypes intrude on the personality *from without.* Substantially alien to the personality, collectives may, if powerful enough, cause it to split. Collective influences are therefore much more dangerous than those exerted by genuine communities; they may break up the individual form. They invade the psyche of the individual *from consciousness,* in a rational or pseudo-rational way, through the innumerable abstractions of modern life. From consciousness, dim as it may be, these abstractions gradually sink into the unconscious, and in this manner they disrupt personality—for no crucial changes occur in a human being without the medium of the unconscious. The unconscious is the formative, the creative ground of the personality, and not until the unconscious has been affected, can any change take roots in a human disposition.

In this way a layer of the unconscious forms that can rightly be called *collective unconscious.* Here is stored up the residue of a host of mass stereotypes, slogans, conceptual simplifications, suggested or imposed attitudes, which by various means have sunk from consciousness into the unconscious.

We are all aware of instances of this process. Business advertising, for example, starts out from some very simple rational, quasi-argumentative appeal. "Live modern," it tells you, and smoke L&M filter cigarettes which "taste richer, smoke cleaner"; Ballantine beer has "purity, body, flavor"; American Airlines "carries more passengers than any other airline in the world." Once these motives for buying are established, compulsion through ubiquitous, noisy repetition sets in. Constant pounding drives the slogans down into the unconscious where they gradually lose their argumentative character and become immediately, mechanically compelling. Novelty, too, starts out from a thrill of sophistication and ultimately becomes one of the most compulsive unconscious motives for buying.

In similar fashion, Hitler, who had studied carefully the methods of American advertising, set out on his demagogical career by propounding his motley theories (including the really ingenious one of mass indoctrination) and displaying his recklessly assembled evidence that the Jews, the bankers, the department stores and so forth were to blame for everybody's troubles. He found it necessary to write a book which was distributed in millions of copies. Here he presented the crude arguments for his policies. This done, the catchwords were drummed into people's minds until the simple word "Jew" would automatically produce the desired effects.

In the Soviet Union the very complex theories of Karl Marx were ground down to a few hackneyed slogans which were mechanically applied to every human situation and ultimately constituted the equipment for a massive militant collective unconscious.

And correspondingly in America the meaning of the word "communist" has been so broadened and diluted that it may include New Dealer, One Worlder, atheist or Harvard egg-head. The mere uttering of the word can touch off the most irrational reactions.

The first traces of such a transformation of rational arguments into emotional stereotypes may be found in the French Revolution when the theories of natural law and of rationalistic philosophy, the ideas of the physiocrats and the encyclopedists had, in a contracted form, descended into the subliminal sphere of people's minds. As we go further back in history, we find the occasional mass movements less and less determined by external or rational actuation. They issued rather from archaic—ethnic and religious —impulses, that is, from the generic unconscious. The pogroms touched off by the Crusades sprang immediately from religious fanaticism and its anticipation of the fight against the infidel. All the peasant uprisings of the Middle Ages and later, though aimed at relieving unbearable oppression, were animated by religious patterns of expectation.

The various strata of the unconscious—the generic, the individual and the collective—are rarely found in reality in clearly separated or separable form. They pass over into one another, mingle and merge, and a continuous interflow goes on between the conscious and the unconscious. While personal experiences and collective intrusions sink into the unconscious, subliminal contents may rise to the surface of consciousness by means of rationalization or sublimation or in some other way. Strange things can then happen. Mobiloil's "Flying Red Horse," which somehow emerged in the brain of a designer from its archetypal ancestry of Pegasus and the spirited steeds of the medieval magicians, returns to the collective unconscious as a collective stereotype and may subsequently remerge with the submemorial forebears. So, too, collective slogans may stir hidden archaic passions and representations: Nazi anti-Semitism certainly revived the portrait of the Jew as painted by the hostile medieval Church; and communistic patriotism in the Soviet Union touched off national and Panslavic aspirations of old. Collective battlecries may mobilize deep-seated genealogical or individual attitudes and prejudices.

Just as the types of the unconscious merge, so too distinction between community and collective is never as sharply defined in historical reality as it would appear in theory. Historical units are never static; their borderlines are always fluid. There exist fundamental differences between them, which can be felt, demonstrated and formulated. But when we look for distinctions we have to base them on centers rather than on boundaries. Accordingly, the present distinction between community and collective should not be interpreted as though the borderlines between the two group types had always been sharply drawn. All archaic groups, when they settle down and expand on their earthly ground, and become solidly organized, turn partly into collectives. Even primeval, tribal settlements, and later the Oriental kingdoms, the Greek city-republics, deeply rooted as they were in ethnic communities with their specific religions and traditions, all brought forth rudimentary collectives. In fact, antiquity arrives at the stage of a full-grown collective in the elaborate administrative body of the Roman Empire. Whenever a nation develops a state, whenever a religion becomes institutionalized in the form of a church, a collective sprouts from the community. Conversely, a collective may sometimes develop such communal traits as special traditions and a social or cultural atmosphere.

The great change that has occurred during the last two hundred years in the relation between community and collective, the event from which this study sets out, is a change of emphasis, a shift of predominance. In former historical periods the institutional collective, the state, grew out of the ethnic community. Not only was it deeply, firmly implanted in the community, not only did it follow the religious and traditional guidance of the community, but all the subsidiary collectives that evolved in the process of expansion —social, professional and economic, juristic, military and bureaucratic collectives—were still in some way vitally connected with and subordinated to the predominant community. In recent centuries, however, collectives began either to form autonomously on purely economic or technical grounds, or gradually to sever themselves from their ethnic communities. The relationship was reversed, for now unfettered collectives, growing to gigantic proportions, came to influence and control the communities. It is this autonomy, this unlimited expansion and predominance of the collectives, that makes them so pernicious to the individual and his personality.

The result is a gradual disruption of the human self, the individual's growing alienation from his world and ultimately from himself. In the following chapters we shall see how collectivization splits the human self into a collective, functional part and a human, actually individual part which grows more and more atrophied.

The collectives, however, are not the only agents of the disruption of personality. There are other forces working to the same end. They derive from different sources, although in their origins they too were connected with the expansion of the collectives. While collectives tend to split the individual self *from without,* those other, more subtle processes divide or shatter it *from within.* We shall observe them in the development of psychoanalytic and artistic techniques and in the growth of a peculiar new sensibility that penetrates ever deeper into the texture of man's existence and of his phenomenal world; its extreme consequence is the existentialist experience, which questions and shakes the very foundations of human existence.

As we arrive at a coherent picture of the whole process of human transformation in which the present generations are involved, the tragic ambivalence of man's endeavor will become fully visible: his reaching out into transhuman dimensions and his losing the ground from which he grew and which gave him support and meaning as a human. Man's balance is deeply disturbed by the process of transformation. Our task is to help, if only through awareness, to restore it in a new form of existence.

CHAPTER TWO

The Split from Without: I

COLLECTIVIZATION

Wir sind ein Wir, aber nicht weil wir eine Gemeinschaft halten, sondern weil unsere Grenzen ineinander verfliessen.

(We are a "we," but not because we hold communion, rather because our contours flow over into one another.)

HERMANN BROCH

THE COMPLEX interconnected developments that led to the formation of modern democracy, science, technology and industry have been amply explored and described by outstanding scholars so that I need not retrace them in detail. Suffice it to recall that these vast processes began in the Middle Ages within the pale of a still supreme and really "catholic" Church, with the help of Aristotelian logic and in opposition to Aristotelian science; all of them in their different ways contributed to a thorough secularization of the Western world. Modern democracy evolved from the various heretic movements which, linked with national aspirations, engendered the great religious schism and the popular revolutions in the wake of the Protestant reformation; it received support from intricate interpretations of natural law, motivated

15

by the most contradictory power interests. Rational undermin-
ing of the Christian dogma was fostered by Islamic speculation and
ancient knowledge transmitted by Arabian and Jewish scholars
from the cultural reservoir of the Middle East, and this rational sub-
version was the first impetus to stir modern science into being: it
brought about the ascendancy of human reason, which supplanted
the authority of God and came to be considered no less omnipotent than God. There followed the "age of reason," stretching from
the Renaissance to the nineteenth century, in which man woke to
enjoy the use of his unfettered faculties and potentialities in the
face of an unveiled and self-revealing world.

It was the beginning of a radical turn in the human mind, the
beginning of that keen *extraversion of man,* the full extent of which
we are witnessing today. Power-greedy rulers in need of money
encouraged applied science, invention, technology. Technology on
its part stimulated science which, in turn, was fired by the lofty
hopes of rationalism for the achievement of human perfection and
happiness through improvement of man's material conditions.
And all these movements, of course, were also propelled by their
own passions, curiosities, interests, and were carried away by the
lead of quasi self-generating techniques.

When we ponder this huge development, extending over almost
a millennium, we are overwhelmed and even somewhat awed by
its inherent, organic necessity. It took its course, went on beyond
the power of individual men. It spans, as it were, the personalities
and generations who, in carrying it out, attached their passing ideologies to it. Nobody could stop it, although there were always
quite a few who wanted to; but nobody in his senses, even today,
would wish to stop it even if he could: the good that comes from
science and democracy is immense.

The greatest admiration for the achievements of science, however, and the fullest recognition of the indispensability of reason
should not prevent us from realizing historical connections and
present dangers where they exist. It is essential that we acknowledge the paradoxical "law of history"—if we may call it that—or,

to put it even more broadly, the "law of life": that any living thing or movement has beneficial as well as harmful effects; that bad and, indeed, perilous effects are inextricably interwoven with the good, productive ones. This is what we mean when we speak of *les défauts de ses vertus.* Any living thing or movement carries its life and its death within the same body; what drives life to its climax is the very same impulsion that fosters the seeds of death. Any principle, therefore, that is pushed to its extreme and loses its resilience, its adaptability to changing conditions, reverses and defeats itself.

IT IS A TRUISM that the progress of our rational and empirical knowledge is closely connected with the development of technology, industry, and of what we understand by democracy; that all these developments are but different aspects of one and the same process. What is not so commonly recognized is the fact that these thoroughly respectable achievements—science, technology, industry, democracy—were the very ones that inevitably brought about that ill-famed collectivism and are about to promote it even further. One should cease to identify collectivism purely and simply with socialism and communism. All social and economic forms of our modern life tend equally to be collectivistic and to develop and foster collectivism. For all of them ultimately derive from rationalistic science and technology and their manifold implications. *The roots of collectivism are to be found in rationalism and technology and not in any specific social or economic doctrine.* A consistent individualist would have to advocate abolition of the whole apparatus of modern life, abolition of modern science, industry, technology—which would be equivalent to reversing the general trend of human life itself.

Let us briefly survey the rise of collectivism out of rationalism. *Rationalism* led to *rationalization,* both scientific and economico-technological.[1] Rationalization means, among other things, *classification* and *quantification,* dissection of unique individual beings and phenomena into abstracted features and functions which they have in common and which can be quantitatively manipulated. In this way, by means of theoretical devices (terms) and technical devices (machines), our physical world and, more recently, also our psychic world are explored, mainly for the mastery and practical exploitation of nature. *"Scientia non est individuorum."* ("Science is not concerned with individuals.") To be sure, science, positivistic science, starts from the individual since, as mentioned before, the individual constitutes the only quite real, because immediately evident, datum. But science does not leave the concrete individual entity intact; science uses it to derive from it, or from a number of them, common properties, property abstractions, statistical laws or laws of nature, thereby cutting up, dissecting the concrete and unique individual or phenomenon. This proceeding necessarily leads to a thoroughly quantitative conception of reality. We all know that not only natural science but also the sciences dealing with human affairs, anxious as they are to prove themselves true sciences, exhibit an ever-growing tendency toward metrics— socio-metrics, psycho-metrics, statistics, indexing, polling and testing methods and so forth; in other words, toward extracting from the qualitatively unique individuals and phenomena those elements that lend themselves to quantitative methods of comprehension.[2] We even notice an inclination to drive terminological abstraction so far as to contract, as much as possible, verbal language into mathematical symbols and formulas. There are sociologists who boast that their science will soon have arrived at a point where it will be able to dispense with individual thinking altogether because facts in combination with business machines will do the job by themselves.

THIS TENDENCY is not confined to science proper; it is about to extend its sway over all of our life which is increasingly subjected to *scientification*. The Kinsey Reports, for instance, attempt to pin down in abstract facts and figures the most delicate, the most personal, the most inexpressibly subtle relationship between human beings. In the spring of 1952 the American Physical Society, discussing a new mathematical theory of communication, seems to have reached the conclusion that, from the thermodynamic point of view, the writing, distribution and reading of books are never worth the energy that is put into them. Now with all the deepest respect for the science of physics, I venture to doubt whether the creative effort of writing a book and the chain-reaction of responses it may unleash in the reader—sometimes through one kindling spark and sometimes with far-reaching practical consequences—can be measured in thermodynamic terms. The problem may have an odd specific interest for the scientists concerned but, nevertheless, it shows the absurdity of applying concepts of one level to an entirely different level of existence. The frequent denial of such difference on the part of scientists is exactly the very consequential issue.

We can apparently measure almost everything today. We can measure the degree of laughter of an audience in response to a comedian. We can tell metrically whether a speaker is boring. And even the qualification for a public office seems to be amenable to quantification: "Francis B. Allegretti," so the Chicago Bar Association's report says, "is 49.63 percent of what a Superior Court judge should be." That after twenty-three years on the bench. On the same score card Rudolph F. Desort, who has been on the bench seventeen years was rated at 52.78 and William J. Lindsay, with twenty-four years' judicial experience, at 56.7. This is only an extreme example of the manifold applications of testing, indexing, and I. Q. scoring, all of which single out certain specifically required, collectively usable aptitudes from the whole of the unique personality, disregarding the fact that a person is more than just a bunch of functional properties and can make up by other qualities for the lack of the tested ones.

Systematic research in its limitless expansion sets out to ascertain everything scientifically, even facts which any person with common sense and a little bit of observation has been aware of in his day-to-day life. From a wealth of instances I just pick a few.

There is an age-old experience, treated by many authors and

often expressed by the personalities concerned, that prominence is bound to isolate a man. It remained for modern sociology to prove this well-known fact by sociometric methods. I quote the abstract of an article bearing a duly departmental title which makes it perfectly unrecognizable that the article deals with human beings: *"Sociometric Stars as Isolates."* [3] The abstract reads as follows: "Conventional sociometric diagrams represent 'stars' or leaders as the persons most often chosen as the center of a circle of admiring friends. When the data of such heuristic diagrams consist of (1) number of incoming choices; (2) number of outgoing choices; and (3) social status scores or some other rating, and are plotted in a three-dimensional model instead of drawn on a two-dimensional flat surface, the 'stars' no longer appear as in the center but as on the periphery of the total group structures. Thus, in social space (not mere direction of choices), 'stars' conform to Cooley's concept of the isolation of the leader."

An animal psychologist, Dr. W. T. James in Athens, Georgia, found out after ten years of experiments that timid dogs go hungry while the top dogs grow fat. "Dr. James has been placing dogs of various temperaments in a run. At the end of the run is a food box from which only one dog can eat at a time. The timid dog will cower in a corner, while the aggressive type moves straight ahead. Two of the domineering type promptly start fighting until the superiority of one is established. If a top, middle and underdog are in the run at the same time, the top dog proceeds to eat his fill. Occasionally the middle-class dog, out of frustration and rage over his secondary position, will take out his spite on the underdog." [4] What apparatus to evidence the evident!

A Ph.D. thesis of 439 pages submitted in 1944 to the faculty of the Graduate School of Cornell University has the following title: "Posture and Other Physiological Responses of the Worker in Relation to the Height of Working Surface used in Household Ironing." It contains 138 statistical graphs, figures, measurements, "kymographic records." Now, an investigation into what constitutes desirable ironing equipment for the greatest number of housewives is a perfectly reasonable and useful procedure for an industrial firm developing new styles of such equipment. An investigator might be asked to make the rounds and interview housewives as to their requirements and preferences, things every woman knows through common sense and habit. To go to such lengths, however, as to measure the height and girth of shoulder, bust, waist, hip, knee, "forces exerted on the ironing board," "postural sway of the subject while ironing," subject's metabolic rate, heart rate, respiration and blood pressure, to take motion pictures of different positions taken by the subject while ironing, and so forth—this is a caricature of real science.

All this scientification is collectivization—not only because it dissects the whole, unique personality and phenomenon into common fractional properties but because it invalidates and eventually atrophies the intuitive faculty, the personal common sense and taste of the individual who becomes afraid of using his own faculties. He does not trust himself any longer. Science is the supreme, impersonal, collective authority and if he feels any personal impulses rising against it he suppresses them. What was known as human wisdom is on the wane.

THEORETICAL ABSTRACTIONS, such as strict terms, mathematical symbols and formulae, correspond to *practical abstractions,* i.e., machines and gadgets. Conceptual abstractions are nothing else than theoretical machines used for the intellectual mastery of the world. Machines are nothing else than materialized, materially applied conceptual abstractions used for the purpose of manipulating and utilizing the physical world. This interrelation becomes most obvious at places where both procedures interlock: in the scientific apparatuses of our research institutes and observatories, in cyclotrons, synchrotrons, computing machines, electromicroscopes, and so forth; and in enterprises where even both purposes meet, like the Radio Corporation of America and the Rand Corporation. Technological processes, which are indefinitely reproducible, reflect scientific laws, which express infinite applicability.

Just as technology is penetrated with science, so, to the same degree, industry is penetrated with technology and with science directly. The result is economic rationalization which was also due to follow autonomously from the expansion of capitalistic enterprise: growth of organization means growth of rationalization.

All these developments, the development of science, technology and industry, and their interpenetration, are but different aspects or ramifications of one evolutionary process; all of them lead eventually to collectivization and deindividualization. They split or invalidate the individual in various ways: apart from scientification, through *specialization, functionalization, standardization, anonymization.*

The chain reaction released by collectivizing rationalization, inherent in science, technology and industry, starts with specialization. Specialization involves functionalization; functionalization brings about standardization—these are the three primary carriers of collective controls. And by means of these consecutive effects rationalization paradoxically ends up, as we shall see, in depriving the individual of his rational faculty.

What does *specialization* do to the individual? It does not appeal to him as a whole, organic being, as a human being, as an individually unique being; it appeals to, it calls forth in him, some specific technical function, some functional qualification which he has in common with other people thus qualified. Such functions correspond exactly to the conceptual abstractions, general property abstractions, which science derives from concrete beings and phenomena. In fact, these abstractions may turn directly into functional beings: certain scientific specialists may actually be regarded as personalized functions. Specialization overemphasizes and overdevelops this functional quality of the individual, singles it out while leaving other qualities and his essentially human qualities to atrophy since they are hardly required in his work any longer. Individuality, as we know, means indivisibility, something that cannot be divided. Now this is exactly what specialization does: it divides the man, it ranges that part of him which it calls forth into some abstract functional order, into the rank and file of some operational combine, into some category of occupational concern with all its paraphernalia: code of behavior, standards of opinion, lingo, and so forth. In this way, the concrete human particularity of the unique individual is displaced by the abstract particularity of the collectively specialized function.

The collective, functional part of the personality grows at the expense of the individual and human part. The working day of the man is filled with his functionally limited occupation and all its implications of restrictive handling, interests and attitudes. The problems of the dreariness of industrial work and the dehumanization attaching to it, "alienation," *Entfremdung*, in the Marxian sense of the word, have been pondered by many people since Karl Marx; for a long time they have not concerned workers alone. To be sure, a great change has taken place, from Frederick Winslow Taylor's *System of Scientific Management*, perfected by Henry Ford, which attempted to adjust man to the machine, indeed to turn him into a link of the machine, to the modern conception of working conditions based on current tests and interviews by corporation sociologists and "psycho-engineers." Modern management has come to recognize that workers are human beings and that it serves the interest of the corporation better to adjust not only the bodies but the minds of people to the complex collective function of the factory; to adjust them not through force and deceptive tricks—for instance, secretly accelerating the speed of the transmitter belt—but through harnessing the good will of the workers by all possible means. No doubt, the workers' situation has improved tremendously in recent decades. Workers in certain industrial areas, in the automobile industry for example, enjoy higher wages and a much greater amount of security than people in intellectual and professional fields. In addition, managements try to improve conditions for their employees with many new conveniences: brighter lighting, better air, more rest periods, shorter working hours, music, clubs with recreational and sporting facilities. Recently even more emphasis has been put on "human relations in industry"—good relations within the factory hierarchy and between workers and management—on teamwork, on a pleasant social climate of work. And yet, as Gordon Rattray Taylor states in his excellent book, *Are Workers Human?* [5] industry is still "ailing"; it has "contrived a state of affairs in which friction is chronic." Taylor wonders at an apparent incompatibility of human attitudes: "Men are often by nature so industrious and energetic that it is almost impossible to restrain them from activity. . . . They are so careless of discomfort and fatigue that they will sail small boats in all weathers for pleasure, that they get up expeditions to the most uncomfortable corners of the earth, and even play football in inadequate clothing in the wind and mud of a November afternoon. But . . . when industry asks them to endure conditions much less disagreeable, a howl of resentment is the response. Why does a man who tells you frankly that he hates work and only looks forward to retiring, go home and spend the rest of the day and all his week end digging in his garden until the sweat streams off his face? To this really crucial question industry appears to have no answer." Taylor believes that this state of affairs is of industry's own making and he deplores the widespread "apathy" which slackens efforts to follow through the recommendations of their research sociologists and psychologists. However, when we study the reports of the counselors and research workers who turned into confessors and psychoanalysts in the famous Hawthorne Plant experiments of Western Electric in Chicago,[6] we realize the bewildering complexity of the problem and we sense at the bottom of the interplay of manifold factors the basic trouble inherent in the situation. "The biggest trouble with industry," said John M. Caffrey, President of International Harvester Co., "is that it is full of human beings." The answer to Taylor's question is, I believe, the individual's need for self-determination, for selfhood, for the satisfaction of producing a whole piece of work and one that is worth producing, or for contributing to a task which he can comprehend in its entirety, with which he can identify himself, i.e., for doing meaningful work. Nothing, not the best of conveniences, can fully replace this elementary satisfaction. The fundamental fact is that the workers serve a purpose which is alien to their essentially own; they serve the purpose of a commercial collective. And even to the extent that modern management genuinely does its best to make work acceptable and smooth for its employees, there remain certain economic and technical limitations which the purpose of an industrial enterprise, by its very nature, imposes on reforms. For instance, some experiments made by Cadillac Motors during the war yielded excellent results: "Completely unskilled Negro women made a precision aluminium component for aircraft engines, each one turning out a finished product." These women did more efficient work than could have been achieved in an assembly line.[7] But unfortunately there are all too few occasions in the vast and complicated production processes of modern industry where such methods could be applied. There are other requirements stemming from the individual, human residue in people which cannot be reconciled with the profitable operation of a big industrial enterprise. Teamwork, for instance, close human relations in a working group, were seen to improve both the willingness to work and the workers' efficiency. But Elton Mayo writes in his book, *The Social Problems of an Industrial Civilization*:[8] "Where groups change ceaselessly as jobs and mechanical processes change, the individual inevitably experiences a sense of void, of emptiness, where his fathers knew the joy of comradeship and security. And in such situations, his anxieties—many, no doubt, irrational or ill-founded —increase and he becomes more difficult both to fellow workers and to supervisors. The extreme of this is perhaps rarely encountered as yet, but increasingly we move in this direction as the tempo of industrial change is speeded by scientific and technical discoveries."

Similar conditions prevail among white-collar workers, among people in various walks of life. The "New Office," as we find it described in C. Wright Mills' book, *White Collar,* "with its tens of thousands of square feet and its factory-like flow of work is not an informal, friendly place. The drag and beat of work, the 'production unit' tempo, require that time consumed by anything but business at hand be explained and apologized for. Dictation was once a private meeting of executive and secretary. Now the executive phones a pool of dictaphone transcribers whom he never sees and who know him merely as a voice. Many old types of personnel have become machine operators, many new types began as machine operators. . . . The rationalization of the office, on the one hand, attracts and creates a new mass of clerks and machine operators, and their work increasingly approximates the factory operative in light manufacturing. On the other hand, this new office requires the office manager who operates the human machinery. . . . Finger dexterity is often more important than creative thinking. Promotions consequently become relatively rare. . . . Some large office managers actually prefer to hire girls who are content to remain simply clerks, who will attempt to rise no higher than their initial level." [9]

The growing bureaucratization of business has somewhat reduced the difference between the situation of workers and executives. To be sure executives may still enjoy the satisfactions and advantages of their elevated position and the largely social character of their functions; but they also work mostly in a group and as a group. And much of what has been said of the workers also applies to the executives. Their dead ends, their frustrations and their particular anxieties we find depicted in John Marquand's *Point of No Return*: "The Stuyvesant [Bank] was the aggregate of the character of many individuals who merged a part of their personal strivings and ambitions into a common effort. It was like a head of living coral rising above the surf, a small outcropping of a greater reef. He only knew that in the end it was stronger than any one person. In the end, no matter what the rewards might be, a part of one's life remained built into that complicated structure. They were all asses following their bundles of hay, the clerks, the tellers, the department heads, the vice-presidents, the president, and the directors . . . they were all on an assembly line, but you could not blame the line. It was too cumbersome, too inhumanly human for anyone to blame." [10]

Another revealing document is an interview with an executive which Riesman reports in his book, *Faces in the Crowd*. What stands out in this interview is the conflict between the business that absorbs the man almost completely and the family toward which he has a bad conscience because he has not given it enough time and attention. "It may well be," says Riesman, "that wife and children stand for him as a symbol for his own unlived life— that his socially approved obligations toward them screen his feelings of not having fulfilled his obligations toward himself." [11]

We recall what Brewsie says in Gertrude Stein's book, *Brewsie and Willie*: "What's rushing around so fast you can't hear yourself think, what will happen, you'll be old and you never lived, and you kind of feel silly to lie down and die and to never have lived, to have been a job chaser and never have lived." Whereupon Willie puts the crucial question: "Can you be a job chaser and live at the same time?" [12]

When a man comes home from his working day, he is of course utterly unable to enjoy true leisure for which he has lost all inner disposition. You cannot expect somebody suddenly to shift from the tempo and turmoil of a modern working day, from the incessant external demands besieging his fleeting consciousness to the calm and composure in which alone real leisure can grow. You cannot expect a man, after having served as a function for eight hours, to turn into a complete and personal human being in an hour or so. So he turns from his working function to his home functions, from his machines to his gadgets. As soon as he leaves his shop or office he is awaited by other abstract, mechanical devices, functions answering his own functions, again appealing to his functional skill and susceptibility. He drives a car, he turns switches, and not only is he served by machines but here again he is induced to serve them in turn, to accommodate himself to the machines. I remember a picture in *The New Yorker* of a man in what could be called a "total kitchen," one of those completely mechanized kitchen units, and this man happens to have an individual fancy for an additional towel which he wants to hang up somewhere, and he does not find a place in the whole room where he could drive in a nail. This picture struck me as a symbol of the situation of the individual in our modern world.

For entertainment the man turns on his radio or his TV, he goes to the movies where again, for the most part, he is served specialized, functionalized events, attitudes, feelings—attitudes and feelings which are utterly untrue in a human sense, but which are shaped according to what Hollywood considers the desires, the predilections, the notions of the masses. Now it can hardly be denied that the masses of people do relish a beautiful car, a gorgeous estate, a sweet romance, and the thrill of a juicy crime; they are certainly longing to satisfy vicariously their sadistic drives and their gambling itches, and finally, after all these gratifications have been amply indulged in, they still want to see justice triumph. And while these are doubtless popular wishes which the entertainment industry feels it must satisfy, the film and TV producers' usual response is to *outdo* such sentiments and attitudes in a distinct direction. They isolate them, take them out of their human context and texture, denaturalize, dehumanize, functionalize them, reduce them to their bare effects; so that we see a crime as such, a romance as such, an alcoholic as such, a capitalistic career as such, and the characters are treated as mere appendages, as mannequins specially adjusted to their prefabricated experiences. These typified experiences seem to have emerged from sectionalized subject files which are labeled according to collectively functional attitudes. As a consequence the most mysterious, intimate phases of life are turned in the minds of people into labeled stereotypes. A little boy, again in a *New Yorker* cartoon, reveals the situation in a flash. Walking through Central Park with his mother, he points at a loving couple sitting on a bench: "Look, Mummy, movies!" An elementary human situation comes to the mind first as a collective cliché.

It is just that which is most harmfully consequential: the reflexive effect of this stereotyping. The dehumanized stereotypes, supposedly representing people's genuine concepts of life, act upon their imagination in such a manner as to *make* them into what they were expected to *be* from the start; people come to behave and react, to feel and experience like the suggested stereotypes. In this way, Hollywood, as well as magazine and best-seller fiction, actually shape people's characters. A person cannot be persistently and helplessly exposed to such crude influences without gradually succumbing to them.

WE SAW THAT SPECIALIZATION is intrinsically one with functionalization, and we have just begun to observe how functionalization passes over into standardization. The ghostly, frightening phenomenon of *standardization* pervades our whole society. We find it arising through functionalization from the various abstractions of our age: conceptual, technological, commercial abstractions. Scientific methods streamline our thinking; machines and gadgets and typified mass products streamline our daily moves; commercial fashions and functional simplifications streamline attitudes and characters.

Fashions of previous ages evolved naturally from human centers: either from long-established local and ethnic customs, or from the slowly changing style of life of a representative elite. Today's fashions are collective types, artificially instigated by the commercial requirements of novelty and without regard for any genuine human need or wish; in fact, the compulsion to produce something new incessantly tends to remove objects further and further from the truly useful, from human and practical requirements. Modern fashions are not local and human, but temporal and abstract variations. Artificially, commercially launched as they are, they retroactively influence the life and behavior of people. The streamlined faces of Hollywood actresses, of beauty-parlor products and fashion models introduced a collectivization of looks: make-up as well as red and clawlike fingernails depersonalize face and hands and destroy their unique, characteristic physiognomy. The result is those crowds of standardized beauties grinning at us wherever we go and ride, on highways and sidewalks, from ads and posters, and at social gatherings. In musicals, at ball games and public ceremonies we see those dance regiments, after the pattern of the Rockettes, forming figurations and performing evolutions of all kinds. The individual is lost in them; the single figures all look exactly alike and we cannot recognize a personal face any longer; we just see so many yards of beautiful girl. This is, if we care to think about it, an indignity inflicted on the human individual. And if we had not, in our daily life, lost the capacity for seeing symbolically, for noticing symbolic situations, we should recognize this as a symbol of accomplished collectivization: the unit here is no longer the individual but the group formation.[13]

Equivalent to this, in our surroundings, are the new housing projects, those "dwelling machines you'll be able to pick off the rack." Again I must refer to a cartoon, this one by Robert Day, in which a dear old lady stands lost in the midst of such a new housing development and has to ask the mailman where she lives. There, in these projects, grow up the "Homogenized Children of New Suburbia" as described in a report by Sidonie M. Gruenberg.[14]

Gertrude Stein worried about the forebodings of the present generation when she met the American GIs in Paris after the Second World War. She put down her experiences in her lovable book, *Brewsie and Willie*. "Ah, those poor American boys," she once said to Richard Wright,[15] "Why did they come to see *me*? Well, it is because they knew dimly that I am an individual. And, somehow, they all wanted dimly to be individuals. But they were scared. I just kept asking them, 'Boys, what in hell is it that you are scared of?' And they could not answer. . . . I kept asking each and every one of them 'What in hell do you own? What on earth are you scared of losing?' And they would just stare at me. They could not answer. And the more I would ask them about what they owned, the more afraid they would become. I told them all to go back home and learn to be martyrs, learn to fight and to live. I told them to be pioneers again . . . to learn to think as individuals. The only thing that makes me hopeful about them is that they are lost and sad and that they know it."

The young generation of our day has been depicted by that expert on youth, J. D. Salinger: the teen-agers in *The Catcher in the Rye* and college youth in his later short story *Franny*.[16] In both stories a very young person, deeply enmeshed in the atmosphere, the idiom, the conventionally accepted, standardized conceptions of schoolmates, is stirred by a somewhat illegitimate personal sensibility which fights its way out through tragic conflicts. Franny, one of those college girls we see flocking into Princeton or Yale for Junior Proms and house parties, announces her arrival to her boy friend in a letter in which nothing unusual could be detected. She pours out to him, with that kind of spirited stupidity of which these winsome young morosophs are capable, the medley of facts of dormitory life and of her own confused school mind, intermingled with week-end expectations and the due singsong of love—a jargon which he swallows with ease. She arrives and the week-end routine is taking its course: the station-platform kiss, the lacing of fingers in the cab, the showing of the room, sitting down for lunch and sipping martinis with the anticipation of the ball game and the dances. Everything seems just "lovely." It is what goes under the name of "having a wonderful time." Then, all of a sudden, when he starts some shop talk about a paper of his, she gets into an argument with him about his academic clannishness, his having a sectional mind, his being one of those overanalyzers who ruin poetry and leave just some verbal debris on the spot. She tries to pierce through his departmental mentality and to convey to him, quite unsuccessfully, a sense of poetry, a flurry of human movability, of personal sensibility, which a mystical book that has touched her deeply has aroused in her, and which now stirs in her dimly and inexpressibly and struggles against her susceptibility to conform. And slowly it begins to dawn on her consciousness what she had felt underneath for a long time and had dreaded to know: that all this was a lie, that she had nothing in common with this boy, with his week-end show-off, his working routine and his crowd; that she disagrees with him, that she does not love him, although in her poor, desperate incertitude she clings to the reassertion of this love and keeps stroking his hand helplessly in the midst of the debacle. And at the mention of a friend of his whom they were supposed to pick up for the ball game, it bursts out of her and carries her away, a long accumulated irritation: not because of anything especially bad or objectionable about this boy, but because of her experience throughout her college years that there are so many of him, just alike. They appear almost indistinguishable. Their every move, every reaction—what they will say and do in certain circumstances—is predictable and anticipated by her: she knows the exact moment when they will tell her nasty stories about some girl in the college, when, with feigned nonchalance, they will start name-dropping and boasting of their connections, when they will ask her about her last vacation, when they will turn on their most engaging air. And the girls too are that way: she meets the same girl at every turn. Even Bohemianism is no longer an escape from conformity; even eccentricity has become commonplace, has developed canonical forms of informality. It is not so much what everybody does, she feels, as that *whatever* they do (whether they are kind or not, clever or not, "interesting" or not, it does not matter) it all seems to have no importance, no meaning, no joy in it.

She wants to break out of this eery circle of sameness. She tries to penetrate through the conventional standards of her boy friend, to override his determination to have his normal, *comme-il-faut* week end undisturbed; she wants to get some personal response out of him. Finally, to relieve the strain on her nerves she goes to the ladies' room, to cry; she comes back and still attempts to rescue a hopeless situation. After a time she gets up again and faints, and then, only then, in the form of real worry, she draws a spark of genuine response out of the boy.

Franny is not alone in her aloneness. Hers is the state of mind of many a young individual apprehensive of the loss of individuality and selfhood, disgusted with the apparently inescapable conformity, and at the same time afraid of the alternative, afraid of being left alone, of being excluded from the company of peers. It is the same longing for a life of one's own, the same desolation and the same sadness that Gertrude Stein sensed in the American GIs. It is the same experience of the ghostliness of monotony that Strindberg conveyed in his chamber plays and Alberto Moravia in his novel, *Gli Indifferenti*. It is the same inner condition that Elisabeth Langgässer expresses in her novel *Das unauslöschliche Siegel:* "I can no longer stand repetition."

The whole tendency of our educational institutions is directed toward streamlining children and young people so as to fit them most completely into their environment; they encourage conformity by all possible means. "Adjustment," "the regular fellow," are the catchwords of our day. In so doing, education only follows a trend already powerful and unchecked in the young themselves, as Riesman has demonstrated with abundant evidence. Such emphasis on adjustment prepares youth for the present world of adults where conformity is the order of the day as well. The reverse side of this is that uniqueness, which we found to be one of the essential characteristics of the individual, is not required nor even desired any longer. Everybody is considered replaceable, a tenet that arises from a misinterpretation of democracy. "The idea," says Erich Fromm, "that all men are created equal implied that all men have the same fundamental right to be considered as ends in themselves and not as means. Today, equality has become equivalent to *interchangeability* and is the very negation of individuality. Equality, instead of being the condition for the development of each man's peculiarity, means the extinction of individuality. . . ." [17]

Conformity, lack of uniqueness, further implies *anonymity*, which, to be sure, evolved also from other origins, from the inevitable bureaucratization of our institutions and from the crowding of daily events. Names pop up in our newspapers, stay in the sharpest limelight for a time until one day they are swept into oblivion, such complete oblivion as never before. New names crowd them out day by day. How can people nowadays, flooded by the perpetual outpouring of radio, TV, movies, magazines, by ceaseless news "every hour on the hour," how should they be able to keep a memory, a lasting notion of the true identity of a person or an event!

In big corporations and in modern governments decisions are no longer made by one man alone; they are the result of joint deliberation of a group of people assisted by experts. It is almost impossible to locate the distinct origin of a decision which has become anonymous. What tipped the scale may have been a clever formulation by some otherwise less important man, or the convincing opinion of an expert—who knows. Of course, there still exist here and there powerful men who exert a personal influence on their groups, but they become conspicuously rarer. One comes to feel, especially with regard to government, like the man in Kafka's *The Castle*: declarations, often contradictory or involved, are handed down, one cannot exactly make out from where.

Even in art, recent developments of non-objective painting favor anonymization. Paradoxically, pictures like those by the Jackson Pollock group, where the criterion is supposed to be vitality, the subjective presentation of the artist's impulses *per se* as expressed in color and line combinations—curiously enough these pictures appear particularly impersonal; the individual distinction in them seems minimal.

DEEPLY CONNECTED with functionalization, standardization, and anonymization, is another predominant tenor of our age, a tendency which may be considered one of the prime contributors to the disruption of personality: this is *commercialization*. The principle of *supply and demand* dominates our society in matters cultural and political no less than in economy, and there is hardly a corner of our life that has remained untouched by the commercial point of view. This trend, detrimental in all aspects, has in combination with collectivization proper most harmfully affected the character of *democracy*.

An adequate analysis of the infinitely complex problems of modern democracy lies beyond the scope of this book. Only a few points pertinent to our subject must be stressed. The development of modern democracy and the development of free commercial enterprise are intricately intertwined. Rising commerce promoted democracy; it demanded equality of partners in trade. In the medieval cities of Europe which were the centers of trade this governing principle of trade freed the peasants who entered the city gates from all bondage and dues to their lords: there was a saying that "city air makes free." The French Revolution was an economic rather than a political revolution; what it actually liberated—all over Europe—was the economic enterprise. What was achieved was freedom from taxes, from conditions of serfdom which under the *Ancien Régime* had already been converted for the most part into disbursements of money and kind, from limitations of property, guild regulations, and so forth. But while at first democracy had been furthered by trade it was later gradually ruined by trade, indeed, it became itself a kind of trade. The spread of the commercial point of view is one of the prime factors that contributed to the degeneration of the democratic process.

Democracy unleashed the full force of capitalistic enterprise, of industry, technology, applied science. Enterprise at last was really free, unlimited by any interference alien to its objectives, and thus, unobstructed as it was, it bred the various kinds of autonomous collectives which we have listed. The adulteration of democracy by the combined forces of collectivization and commercialization can be observed when we compare an earlier stage of democracy, as it is still extant in some small European countries, with the state of democratic structure and process as it prevails today in America and in other large countries.

In the early stages of American democracy, and in small

democracies like Switzerland, Holland, the Scandinavian countries
even today, the people constituting the electorate can be considered more or less identical with the people of the country,
that is to say with the group of individuals forming a national
community. Foreign policy being negligible, the domestic concerns as well as the men running for office are pretty familiar to
every one. The voters are able to understand the issues and when
they cast their votes for a candidate they implicitly decide on
real issues. (Besides, in some countries there exists the institution of the referendum whereby people decide on issues directly.)
Since in these small democracies, just as in early American democracy, the constituency is still fairly identical with the people,
the demand of the constituency coincides, or let us say, can
coincide with the real need of the people.

In present American and in some of the large European
democracies, however, a partition has taken place. Owing to the
overgrowth and increasing predominance of the collectives, which,
incidentally, even interfere with government directly through their
influential lobbies, the constituency itself is no longer identical
with the people, with the national community of individuals. The
constituents are only partly individuals; they may be called that
only as far as their life within family and among friends is
concerned. Even here, however, in private life, the collectives
have made deep inroads as we have seen, and even friends are
mostly co-workers. For the most part these "individual" constituents act and react as members of collectives, of associations,
unions, business interests, parties, and so forth. They may even
simultaneously belong to several such collectives: a social class,
a professional group, a class of consumers, a regional unit, a
party, and so forth. Their criteria, accordingly, are bound to be
an expression of their specialized and standardized group interests,
single or mutually compromising.

As matters stand, "individual" constituents are, as are even
their representatives, unable to grasp the status and the real

needs of the country as a whole, of the people, the national community of individuals. The present constituency is *not the people;* it is what we call *the public;* a momentary, anonymous, amorphous medley of the most varied elements and interests, collectives and scattered individuals, a mass fundamentally unaware of the actual situation and therefore answering short-term problems with short-term reactions which are oriented according to the all-pervading commercial point of view. Often the country is wrongly identified with and pictured as a huge business enterprise, and it is argued that the business of government should be handled by the same people and according to the same principles that govern business. When it comes to elections, the public follows the law of supply and demand just as in other concerns, and this insufficiently informed demand is like a mean between the most diverse instantaneous interests and no longer coincides with the real need of the people. The public follows the candidate who is best able to "sell" his ideas and his "personality," the platform that promises the most at the lowest cost.

Not only the politician, but nearly everybody in our society has to sell his "personality." Let us look at what commercialization, the general application of the principle of supply and demand, does to the individual. Erich Fromm has studied this problem thoroughly and we cannot do better than follow his argument:[18] "The market concept of value," he writes, "the emphasis on exchange value rather than use value," as applied to goods, "has led to a similar concept of value with regard to people and particularly to oneself. The character orientation which is rooted in the experience of oneself as a commodity and of one's value as exchange value," this "marketing orientation," has been growing rapidly in our time, together with the development of a new market which Fromm calls "the personality market." What he refers to as "personality," a kind of commercial *persona,* is just as much a functional capacity as any other professional skill, the capacity to repair telephones or to drive a truck. "Success depends largely on how well a person sells himself on the market . . . how nice a 'package' he is; whether he is 'cheerful,' 'sound,' 'aggressive,' 'reliable,' 'ambitious' . . . a stockbroker, a salesman, a secretary, a railroad executive, a college professor, or a hotel manager must each offer different kinds of personality that, regardless of their differences, must fulfill one condition: to be in demand. . . . Since modern man experiences himself both as the seller and as the commodity to be sold on the market, his self-esteem depends on conditions beyond his control. If he is 'successful,' he is valuable; if he is not, he is worthless. The degree of insecurity which results from this orientation can hardly be overestimated. If one feels that one's own value is not constituted primarily by the human qualities one possesses, but by one's success on a competitive market with ever-changing conditions, one's self-esteem is bound to be shaky and in constant need of confirmation by others. . . . If the vicissitudes of the market are judges of one's value, the sense of dignity and pride is destroyed. But the problem is not only that of self-evaluation and self-esteem but of one's experience of oneself as an independent entity, of one's *identity with oneself*. . . . In the marketing orientation man encounters his own powers as commodities alienated from him. He is not one with them but they are masked from him because what matters is not his self-realization in the process of using them but his success in the process of selling them . . . thus his feeling of identity becomes as shaky as his self-esteem; it is constituted by the sum total of roles one can play: *'I am as you desire me.'* . . . Others are experienced as commodities like oneself; they too do not present *themselves* but their salable part. . . . The premise of the marketing orientation is emptiness, the lack of any specific quality which could not be subject to change, since any persistent trait of character might conflict some day with the requirements of the market. Some roles would not fit in with the peculiarities of the person; therefore we must do away with them—not with the roles but with the peculiarities. The marketing personality must be free, free of all individuality."

NOW WHAT FROMM TERMS the "commodity" or "sales" value of a human being, is in my terms his functional, non-individual value, that collectively standardized property that flourishes on total inner emptiness. And this leads us to a further attribute of our civilization, one that again is deeply intertwined with those already mentioned: *alienation.*

The concept of alienation recurring throughout this book in various forms requires a brief historical explanation. As originally used by Hegel and elaborated by Marx it meant a cleavage inherent in human nature: man being isolated and detached from universal nature is driven into opposition not only to all natural being but implicitly to his own being; he parts with it through self-reflection (i.e. through knowledge), and through labor. Since man, unlike the animal, cannot live on nature alone and does not find his means of subsistence directly in his environment, he is forced into an intermediary task: he must produce them through labor. *Labor,* then, is the first source of alienation, self-alienation and alienation from his environment. This original factum of human life becomes particularly intensified and dangerous through an additional result of social evolution: *the division of labor* which, as Marx points out, makes individual men dependent on each other and creates "a conflict between the interest of the single individual . . . and the common interest of all individuals." As a result of this conflict, "the common interest assumes an independent character in the form of the state, separate from the actual individual and common interests, and at the same time as a delusive common interest. . . ." Thus, "man's own accomplishments turn into a power alien and opposed to him, which come to subjugate him instead of being controlled by him." According to Marx, this "consolidation of our own product into an objective power beyond us which escapes our control, obstructs our expectations, and makes void our calculations" [19] is the basic factor of social alienation. The "classless society" as conceived by Marx, is by no means identical with the total state represented by Soviet communism: indeed, communism as it is generally understood today, the "socialization of the means of production" and the "expropriation of the expropriators," is in itself not the ultimate goal of history for him. Such communism Marx calls "only a generalization and perfection of private property;" it is just "the total (*allgemeine*) capitalist." Prophetically, as if he had foreseen the abuse of his theory, he considered such communism to be so dominated by the obsession of material property "that it wants to destroy everything which is incapable of being the private property of all" (i.e., of the collective). "Material, immediate property, is regarded by [this communism] as the only goal of life and existence; the predicament of the worker is not abolished but extended to all men. . . ." [20] Thus, what Marx understood by his ideal classless society is not the transformation of the whole of society into a production mechanism, but the liberation of human life from its subjection to "alien forces." Man should cease to be a product of organizational and institutional "circumstances"; "circumstances" rather should again become a product of man. Among these "circumstances" that enslave man, *money* is the most powerful agent of alienation, money, that "common whore," that "procurer" of everything: "What I as man cannot do, that which all my individually inherent powers cannot bring about, that I can bring about through money. . . . I, who through money can bring about all that a human heart desires, do I not possess all human potentialities? Does not money transform all my impotence into its opposite? . . . that which money can buy, that I *am*. . . ." [21]

Technology, which had not yet reached its all-penetrating power in Marx's time, has become in many respects another agent of alienation. That the machine has driven a wedge between man and nature is all too evident. But, omnipresent as it is in modern life, it has so overwhelmingly besieged man's consciousness that it has profoundly disturbed also his contact with himself. People are never quite alone with themselves any longer and they are increasingly losing the faculty of facing themselves without such silent presence of the machine, not to speak of the constant noisy interference of radios, urban turmoil and ubiquitous publicity; all this must eventually result in people's inability to face themselves at all. Regarding the communication between man and man, the role of technology is always of an ambivalent nature. Technology has potentially, indeed inherently, a unifying tendency. It has almost abolished distances between countries and continents, has by its manifold means of communication— radio, television, airplane—and through economic and cultural interrelation established the one world in which we are irresistibly bound together. The machine has on the one hand disrupted immediate contacts between *individuals,* as in the situation mentioned earlier of the executive communicating through the dictaphone with secretaries "whom he never sees and who know him merely as a voice"; or in the case of the motion-picture camera and the gramophone which eliminated the unique and mutually inspiring contact of actors and musicians with their audiences. But it has, on the other hand, greatly furthered the *general* contact of the "unseen audiences" with artistic expression, particularly music. Whether the unifying or the alienating force of technology will prevail will depend on that crucial alternative on which the whole of our human destiny hinges: whether man will succeed in gaining control of his creations instead of being controlled by them.

The estrangement between human beings in daily life, the lack of immediacy in human contacts and the resulting loneliness we frequently witness today, have their roots in man's alienation from his own personal human center. Since his "commodity" or functional self has taken on such importance, his individually human self is left to wane. The perfectly legitimate question, "who are you?", which has come to be taken as an almost personal assault, is usually answered with a description of one's work; while a feeling of emptiness and falsehood, a feeling that one has not at all given an answer to the question usually remains. Identification of one's function is the admittance ticket granting the right to exist. And so people tend more and more to touch each other with that externally established functional part of the self, that part of the self that has the right to exist, while their individually human parts, for which no legitimate place is provided in our social structure, become increasingly isolated, unrelated and alienated from each other.

The disruption or curtailment of common human *language,* the dispersion of language into manifold remoteness from the human center, has its share in the estrangement between human beings. We scarcely have a common human language any longer. Various collectively sectional vocabularies have developed a multitude of scientific, technological, professional, commercial and journalistic slangs, and that means so many fractional abstractions. The very same term has split into most diverse significations as used in different fields and contexts. The result is that Tower of Babel situation that makes it difficult sometimes to carry on a discussion of general problems without first defining terms, digging all too deep into the meaning of formerly unequivocal words. On the other hand, it happens that plain, ordinary people in extraordinary moments of life, when it is a matter of conveying human feelings, are afraid and somewhat ashamed of using natural human language. They are unable to express themselves otherwise than through shy little gestures because their true and familiar language is a functional lingo. Just the simplest and most direct human words take on for them a pompous and insincere tinge.

The *artist,* the *poet,* whose age-old vocation to explore and express the human condition predisposes him to provide in his work and language a common human meeting place, is burdened more heavily than anyone by this alienation. In his effort to reach into common human ground, to reassemble the deviated minds in the human center, he has to penetrate and somehow comprehend so many social and psychic complexities that he is forced to develop his own kind of abstraction, symbolic and parabolic abstraction, which again alienates him from the human community. The alienation of the artist is only a symptom and symbol of the alienation of the individual human being for whom the artist stands and whose last bastion he is. With this particular form of alienation we shall be dealing at a later point in this book and there we shall see how it leads further to the alienation of human existence proper.

The history of man could very well be written as a history of the alienation of man.

IT REMAINS TO POINT to certain *trends in modern literature and art* registering the tendency toward collectivization. The first indications of such a trend may be found far back in the nineteenth century, in Balzac's and Dickens' sociological digressions, and later in Zola's experimental novels and Tolstoy's *War and Peace,* which show in different ways the collectivistic widening of the narrative. Both Zola, in his attempt to make the novel scientific, and Tolstoy, in his attempt to unfold the historic panorama of a gigantic national event thereby illuminating all its social strata, deal no longer as much with individual destinies *per se* as with the interrelation and interdependence between individual and collective happenings. When we compare Stendhal's treatment of the Napoleonic Wars in his *Chartreuse de Parme* (1839) with that of Tolstoy in *War and Peace* (1866) we notice the increased importance which social groups have assumed in Tolstoy's great novel.

In our day, this collectivizing trend has produced a whole new genre, which could be called novelistic reportage, presenting through a novelistic medium accounts of catastrophes, collective events and milieus. Examples, standing for many more of this kind, are: in the United States, Norman Mailer's *The Naked and the Dead* and James Jones's *From Here to Eternity*; in France, David Rousset's *Les jours de notre mort* and Marcel Aymé's *Uranus*; in Germany, Plievier's *Stalingrad* and Bruno Werner's *Galeere*; in

Italy, Silone's *Fontamara,* and Carlo Levi's *Cristo si è fermato a Eboli.*

The same tendency manifests itself from the reverse angle in stories describing the loneliness and forsakenness of the individual amidst our mercilessly overpowering group standards, or his inescapable subjection to them: stories such as Salinger's, discussed earlier, Saul Bellow's *Dangling Man,* Richard Wright's *Outsider,* Ralph Ellison's *Invisible Man,* and others.

Certain developments in the drama are even more pronounced. They are also much more interesting because here the limitations inherent in the genre necessitate a special kind of abstraction, namely, *typification.* A type is a collective abstraction. In naturalistic drama (such as Gerhart Hauptmann's *Die Weber* and *Florian Geyer* and Galsworthy's *Strife*) the protagonists were no longer individuals, but groups. This proved quite unmanageable dramatically. In German expressionist theater, however, in the plays of Georg Kaiser, Ernst Toller, Bertolt Brecht and others, some of which are extremely dramatic, groups are impersonated by immediate types.[22] Figures even lack individual names, appearing as "the executive," "the bank teller," "the worker," "the industrial engineer," "the revolutionary," and so on. The plays are enacted, as it were, by collective individuals. Arthur Miller's *Death of a Salesman* is, Willy Loman's personal tragedy notwithstanding, a clear step in this direction. In Sartre's *Le Diable et le Bon Dieu* the figures, although bearing names, are obvious abstractions.

A parallel to the collectivizing trend in literature can be observed in some products of the plastic arts, particularly in the group sculptures of Henry Moore and Kenneth Armitage. As compared with a plastic composition such as Rodin's *Bourgeois de Calais,* in which the group is still conceived as a combination and relationship of individual figures and forms clearly set apart as such, a group like Kenneth Armitage's *Family Going for a Walk* is seen as an immediately supra-individual unit. The same holds true of Henry Moore's figure combinations where the locus of gravity seems to have moved to the intricate interrelations of the periphery, a periphery which surrounds the lack of a center, an almost symbolically empty core. The technicalization of sections of our sculptural art, an entirely a-functional technicalization (i.e., mechanical constructions *per se*), is too obvious to require special demonstration.

WE SURVEYED the various forms of collectivization—scientification, specialization, functionalization, standardization, anonymization, commercialization—all of them originally springing from rationalization and technicalization and all of them splitting the individual, dividing him into a collective, functional part, and an individual, human part. The collective part keeps extending while the individual part increasingly shrinks. We also noted the psychic concomitants of these processes, the different forms of alienation and the anxiety and desolation they produce.

There are people who like to view the developments we observed as an exclusively and typically American phenomenon. I do not think that they are right. Such processes occur everywhere in our contemporary world to a larger or lesser degree. In the following chapter we shall see that they were pushed to much more extreme, much more horrible consequences in Germany. Today, America is simply the most accomplished exponent, the most advanced outpost of that ever-broadening general trend of Western civilization which may be characterized as *the extraversion of man*. America was, to be sure, predestined to play a particularly predominant role in this process: first, because she was indeed the only great nation which started out from a rational basis, in an age of rationalism and incipient science, and which was formed through explicit covenants and constitutions; and, second, because her settlers faced the tremendous task of penetrating, exploiting, making livable a vast and wild continent partly populated by hostile tribes. This task, up to the closing of the frontier, that is, up to the end of the nineteenth century, turned all their energies *outward* and absorbed all their attention. It necessarily called for the development of America's thorough-going capitalistic system of mass production and mechanization of techniques, goods and services which we see in full swing today. It instilled in the American people boundless confidence in rationalism, science and technology. And because of all this, America promoted immeasurably the extraversion of Western Man.

America, however, is not the *causa causarum*—if there is such a thing at all, which I doubt—America is not the originator of this great process. The origins may be found—if we have to predicate a beginning—in the rise of modern rational man from the depth of the Middle Ages. The productive side of this process—the enormous advances in man's outer conditions, health and hygiene, comforts, facilities, standards of living, and the rights of man—is an achievement which is praised every day of the week, and rightly so. But, as indicated before, the same development which extended the reach of man as a genus into previously inconceivable cosmic and psychic spheres escaped the control of individual man and like a Frankenstein threatens to tear him away, together with all the human values he stood for.

The whole development had a somewhat autonomous character; it went on and went beyond the personalities who formed it, although in the first centuries of the modern era, indeed, up to the nineteenth century, it was personalities, individuals, who carried it out. In those centuries government was the signorial affair of a few princes and statesmen; now it has become a huge anonymous apparatus. The magic and genius of one man was often decisive in military campaigns, trade and industry were in the hands of single powerful entrepreneurs; while today's armies are gigantic impersonal machineries, and business corporations are bureaucratic colossi. Inventions and discoveries, in their fundamental stage still interwoven with philosophical speculation, were so slow and scarce that their originators stand out in the memory of man like landmarks of humanity, a position which today only Einstein and Freud, and perhaps in a more restricted domain Niels Bohr have attained—and this not because today there are any fewer, but, on the contrary, because there are so many brilliant minds at work whose partial efforts concur in the extremely complex advances of our age. Science no longer moves in single strides from one man's to another man's personal thinking and searching; it has become an established wide-range collective institution, which progresses ceaselessly and collectively in a continuous flow of systematic discovery and invention. Any young scientist starting on his career today finds in his overspecialized field a set of problems prepared for him by the present stage of collective research. It is a far cry from the time when a man could endeavor to answer alone his personal intellectual questions and seek out fundamental solutions on his own. In science, too, the individual often works as in an assembly line and is considered easily replaceable. As Professor Richter of Johns Hopkins University said in a 1954 issue of *Science:* "Large funds encourage great enterprises, great experimental designs. They encourage 'great teams of workers' . . . they set up pressures that divert scientists from their own work to devote their energies to the projects of others. . . . It is the project, the design that counts. Who does the work is often relatively unimportant." [23]

This huge corpus of institutionalized knowledge of scientific findings and searchings which no single scientist can encompass within his grasp any longer—it is a truism that many scientists do not even know what goes on in their neighboring field—this huge corpus constitutes what I would call a *collective consciousness.* Knowledge is there, it *is* rational knowledge, ever on the move as it may be, but no individual at present can seize it in its entirety and understand its huge, dynamic network. It is known, but no single person knows it. This is particularly important to note because it reveals another tragic split in the modern personality. A man who formerly could try to find for himself an answer to his philosophico-scientific questions had some possibility of establishing connections between his personal life and his scientific problems; he was able to look for some rational coherence between his various concerns. Today the scientist is hardly in

a position to hope for such a coherence. And so it happens sometimes that a man is working in his laboratory or in his study on
the most intricate and subtle rational problems while politically
or personally he is completely emotional and lacks all common
sense. "Rational" is no longer identical with "reasonable," as
generations of rationalists liked to believe. Surely, there existed
such internal schisms before, as in the times of dual verities; but
at that time people struggled against, or in any case saw this
incompatibility clearly. Today they are hardly aware of the contradictions between one and the other sphere of their existence.
They live in what Hermann Broch called "the twilight condition,"
which is a general condition of man: Human inertia, human gravi-
tation toward habits, established circumstances and conventions—
this is the natural state of man; it keeps us moving in tracks and
under the spell of a benumbing routine. This human situation obtains even in the most rational, rationally defined mental states.
It is only in the rare moments of creation, in the shock and thrust
of genuine creation that man reaches the sublime flash of actual
clarity and freedom. Whenever conditions, methods of procedure,
modes of thinking become rigid, be they as rationally advanced as
they may, we are sunk in that "twilight condition," and it needs a
real effort, a creative effort, to attain the light of full awareness
and self-awareness again.

If we were able to know what we know, if we were able to see
our human situation as a whole, then, I believe, we would be saved.

CHAPTER THREE

The Split from Without: II

TOTALIZATION AND TERROR

Les hommes normaux ne savent pas que tout est possible. Même si les témoignages forcent leur intelligence à admettre, leurs muscles ne croient pas. Les concentrationnaires savent.

(The ordinary people don't know that everything is possible. Even when the testimonies compel their intelligence to admission, their muscles do not believe. The inmates know.)

DAVID ROUSSET

WE HAVE DISCUSSED the various forms of collectivization which have developed as a consequence of rationalization and technicalization. As we have seen, these various forms of collectivization produce, each in its own way, a split in the human personality; they divide the personality into a collective, functional part and an individual, human part.

The course of our analysis will now carry us a step further in this direction: from collectivization to totalization and its peculiar, horrible methods of disrupting the individual. I speak of "methods" because here we are no longer dealing with involuntary effects of social and economic processes, but with definite intentions on the part of the supreme collective, the state, to wreck the structure of the individual.

The study of this phenomenon takes us to Germany. Just as America appears to have been specially predisposed, by her origins and her tremendous tasks, to play such a prominent role in the extraversion of man and the multiform collectivization which this involved, so, in a similar way, Germany seemed predestined by her character and her history—for the history of a nation is nothing else than its character unfolded in time—to that particularly radical turn which the collectivistic tendency of our age took in that country. (The case of Russia is of a different nature, as we shall see later.)

Let it be emphasized from the outset that the story presented in the following pages is not directed against the German people as such and as a whole, nor should it be so interpreted. The purpose of our study makes it necessary to single out from a very complex character structure certain striking and relevant tendencies and their results. Although it is no accident that these things happened in Germany, it is, in the last analysis, irrelevant where they happened. Important alone is *that* they happened, and that they happened *in our epoch*. The stress must not be put on the fact that they happened among Germans, but rather on the fact that they happened among human beings.

THERE ARE two main historical determinants which set the Germans on their fateful road to totalization. One of them is the *special German disposition for total state control,* and the other is the likewise characteristically *German disposition for the splitting of personality*. The crucial figure in both these developments is Martin Luther.

From the outset, and throughout its course, German history has been a *history of splits,* beginning with the *Roman Limes* which cut the country into two sections, one Romanized and the other remaining thoroughly Nordic, carrying strong pagan and at least some semi-barbarian psychic undercurrents. Later, this geographical and cultural partition settled down and deepened into a religious rift between a Catholic and a Protestant region whose borderlines roughly coincide with the *Limes*; and in a secular age this schism took the form of ineradicable antagonism between two distinct mentalities and ways of life: a South- and West-German and a North-German one.

There is another *split between universal and national aims*. All other Western nations evolved from the basis of their own possessions, were they ever so small, pursuing their own specific interests, and gradually consolidating their national domain and personality. And only through the cultural and intellectual sublimation of their national concerns did they finally attain European, or even broadly human significance. All these nations, then, developed *centrifugally,* from their individual center, usually an established capital and royal residence, to their national, and finally European, or universal range. They developed as any being naturally tends to develop, as a child grows into a mature adult. The national concerns preceded universal involvements and gradually passed over into them; national aims did not contradict universal aims.

Conversely, Germany was, from the very beginning, tied up with a framework that was universal in scope. Complex circumstances imposed the inheritance of an overcivilized world empire on the semi-primitive German tribes who were wholly unprepared for the tremendous task of championing a universal idea. This produced a complete reversal of what should have been Germany's natural process of development. Her spontaneous evolution as a nation was stunted at the roots; foreign tasks and foreign interests kept absorbing the energies of her rulers before they were able to consolidate their rule at home. Here the universal aims preceded the national aims and were mostly in conflict with them. Germany, accordingly, developed *centripetally,* from the periphery of a vaguely outlined, substantially empty and disintegrated empire to the national core, the national consolidation, which was hardly ever reached; from the universal scope to the national concern.

National integration was the end instead of the beginning of German development; it was the eternal aim and not the point of departure. It lay in the future and not in the past and, accordingly, was not the substratum of an unconsciously sustaining national tradition; it was a consciously strived-for objective. Even the external unification of Germany was only achieved in 1871 and has been undone again in 1945. And even the German Reich of 1871, usually called the Second, but actually the first truly German Reich, represented only a state but not a nation.

Here we have one important result of the rift between the universal and the national. National consolidation being the goal and not the beginning of German development, it was inevitable that in that country nation fused with state, and was confused with state; *a community was immediately conceived as a collective.* The Germans believed that they could achieve nationality by means of the state: the stricter, the more rigid the control of the state, the firmer, the faster, so they thought, they would hold their nationality. This among other factors was the driving force that carried Prussia, and later Hitler, into power.

But that initial split between the universal and the national engendered countless further splits: there was the unparalleled *splitting and splintering of territories, authorities, rights and claims* due to the incompletion of the feudal system in Germany, which, in turn, was a result of the incapacity of the ever-campaigning emperors to perpetuate a dynasty and to curb their peers. All human dependencies, dependencies originally based on human relationships, between lord and vassal, official and subject, landed proprietor and servant, were being cut off from their human source, from their personal, traditional holders, and became loose, detached, impersonal rights or claims, which could be bartered, mortgaged, given in fief and sub-fief, and so forth. All this eventually brought about that famous German *Kleinstaaterei,* the fateful dispersion and splintering of territories and dominions under a motley multiplicity of little rulers, which broke up all organic, ethnic coherence of lands and populations.

There was, in addition, the *split between city and country,* between burghers and noblemen. The cities developed rather late on purely economic lines: no capital city, no permanent royal residence could establish itself to serve as a nucleus for a leading national society and a forming national tradition. Every little knight in his castle wanted to be a ruler by himself. Up to the fifteenth century the noblemen refused to descend into the cities and to participate in commerce and learning.

The royal and princely courts of the Western and Southern nations were the leaders not only of social life but of intellectual life as well; in fact, one was inseparable from the other. Intellectual life was an integral part of the new courtly civilization, and a link between the different social ranks and classes. In this way the intelligentsia moved in a wide social arena and gained a proper sense of national and public affairs; ideology and reality were well balanced and connected in the mind. And the ruling class, on the other hand, was taught by tradition to appreciate the values of matters cultural. In Germany, the boorishness, the stubborn anti-urbanity and anti-intellectualism of the nobility left the cities to pursue their narrow economic aims and to develop a pure-bred middle-class spirit which took the lead in intellectual life and, later, through the channels of Protestantism, in German life in general. It was a spirit fluctuating between the homely narrowness of parochial surroundings and the suspended infinity of fantasy and speculation, between pedantry and romanticism. Such sharp contrasts are quite manifest in German literature and German painting, where the minute elaboration of details, an excessive closeness to the visual material, clashes harshly at times with the irruption of the infinite and the spiritual. We find these combinations in the narrative of Grimmelshausen and in the novels of Jean Paul. And one recalls Grünewald's picture of Holy Mary on the Isenheim altar, where the Madonna is seen sitting with little Jesus in her arms surrounded by her homely utensils, bed, tub and chamberpot, in the midst of a cosmic scenery with God the Father radiant through the clouds and angels playing and flying about. Such

abrupt alternating of realism and transcendentalism, frequently inherent in the very concept of earlier German painting, later occurs
as stylistic treatment in such painters as Philipp Otto Runge and
Otto Dix.

That early split between nobility and middle class laid the
ground for the extreme departmentalization and functionalization
of German society and for the social homelessness of the intellectual. One of Germany's greatest poets, in fact one of the world's
greatest poets, Hölderlin, pictures the situation in the famous
lament of his Hyperion: "It is a bitter word, and still I have to say
it, because it is the truth: I could not imagine a people more torn
than the Germans. You see craftsmen, but no human beings,
thinkers, but no human beings, priests, but no human beings,
masters and servants, people young and old, but no human beings. Does this not resemble a battlefield where arms and hands and
all limbs are strewn about in fragments while the shed blood of life
soaks into the sand?"

Finally, there is Martin Luther, whose fateful influence on
German development cannot be overrated. He is the actual shaper
of modern Germany: the Germans after Luther were a different
people from what they had been before. Luther established, at one
stroke, the specifically authoritarian mentality of German governments, and the specifically submissive state of mind of the German
middle class, the *Obrigkeit* and the *Untertan*. The peculiar form
and extent of state control in the Prussia of Frederick William I
is inconceivable without Luther. This, however, is not the whole
story.

Luther was foremost a theologian. His real concerns were
strictly religious, and he did not at all like to overstep the religious
domain and interfere with worldly affairs, which, however, he was
constantly forced to do. This sharp separation of religious and
practical life, which distinguished Luther from Calvin, followed
from his basic Pauline tenet, from the belief that had freed him
from the agony of his youth, the feeling of ineradicable sinfulness:[1]
justification by faith and by faith alone, as against justification by

works, which at that time meant Church services and services rendered to the Church. The protest against the misuse of these "holy works" confirmed Luther in his overemphasis on faith and on the unmediated grace of an omnipotent, indeed, almost arbitrary God. And since the authority of the Church was to be denied and removed, and since there had to be an authority on earth, he turned this authority over to the secular rulers. Thus, the liberation from the rule of the Church, the "freedom of Christian man," meant in reality a twofold submission: submission to the inscrutable will of God, which could only be derived from His word in the Bible, and submission to the rule of secular authority, which was supposed to have been instituted by God as a perpetual rod of correction for sinful, inordinate man. In point of fact, however, submission to the word of God—which is identical with faith— has remained entirely within the spiritual, theoretical sphere, the inner sphere of man, while outwardly, in practical life, it could only express itself through civic obedience, through compliance with the commands of God-authorized secular authority. In other words, there was no way of living one's faith in action other than conformity to current middle-class morality and submission to the will and whims of the rulers.

In such a way Luther deepened the old Christian rift between soul and body into a radical split: he divided the human being into a spiritual, theoretical section, and a physical, practical section; into an inner, entirely theoretical freedom and an outer, practical subjection to a worldly authority which was even worse than the quasi-spiritual authority of the Church. Man was believed to consist of a double nature, spiritual and corporeal; and these two were opposed to each other, the spirit fighting the flesh, and the flesh fighting the spirit. And from this Luther concluded: "But it is clear that external things have no effect on Christian liberty. . . . Good works," he says, "do not make a good man, but a good man produces good works." There is certainly some truth in that, inasmuch as it is the spirit, the intention of a man that counts. And yet it is only partly true since good acts, in turn, are capable of developing the taste for the good, for the beauty of goodness. And if you keep teaching people that it is only faith that counts, it induces them to take acts lightly, and this is what actually happened with the Germans. The consequences of this attitude became manifest even in Luther's time in the theoretical disputes of the Antinomian sect who denied the relevance of the Biblical law for the faithful. They made themselves increasingly felt in German public life with generations of Protestant ministers teaching the people to accept, without as much as a whimper, whatever their governments imposed upon them. And the climax of Lutheranism may be found in the behavior of Pastor Niemoeller who swallowed all the Nazi atrocities until the doctrine of the Protestant faith itself was jeopardized. Only then did he take a stand against the Hitler regime.

Luther encouraged the secular rulers in an unlimited use of their prerogatives and, as if he had not done enough for them, he helped them with an additional distinction between the official function of the ruler and his private personality. He severed the function from the man: "A prince can be a Christian," he wrote, "but he is not bound to rule as a Christian. . . . His personality is Christian, but his office or principality has no concern with his being a Christian." [2] To what extremes Luther was driven by his cutting the human being into separate sections can be seen from his furious arguments against the peasants' attempts to free themselves from bondage: "There is to be no bondage, since Christ has freed us all? What is all this? This only makes Christian freedom fleshly! This is therefore against the Gospels, it is an act of piracy, in that each one robs his master of his body.[3] . . . All this talk is directed toward making men equal and making a worldly, external kingdom of the spiritual kingdom of Christ. And this is impossible. For a worldly kingdom can not persist unless there is inequality, so that some are free and others captive, some are lords and others subjects." [4] He even went so far as to forbid the Christians, enslaved by the Turks, to strive for their freedom. "For you are robbing and stealing your body from your master, your body, that he has bought or acquired in some other way, so that it be no longer yours, but his property, like cattle or other goods." [5] *Like cattle or other goods* . . . splitting the personality took Luther pretty far ahead into the German future!

Thus both trends, the tendency toward total state control and the tendency toward invalidation and disruption of the personality are present and intricately interconnected in Luther's doctrine.

What happened next was this: The chaotic condition of the Holy Roman Empire, the multiplicity and ethnic incoherence of dominions, the lack of a national tradition, of a national society and style of life, the complexity and instability of people's circumstances, produced at first an extreme individualism. Luther had paralyzed outer life, practical political life, community life, by depriving it of all avenues of expression and had referred man exclusively to his inner sphere. As a consequence, this inner life, the famous German *Innerlichkeit,* began to sprout emotionally as well as intellectually, and opened up into boundless imagination and speculation, into a striving toward abstract universal ideals. This became a pervasive characteristic of German philosophy, German classic and romantic literature. In the sphere of active life, it served merely to further complicate the German situation. And if, as we shall see later, there exist in our age many general motivations for the profound feeling of insecurity and desolation in the individual, for the desire to "escape from freedom," the Germans certainly had their additional, particular reasons for such a state of mind. Just because the Germans, in the midst of their complexities, were such lonely, such absolute individuals, they were the first and foremost to yearn for the status of rank and file, for putting an end to all problems and impossible decisions by unconditional obedience to a command. It is the same impulse that also drives them to seek an inner support in work, exacting work which silences all personal thinking. When Hermann Rauschning, former Nazi chief of Danzig, after having deserted Hitler and escaped to this country, was asked by reporters why he had joined the party in the first place, he answered: "In the presence of Hitler everything seemed so simple and, you know, we are such a complicated people!"

The German poet Immermann in his novel, *Münchhausen* (1839), tells a little story, a very German story, illustrating the grotesque perplexities in which Germans could get involved: During the Napoleonic Wars, a German captain served in the French army until the battle of Leipzig. He fought so bravely that he was awarded the Legion of Honor. Afterward, when his army corps was dissolved, he joined the Prussian army, and again he did so well that he got the Iron Cross. At the termination of the war he was seized with an inner cleavage and confusion which drove him almost insane. He could not "harbor it in himself" (*in sich beherbergen*) that within a year he had been a valiant Frenchman and a valiant Prussian, that "until October he had to scourge *la perfidie du cabinet de Berlin,* and after October he had to save the Fatherland." So he fixed himself two rooms, one French, containing all kinds of Napoleonic paraphernalia, and the other Prussian, exhibiting all kinds of German military trophies, and lived alternately one week in the former and one week in the latter. In the French room he assembled all the souvenirs of the French Empire and in the Prussian room he kept pictures and books concerning the German wars of liberation. In this way, so Immermann puts it, "he established a military order in his memories." [6]

The perpetual fragmentation of the German situation probably is responsible for another kind of incongruity in Germans, a peculiar psychic incoherence which has been frequently noted. An interesting case of this sort is described by Jean Stafford in her story "The Maiden." [7] Here, a charming and sensitive German couple, deeply in love and utterly sympathetic, is discovered to have shown an amused callousness toward a most gruesome execution of some poor devil, the husband's first legal case, to which he had been invited as a special guest. Ceremonially dressed in all the prescribed finery, he found this bloody spectacle so elating that immediately after the gory deed he proposed to his future wife. The delight and relish he shows while recounting this happy memory at a dinner party estranges and dumfounds an American girl present, who had before been completely enchanted, almost in love, with that endearing and delightful couple.

THE FIRST FORM in which the *total state* appeared—the total state, not just an authoritarian state—was Prussia under King Frederick William I (1713-1740). It was just as much an exemplification of Luther's doctrine as it was a prefiguration of the Third Reich. In other countries during that period the power of the state interfered with the lives of its subjects rather casually and arbitrarily, according to the caprice of the rulers. Here, in Frederick William's Prussia, the power of the state was systematically organized, was made into a gapless institutional system. What is particularly striking as anticipating Nazi rule is the levelling down, in certain respects, of the old feudal and official ranks before the law which was identified with the interests of the state. For instance, recruiting by force, as well as corporal punishment, was applied not only to peasants and "people of mean extraction," but also to the sons of nobles. The king's police took them forcibly from their estates and families into the cadet corps. Another feature reminiscent of the Nazis was the new drilling methods deliberately designed to break the individual will and to produce uniformity of collective functioning, irrespective of tactical need. Here too, officers were subject to no less rigid discipline than the privates; they had to live with their soldiers, unlike French officers who lived at the royal court. They had to wear uniforms all the time. The most minute details of their life were regulated and controlled: their religion, their social intercourse, their expenditures. Even royal princes underwent exactly the same treatment. The regulations of 1726 read: "When one takes the oath to the flag, one renounces oneself and surrenders entirely, even one's life and all, to the monarch, in order to fulfill the Lord's will; and through this blind obedience one receives the grace and the confirmation of the title of soldier." [8] Unannounced inspectors and spies checked up on the reliability of officials. An official guilty of false reports, delays or bribery, was publicly struck in the face and imprisoned for life, if not hanged.

Craftsmen, farmers and experts in special fields were trans-planted by force from one province or district to another, according to economic need. Even a project for the systematic breeding of a new, particularly vigorous race of men was started by Frederick William I. Especially robust human specimens, grenadiers and Dutch peasant girls, were selected and ordered to marry and pro-duce many children. Human beings were treated "like cattle," or other state material. Cultural life was similarly controlled. The sci-ences were promoted only in so far as they could serve official pur-poses. It was only with difficulty that the King could be prevented from abolishing the Academy of Science which his father had founded on the French pattern. The funds necessary for its main-tenance, which he considered entirely superfluous, he entered under the heading "Expenditures for the King's Fools." (The Nazis, similarly, scorned the *Intelligenzbestien,* "intellectual beasts.") Theological controversies were prohibited. "Salvation in heaven is God's province; all the rest is mine." This was the strictly Lutheran device of Frederick William I.

Now, the Third Reich was certainly not such a paragon of rigor-ous order as this Prussian state had been. The Nazi Reich arose from a variety of origins and had a much more complex character; its totalitarianism was intermingled with romantic savagery and even authorized corruption. In fact, it would be more correct to say that the brutish drives, the atrocities and the corruption, were built in, were as such deliberately incorporated into the state sys-tem; they were wilfully institutionalized: irrationality and inco-herence themselves were rationalized. Only to the extent that the Nazi Reich was totalitarian, that it used coercion, organization, comprehensive systematization, only insofar did it follow and carry to the extreme the old Prussian pattern. The rest, however, was new and produced entirely novel psychic phenomena.

Toward the end of the nineteenth century, the Prussian historian Heinrich von Treitschke formulated the principle of the Prussian state as follows: "The core of the state is power. The state is not there for the citizens. It is an end in itself. Since the state is power, it obviously can draw into its sphere of influence all human activities in so far as they are apparent in the external lives of men. . . . Under certain conditions, the state will control human life as much as it is able to do." [9]

Such "certain conditions" presented themselves after the First World War, when the Germans had undergone three devastating experiences: defeat, inflation, unemployment. This was the setting from which the Nazis embarked on their vast adventure of power, and for its smooth internal operation they needed really total, outer and inner standardization, a streamlining, *Gleichschaltung,* of the people. And in their effort to secure this *Gleichschaltung,* the Nazis indeed discovered new methods of control, extending the sway of the state over spheres of human life which had never before been accessible to such external control. Compared with these new methods those of old Prussia seem infantile. To be sure, the Nazis were able to profit from the technological and socio-psychological innovations of our time: radio, modern arms, military and industrial techniques, new police methods and police controls, and the lesson of Russia's revolutionary secret police whose range of activity, as is well known, by far surpassed even that of the Czarist *ochrana.* Nevertheless, some of the new instruments of state control were genuine Nazi inventions. One, the most effective, was the systematization of Terror.

TERROR as such is, of course, not new. It formed part of the French as well as of the Russian Revolution, not only as an effect, or by-effect, of revolutionary action, as a revolutionary act itself, but also as an intentional deterrent used against the opponents of the movements, or to whip up the fury of the people. In 1793 the Hébertist Royer harangued the Jacobins: *"Qu'on place la Terreur à l'ordre du jour! C'est le seul moyen de donner l'éveil au peuple et de le forcer à se sauver lui-même!"* ("Make terror the order of the day! It's the only means to arouse the people and to compel it to save itself!") The Terror in Russia has wiped out almost the whole of Russian nobility and Czarist officialdom. Here, as everywhere, this ghastly revolutionary practice made no distinction as to individual guilt; it only knew class guilt, collective guilt. But in Russia, as in France, the Terror started in reaction to setbacks and counterrevolutionary moves; in France four years, in Russia eight months after the actual overthrow of the old regime. In Russia it was later suspended for a period of six years— between 1922 and 1928. In 1931, when the battle over collectivization was at its peak, the dramatist Alexander Afinogeniev wrote a play called *Fear,* in which the subject is treated from what is doubtless an official, or officially approved, point of view. In this play, an old woman, member of the Commission of Party Control, declares: "When we break the resistance of the last oppressor on earth, then our children will look for the explanation of the word 'fear' in a dictionary." And she adds that the Terror has been tolerated because it has not touched the masses. When and if it touches them the regime will be in danger.[10] So, however horrible the results, French and Russian Terror was directed against actual or potential enemies of the regime, or scapegoats substituted for these enemies.

The Nazis, in contradistinction, not only started with the use of terror even before they had risen to power, indeed, from the very beginning of the movement, but with them terror acquired a new meaning and purpose. For this Hitler himself is responsible. He wanted to use terror not merely against opponents, and not merely as a deterrent, or momentary stimulant, but as a permanent educational instrument aimed at the German people as a whole— followers as well as enemies—for the purpose of extirpating inconvenient values. The concentration camps were intended not only to "break the prisoners as individuals" and to "spread terror among the rest of the population by using the prisoners as hostages for good behavior," but also to "provide the Gestapo members with a training ground in which they are so educated that they lose all human emotions and attitudes." [11]

In his talks with Rauschning, even before his rise to the chancellorship, Hitler said: "We must be ruthless. We must regain our clear conscience as to ruthlessness. Only thus shall we purge our people of their softness and sentimental philistinism, of their *Gemütlichkeit* and their degenerate delight in beer-swilling. We have no time any more for fine sentiments." And later again: "I don't want the concentration camps transformed into penitentiary institutions. Terror is the most effective political instrument. I shall not permit myself to be robbed of it simply because a lot of stupid, bourgeois mollycoddlers choose to be offended by it. It is my duty to make use of every means of training the German people to cruelty, and to prepare them for war. . . . A violently active, dominating, intrepid, brutal youth—that is what I am after. Youth must be all this. It must be indifferent to pain. There must be no weakness or tenderness in it. I want to see once more in its eyes the gleam of pride and independence of the beast of prey. . . . Anybody who is such a poltroon that he can't bear the thought of someone nearby having to suffer pain had better join a sewing circle, but not my party." [12]

The impact of Nietzschean, Wagnerian, Spenglerian ideas is all too obvious in these pronouncements which clearly reveal the ultimate motives of the Nazis' institutionalization of terror: that is, of atrocities and horrors, meticulously designed and bureaucratically administered. This systematization and bureaucratization of crime and its quasi-pedagogical motive, this is one of the novel features of Nazi terror.

Equally novel are the disruptive effects of this use of terror on the structure of personality. Here we have to distinguish between the premeditated effects on victims and potential victims, that is, on the people at large, and effects developing automatically in the perpetrators of the atrocities. These two kinds of effects are different in character. What the Nazi terror intentionally did to victims, in concentration camps or Gestapo cellars, was an outright destruction of personality, destruction not only of the person's life, but of his mind and identity. What it produced in the executors of these horrors, on the other hand, was a peculiar kind of schizophrenia.[13] These two different effects, on victims and on executors, are, as far as I can see, entirely new. Hardly anything like it has ever happened before.

LET US FIRST briefly consider the *effects on victims*. They are most exhaustively described in an article called "Terror's Atomization of Man" by Leo Lowenthal.[14] "Terror," Lowenthal says, "accomplishes its work of dehumanization through the total integration of the population into collectivities, then depriving them of the psychological means of direct communication in spite of— or rather because of—the tremendous communications apparatus to which they are exposed. The individual under terrorist conditions is never alone and always alone. He becomes numb and rigid not only in relation to his neighbor but also in relation to himself; fear robs him of the power of spontaneous emotional or mental reaction. Thinking becomes a stupid crime; it endangers his life."

The main features of Nazi terror in action, according to Lowenthal, are the following: "1—*Directness and Omnipotence*. One of the basic functions of terror is to wipe out the rational connection between government decisions and individual fate. The wholesale arrests of people during the first stages of totalitarian terror, the mixing in the concentration camps of the most diverse elements of the population for the most diverse reasons, fulfills precisely this function of elimination of individual differences and claims before the apparatus of power. The qualitative difference between the imprisoned lawbreaker and the rest of the population does not exist between the victims of terror within the concentration camps and those outside. The principle of selection of the forced workers of the camps is direct terroristic calculation. They are in the majority trapped in mass arrests, with no question of individual guilt involved and no hope of limited punishment. . . . This interruption of the causal relation between what a person does and what happens to him fulfills one of the chief aims of modern terror. . . . 2—*The Breakdown of the Continuum of Experience*. With the breakdown of legal rationality and its clear relation to the individual fate, this fate itself becomes so enigmatic as to lose all meaning. The individual does not know what he may experience; and what he has already experienced is no longer important for his person or his future. The normal rhythm of youth, manhood, old age, of education, career, success or failure, is completely disrupted. The creative faculties of fantasy, imagination, memory, become meaningless and tend to atrophy where they can no longer bring about any desired change in the individual's fate. . . . Thus life becomes a chain of expected, avoided or materialized shocks, and thus the atomized experiences heighten the atomization of the individual. . . . In a terrorist society, in which everything is most carefully planned, the plan for the individual is—to have none; to become and to remain a mere object, a bundle of conditioned reflexes which amply respond to a series of manipulated and calculated shocks. 3—*The Breakdown of Personality*. In a system which reduces life to a chain of disconnected reactions to shock, personal communication tends to lose all meaning. The super-ego —the agency of conscience—in which people have stored the mechanism of moral decency, is repressed by what I may call a Hitler-ego, meaning that the inhibitions produced by conscience yield to inhibitions or drives produced by mechanical reactions and imitations. [This belongs to what in the present study has been termed "the collective unconscious."] Neither the terrorized nor the terrorist is any longer a personality in the traditional sense. They are mere material conforming to situations created by power utterly independent of themselves. An underground report by a prisoner escaped from Oswiecim (Auschwitz) tells how the camp system 'destroyed every social tie in a victim and reduced his spiritual life to a fear-driven desire to prolong existence, be it only for a day or an hour.' And a keen observer with personal experience in two camps, Dr. Bruno Bettelheim, now with the University of Chicago, has studied this deterioration to its end in loss of the vital passions: 'This outside world which continued to live as if nothing had happened was in the minds of the new prisoners represented by those whom they used to know, namely, by their relatives and friends. But even this hatred was very subdued in the old prisoners. It seemed that, as much as they had forgotten to love their kin, they had lost the ability to hate them . . . they were unable to feel strongly about anybody.' (Individual and Mass Behavior in Extreme Situations, *Journal of Abnormal and Social Psychology,* 1943.) A similar shrinking of the personality to a cluster of conditioned reflexes has been observed among the guards. In his report, 'A Year in Treblinka,' Yankel Wiernik describes the practitioners of terror as automata devoid of passion or remorse, who performed their given tasks as soon as some higher-up pressed a button. . . . These automata themselves . . . admit the most atrocious crimes but show not the slightest sense of guilt. Their inhuman conduct was justified, they maintain, because it was ordered by their superiors. 4—*The Struggle for Survival.* 'The urge of self-preservation, bestial fear, hunger and thirst led to a complete transformation of the majority of the prisoners. . . . In many cases the sense of responsibility toward others disappeared entirely, as well as the least feeling of consideration of their common lot. Many a prisoner carried on a wild, ruthless, and thoroughly senseless struggle for his individual survival.' (Kurt Bondy, 'Problems of Internment Camps,' *Journal of Abnormal and Social Psychology,* 1943.) 5—*Reduction to Natural Material.* What the terrorist masters fear most is that their victims may recover their awareness of belonging to a whole, to human history. The complete victory of totalitarianism would be identical with the complete forgetting of history; that is, with a mankind become void of reflection, or in other words with a mankind solely become natural material. . . . Mankind, having become domesticated again, becomes part of the overabundance of nature. It thus becomes material indeed, for exploitation where needed and for annihilation where not—in any case, mere material to be *processed.* Modern terror always looks at people with the eyes either of the big monopolist surveying raw materials or of the undertaker anticipating the disposal of the useless human corpse. . . . There is a striking analogy between this treatment of human beings and that of merchandise shipped into the inventory rooms of a large department store or factory. It is a planful handling of materials for certain purposes. According to the witnesses, the system became so streamlined that only the really useful human merchandise was tagged. He who got no number was a reject; he was disposed of. And as in any oversized administrative unit, no one cared to take the blame for mistakes. Even if the merchandise had been rejected by mistake, it was destroyed. 'Since the prisoners were checked according to numbers and not according to their names, an error could easily be made which would be disastrous. If the 'block-writer' had marked 'dead' a number which in reality was still alive—a thing which can happen in these extreme cases of great mortality—the mistake was corrected by putting to death the holder of the number.' ('Die Judenausrottung in Polen,' *Augenzeugenberichte, Dritte Serie,* Geneva, 1944.) 6—*Assimilation to the Terrorists.* Terror reaches its peak of success when the victim loses his awareness of the gulf between himself and his tormentors. With the complete breakdown of the personality the most primitive historical force, imitation, becomes openly prevalent in the dehumanized atmosphere of totalitarianism. This ultimate stage in regression is described by Dr. Bettelheim: 'A prisoner had reached the final stage of adjustment to the camp situation when he had changed his personality so as to accept as his own the values of the Gestapo. . . . Old prisoners who seemed to have a tendency to identify themselves with the Gestapo did so not only in respect to aggressive behavior. They would try to arrogate to themselves old pieces of Gestapo uniforms. . . . This identification with their torturers went so far as copying their leisure-time activities. One of the games played by the guards was to find out who could stand to be hit longest without uttering a complaint. This game was copied by the old prisoners, as though they had not been hit often enough without needing to repeat this experience as a game.'[15] Other problems in which most old prisoners made their peace with the values of the Gestapo included the race problem, although race discrimination had been alien to their scheme of values before they were brought into the camp. Can one imagine a greater triumph for any system than this adoption of its values and behavior by its powerless victims?"

All these effects are not confined to the actual victims—the inmates of concentration camps—but the whole population to a certain degree becomes a victim of these methodical practices. The terror extended from the concentration camps to the German people at large: "If a group of the population got fed up with the Nazi regime, a selected few members of this group would be brought into the concentration camp. If lawyers became restless, a few hundred lawyers were sent to the camp; the same happened to physicians when the medical profession seemed rebellious etc." [16]

It is well known how the elementary community, the family, was broken up by the terror-loaded Nazi collectivities, how youth was regimented and children trained to inform on their parents. People acquired what has been called *der deutsche Blick,* the German look, that uneasy gazing around for suspected spies.

BUT NOW we come to a phenomenon which has much broader significance. It concerns a peculiar mode of *behavior on the part of the executors* of the Nazi crimes, a novel kind of schizophrenia which, in a rudimentary or potential form, is present everywhere in our modern civilization, but has grown to extremes only in the Nazi situation. If we want to understand clearly the novel character of this phenomenon, we have first to dispose of possible confusions. In comparing recent happenings with apparently similar ones of previous ages, the most careful attention must be given to particularities of cultural stage and environment, to motives and mentalities which alone determine the meaning of happenings. First of all, when we consider these phenomena, what matters is not the degree of cruelty, or even the nature of the atrocities as such. History, needless to say, abounds with cruelty and with the most hideous acts of men. The execution of Damiens, the man who attacked Louis XV with a knife, will forever remain a landmark of unsurpassable human cruelty. It was clearly an exhibition of sadism, accompanied as it was by sexual pleasures between the attending ladies and gentlemen of the court. Nor are we concerned with the quantity of victims. At the beginning of the thirteenth century, the victorious sweep of the Mongols under Genghis Khan through the Middle East, Southern Russia and Northern India was connected with a mass-annihilation of tribes and cities, which up to our time stood out as the largest massacres known in history. They were probably exceeded only in our last decades by the Nazis' extermination of millions of Jews, Gypsies, Krimchaks, Poles, Russians, and so forth, and by the mechanical mass extermination of whole cities and populations in modern warfare, not to speak of what may still be in store for mankind, thanks to the relentless efforts of nuclear and biological laboratories.

Therefore, a superficial glance could induce us to see in the Nazi acts merely an increase in the amount of victims. It could be argued that in the past as well as in the present we have had mass atrocities. What difference can there be, except, maybe, in numbers? There are, however, striking differences. The massacres of the thirteenth century were committed by semi-nomadic hordes who had not yet undergone the smoothing and sensibilizing effects of a world religion, who had never been taught the special dignity of the human being, the human quality common to all men, which alone makes individual life precious. Hence, the Mongol atrocities did not constitute a slump from a higher to a lower level, a regression from a broader to a narrower scope of life. Even such advanced civilizations as the Greek and the Roman lacked until late that experience of a common humanity; the so called in-group-out-group relationship—to make use of the sociological jargon—the relationship between Greek, or Roman, and barbarian, was not a mere group difference within the same pale, but a difference between two levels of existence; therefore slavery with all its implications could appear legitimate even to the noblest minds of antiquity.

Moreover, we have to consider that at certain points, and particularly in combination with mechanization and systematization, increase in quantity turns into change of quality. In a single act of murder the destruction of human life may still rebound with its full value from the victim to the slayer. Even in barbarian sagas recounting a savage fight between two warriors—for instance in the moving Old High German song of Hildebrand, the Old English song relating the Battle of Brunanburh or the Irish tale of Cu Chulainn's Fight at the Ford (in the *Ulster Cycle*)—we sense the pulsation of human feelings. In a massacre, the real depth of destruction and suffering cannot be taken in by any individual mind any longer. The Mongols were able at least to refer to the city they destroyed as a *Mou-baligh,* a city of agonies. But the step from hand-to-hand killing to modern regularized mass production of horrors and mass extermination by mechanical weapons brings about such a thorough depreciation of human life that the person who launches a bomb by pushing a button, or the general or states-man who directs the slaughter from afar, faces only targets and numbers, and must, by necessity, lose the ability to value and distinguish human beings.

In an interview, American pilots in Korea spoke of the "mis-understanding between ground and air," of the "abstract view of ground life" they acquired. The reporter, for the sake of contrast, recalled a situation in the Spanish-American War where the com-mander of the battleship *Texas* reprimanded his sailors for being so elated after they had finished off an enemy ship. "Don't cheer, boys," the captain said, "the poor devils are dying." A similar story is related of Napoleon at the battle of Leipzig. The pilots' reports, on the other hand, as issued by the Air Force's public-relations people, "give one the impression that Korea is looked on mainly as a shooting gallery and that fliers have little thought for the mortals broiling in the napalm below. 'When we take a wounded Chinese prisoner on the ground,' the pilots said, 'we smother him with good medical care, but when we are aloft, we become impersonal.' " "Of course," the reporter added, "the pilots involved are, seen close to, the warmest human beings imaginable." [17]

Here we are at the threshold of the new psychic phenomenon

which concerns us. In the case of the fliers in Korea, the incongruity is due to a modern technical situation. The temporary callousness of the pilots is brought about by the abstractness of their visual range. This incongruity turns into schizophrenia when it establishes itself within the human mind. Traces of such happenings are observable everywhere in modern life, but this state of mind assumed monstrous proportions under the impact of Nazi indoctrination. Here are a few examples out of a host of material available.

The first case concerns an incident which occurred during the punitive (erroneously punitive) action carried out by the Elite Guards against the little French town of Oradour-sur-Glane. "The peak of horror," said the Swiss informant, Ernst von Schenck,[18] "is not reached by the fact that as an act of revenge, a whole town has been reduced to ashes, the entire male population shot and all women and children locked up and burned in the church. If such a thing had been done in a delirium of hatred, aroused by a savage fight, it would have been gruesome enough, but somehow humanly understandable. . . . But the Elite Guards who had received this order . . . carried it out with utter calmness and placidity (*seelenruhig*). They assembled the women and children with pronounced kindness. The mothers were moved by so much tender care on the part of these dreaded men who were hugging and fondling the children, playing and joking with them, taking them gently into their arms or putting them carefully into the perambulators. Their behavior was such that the mothers followed them confidently into the church as if they all went to some feast of atonement. After all the women and children had gathered in the church the doors were closed and the mass murder began."

"I am convinced," Mr. von Schenck continues, "that these Elite Guards did not feel the slightest shade of hatred against the French children when they held them in their arms. Some of them, in this moment, might even have thought of home and might have toyed with the idea of fondling their own child. And I am equally convinced that, if a counter order had arrived . . . they would have continued to play daddy. . . . But, an order is an order. What

kind of human beings are these? . . ." Mr. von Schenck shudder-
ingly asks. "Here a limit has been reached where no analogy can
be found in the behavior of any other people up to this time and,
let us hope,—from now on."

The same uncanny suspension of all human sensibility can be
oberved in other situations of the greatest variety. In the Nürnberg trials of the *Einsatzkommandos* (operational details of the
S.D.—*Sicherheitsdienst*—police, designated for the extermination
of Jews, Gypsies, Communists, etc. behind the front of the advancing German armies in the East), "the defendants were," according to the text of the judgment from which I quote:[19]
"not untutored aborigines incapable of appreciation of the finer
values of life. . . . Each man at the bar has had the benefit of
considerable schooling. Eight are lawyers, one a university professor, another a dental physician, still another an expert on art.
. . . This group of educated and well-bred men does not even lack
a former minister, self-unfrocked though he was. It was indeed one
of the many remarkable aspects of this trial that the discussion of
enormous atrocities was constantly interspersed with the academic
titles of the persons mentioned as their perpetrators. . . . Most of
the defendants . . . came of devout parents. Some have told how
they were born in the country and that close to Nature, and at
their mother's knee, they learned the virtues of goodness, charity
and mercy. . . . Though they seemed not to see the frightful contrast between the events of their day and those precepts of the past,
yet they do recognize that the latter are still desirable. . . . Some
of the defendants called witnesses to testify to their good deeds. . . .
The pages of these testimonials fairly glitter with such phrases as,
'honest and truth-loving,' 'straight-thinking and friendly manner,'
'industrious, assiduous and good-natured,' 'of a sensitive nature.'
. . . Nor are the affidavits merely subjective in phrase. They point
out objectively what the defendants did in attacking injustice and
intolerance. . . . Ott, who enforced the Führer-order from beginning to end in Russia, was all kindness and gentleness to the
villagers of Gross-Biederstorff in the Lorraine. . . . Haensch

. . . was the epitome of charity in Denmark where the population in paeans of thanksgiving showered him with adulatory messages and bouquets of flowers. . . . Naumann befriended the Jews [in Holland], got them out of concentration camps and released hostages." In fact, "Most of the defendants in all these proceedings [at the Nürnberg trials] have expressed a great regard for the Jew. . . . They assert they have admired him, befriended him and have deplored the atrocities committed against him. . . . It would seem they were ready to help [him] in every way except to save him from being killed." [20]

Out of the unspeakable horrors which these men committed professionally through several years, I only want to mention one event which is particularly relevant in our context: "In the early part of December [1941] the Commander of the 11th Army, which was located in [the] area [of Simferopol], notified the chief of Einsatzkommando 11b that the Army expected them to kill some several thousand Jews and Gypsies before Christmas. This savage proposal, coming on the eve of one of the holiest days of the year, did not consternate the kommando leader. . . . The only impediment [he] saw in the execution of the order was that he lacked enough men and equipment for so accelerated an assignment, but he would do his best. He called on the army quartermaster and obtained sufficient personnel, trucks, guns and ammunition to do the bloody deed, and it was done. The Jews and Gypsies—men, women and children—were in their graves by Christmas." The massacre completed, "They found themselves in the mood to celebrate their own Christmas party. Their chief, Otto Ohlendorf, made a speech on that occasion. . . ." [21]

The same schizophrenic attitude can be observed in the big executives of the Krupp, Siemens and I. G. Farben corporations. They not only knew and approved of the ruthless exploitation of starved, overworked and torture-driven concentration-camp inmates, among them women as well as children down to the age of six, for the profit and the patriotic and commercial "prestige" of their business; they built factories in the vicinity of the camps of Ravens-

brück, Neuengamme and Auschwitz, in order to save on transportation costs, to have new labor material always at hand and the
gassing facilities ready when the last spill of strength had been
squeezed out of the emaciated bodies. These unfortunate victims
were not known by names; there were too many and there was
no need for individual distinction anyway. They were not people
any longer, but mere "pieces" (*Stück*); as such they bore numbers tattooed on their skin. "Weapons with which [workers] were
beaten were distributed by the Krupp firm," and "the plant leaders
sometimes watched while the people were being beaten." [22] The
loan of work slaves to industry was a two-way business, of equal
profit both to the Nazi chiefs and the industrial corporations. Not
only did this slave trade make the concentration camps self-sup-
porting but it yielded enormous financial gain to stock companies,
"common interests," which sprang up for the purpose of such
exploitation.[23]

Once a point had been reached where human beings lost their
human quality and became just manipulated objects and wares,
no obstacles stood in the way of the ultimate consequence: the
utilization of human "material" by the industrialists as well as by
the Nazi doctors and professors, for chemical, physiological and
vivisectional experiments, without the slightest regard for the life
and suffering of these human guinea pigs. At the I. G. Farben trial
in Nuremberg a correspondence was produced between the I. G.
Farben's Bayer plant and the commandant of the Auschwitz camp,
from which I quote the essential passages: 1. "In contemplation of
experiments of a new soporific drug we would appreciate your pro-
curing for us a number of women." 2. "We received your answer,
but consider the price of 200 marks a woman excessive. We pro-
pose to pay not more than 170 marks a head. If agreeable, we will
take possession of the women. We need approximately 150." 3.
"We acknowledge your accord. Prepare for us 150 women in the
best possible health conditions, and as soon as you advise us you
are ready, we will take charge of them." 4. "Received the order of
150 women. Despite their emaciated condition, they were found

satisfactory. We shall keep you posted on developments concerning this experiment." 5. "The tests were made. All subjects died. We shall contact you on the subject of a new load." [24] For the various medical experiments, suffice it to refer to the amply documented report of Doctors Alexander Mitscherlich and Fred Mielke in their book *Doctors of Infamy*.[25]

These executives, these doctors and university professors—among them famous scientists like Professor Clauberg, heads of medical departments like Hirt, Haagen and Bickenbach of the University of Strasbourg, Gebhardt of the University of Berlin, Rose and Lockemann of the Robert Koch Institute—these men, after having done their gruesome work, after having watched, sometimes closely, the ordeal of their camp laborers—the Krupp executive von Bülow, for instance, had his office right above the working rooms of the prisoners—after having directed and inspected excruciating experiments on humans, went home to their families, parties, classes, delivered lectures, carried on their research, partook of all the modes and manners of our modern civilization without even the slightest sense of the flagrant contrast between the two aspects of their lives. In the diaries of Ambassador Ulrich von Hassel they may be seen moving about in the nice restaurants of the capital, the theaters, social gatherings, reception rooms of officials, scheming, joking, convivially gossiping. The commandant of the Auschwitz camp, Rudolf Hoess, related in his trial how after the conferences with the leading gentlemen of the I. G. Farben concern, "They had their socials, the commandant, the gents from I. G. Farben and their ladies. There was champagne and small tasty sandwiches." [26] And Count Bernadotte in his report on his negotiations in Germany depicts Professor Gebhardt—initiator of the ghastly test infections and transplantations of bones, muscles and nerves on healthy prisoners—showing his clinic of Hohenluechen as a paragon of medical conscientiousness.[27]

The same phenomenon that we observed here in specific cases of actual human behavior may also be found residual in common

practices of the Third Reich. The interrogation of terrified Jews as
a feature of the radio, the mailing of the ashes of murdered people
by parcel post, the use of human bones, fats and hair for the
manufacturing of fertilizers, soap and mattresses, of tattooed human skin for lampshades and handbags, the setting up of advertising posters next to the extermination camps by the firms
which furnished installations—all such combinations of things
human, of death and suffering which, throughout history, have
been surrounded by awe and ritual cultivation, with the mechanized processes of modern industry and technology and the exploitation of matter which they imply—all this reflects the same
weirdly incoherent form of human behavior, which, I contend,
made its first appearance in our epoch.

WHAT IS IT, THEN, that we may regard as new in these happenings? The fateful novelty may be seen, I believe, in that accomplished split in the personality, a split reaching deep enough to
shatter the identity of the human being. Those persons, Elite
Guards, intellectuals, executives, whom we have seen professionally attending to the most gruesome activities, seemed to act
only with a certain part of their being, while another part was
left behind, remained in the background; in fact, their behavior
bears a semblance to technological procedures and can best be
expressed in technological terms. We could say that different
faculties of the human being are switched off or turned on according to requirement; and substantially, these different faculties, or
sections of the personality, seem entirely disconnected from one
another.

To be sure, any human psyche abounds with striking inner
discrepancies. Every one of us harbors in the depth of his nature
characteristics, feelings and reactions which, if he is capable of
viewing them rationally, he will recognize as wholly incompatible.
Who could say of himself that he is thinking, feeling, living quite
consistently? From history, from psychological and criminological
evidence we may gather as many examples as we want of strange

incongruities within one and the same person—not to speak of pathological Dr.-Jekyll-and-Mr.-Hyde cases. The connection between aestheticism and crime is a well-known fact: the subtlest sensitivity to artistic values sometimes makes a person particularly insensitive to ethical values. It is equally well-known that hardboiled gangsters may be the tenderest friends or fathers. Gilles de Rais, the very same man who was a national hero and was ready to give his life for Joan of Arc, slaughtered beautiful children in an unspeakable manner. In all such cases, however, if we search deep enough, we shall detect some organic coherence, however irrational, in the individual character. The Borgia prince who, after an agreeable, convivial meal, impressed his poisoned ring in the palm of a shaken hand, relished his elegant triumph, his *bella vendetta,* which had to be built up long beforehand out of carefully selected circumstances. Gilles de Rais' sadism was deeply intervolved with magic and alchemistic endeavors and constantly struggling with religious qualms. At any rate, these were personal crimes, personal risks, actual as well as moral, taken and accepted in their full weight. And wherever there existed discrepancies in the behavior of such monstrous malefactors, we may still find a personal focus where the discordant parts are linked together.

The frightening new feature in modern atrocities is exactly the lack of such personal focus in which conflicting faculties can still cohere. The split in the personality reaches into unfathomable depths, it is total, it is consummate schizophrenia. While formerly the divergent parts of the personality, being somewhere and somehow deeply connected, both belonged in the orbit of the individual psyche and, therefore, retained some ultimate homogeneity—they were both still human in that they were personal—today these parts are utterly heterogeneous: the part that commits atrocities seems wholly impersonal and, accordingly, in-human in the literal sense of the word; indeed, we should rather call it a-human. Even inhuman behavior, brutality or cruelty derives from impulses which are human, whereas what we are facing in the modern atrocities is the absence of anything human. These Nazi acts and practices did not evolve from genuine cruelty or brutal rage (they were not particularly enjoyed, nor were they abhorred); they were done without pleasure but also without repugnance.[28] They were not done personally at all—no feeling whatsoever was involved. They were done functionally, on order, with extreme factuality, in a thoroughly businesslike manner. *It was the collective that acted in them, the collective intruding and disrupting the personality from without.*[29]

CERTAINLY, similar forms of schizophrenic behavior occurred and keep occurring in the *Russian orbit*, although, as I indicated before, the general situation in Russia proper is altogether different.

First of all, from time immemorial an omnipotent autocratic and implicitly theocratic rule has borne heavily on the Russian people; and the pressure of the Czarist regime has without interruption passed over into the party dictatorship of the Soviets. There never developed an experience of general liberty or, except among intellectuals, accomplished individualism. Industrial and technological civilization was long retarded by the sluggish reluctance of the Czarist regime and the massive inertia of the Russian psyche which was sturdily, piously rooted in its rural homeland and Byzantine past. Between the ruling class—nobility and officialdom—and the benumbed peasantry there existed hardly any middle class. The Russian people at large were identified with the peasants; and this mass of people, held in bondage and suffering through the centuries, was on its part pervaded by a special sort, a primitive sort of Christianity. The mystical trends of Eastern Christianity, particularly the monkish, the *Staretz* way of piety, had penetrated the masses who were the "bearers of the Lord." "Christ roams through the country in the guise of a beggar," says Dostoievsky. This means that poor, tormented and sinful man becomes Christ—the more sinful, the sooner; and a kind of emotional communism was brought forth, a feeling, beneath all brutishness, of the brotherhood of men. Such indistinct, anonymous feeling is reflected intellectually in the writings of the great Russian authors, from Pushkin and Gogol to Dostoievsky, Tolstoy and Gorki who, all of them, "bowed down before the people," as Dostoievsky put it. In his eulogy of Pushkin, Dostoievsky wrote in 1880: "To become a genuine, an integral Russian, may mean—finally—to become a brother of all men, an 'all-man,' if I may say so . . . our calling . . . is to embody the idea of unity on earth, a unity achieved not by the sword, but by the power of brotherly love, and by our brotherly striving for the re-unification of all men."

What happened in Russia cannot be properly evaluated without taking into account these historical premises: the original, emotional propensity toward human community—a religious preparation for and prefiguration of social collectivity—and the age-old acceptance of suffering. It is this which preserved in the depths of the Russian psyche a powerful source and resource of humanity and which may have lessened to a certain degree the disruptive impact of the new Terror, even after the peasants had been transformed into industrial and agricultural workers. Witness thereof are reports like the one of the German minister Helmut Gollwitzer, a confirmed anti-communist, who was a prisoner in Russia for five years.[30]

When the irrational despotism of a theocratic dynasty was supplanted by the rational despotism of an imported doctrine, the Soviet regime faced a threefold task: to mobilize the country and bring it up-to-date; to arouse the people from its inertia and illiteracy and train it for industrialization and technological advance; and simultaneously to ward off the many counterrevolutionary assaults, from without as well as from within. Accordingly, the Russian Terror, reflecting the fear of the regime itself, was intended to crush all opposition, actual and potential, including, as is well known, the ruling group itself; to prevent all hindrance of construction and production, and to whip up the people for speedy, efficient work. However, the gruesome features of Soviet life—the police methods, the omnipresent surveillance, the indiscriminate arrests and deportations and the conditions in prisons and labor camps—all these horrible features are mostly continuations of Czarist practices, intensified by the increased pressure of circumstances.

The ordeals of the labor camps, following the pattern of Czarist deportations to Siberia, are not characterized, like those of the Nazi camps, by active, deliberate cruelty, but rather by utter neglect and indolence. Various reports repeat the same story: slave labor—though not for the benefit of high officials and industrial corporations—unattainable working norms, combined with starvation food rations, inadequate shelter, clothing, heating, hygiene, medical care, but with at least initial, theoretical intentions to provide for indispensable needs. People die of exhaustion, despair and disease, but they are not tortured, hanged, gassed, or beaten to death. Doctors and nurses, although lacking supplies and equipment, are provided to cure and assist inmates, not to kill and vivisect them.[31]

Thus, when we look at the over-all picture of the Russian situation, it does not, in spite of its ghastly features, appear to foster schizophrenia in the same manner as the Nazi state did. The Russians were never as individualistic and middle-class as the Germans; they were conforming, not inversely, like the Germans, *quia absurdum,* but rather naturally, to their huge total state whose boundaries constituted the limits of their world.

It is in the satellite countries, in Czechoslovakia, Poland, Hungary, in Eastern Germany and of course in the rank and file of the Communist parties of the Western countries, where such schizophrenia is much more likely to occur. Sartre in his *Mains Sales* very clearly exposes the problem.

There is, however, one form of disruption of the personality effected by the Soviet regime and its tortuous party line, which in a certain direction surpasses even the Nazi accomplishments. (In recognizing this, we must not disregard the crucial differences in kind between the two: the Soviets betrayed their ends by their means; the Nazis betrayed everything human by the insensate criminality of their very ends.) The discipline of the Communist Party demands of its devotees not only blind obedience to the decisions reaching down from the changing administrators of the party line; not only the sacrifice of all private interests, comforts and pleasures whenever the cause calls for it—in contradistinction to Hitler who authorized corruption—the party line claims not only a comrade's life, but imposes on him even the sacrifice of his honor, that is, his reputation *within* his group. Whenever a culprit or a diversion of the anger of the people is required, the party member must be prepared, innocent and dedicated as he may be, indeed as a token of his dedication, to profess himself a traitor or a bungler. Our generation had enough opportunities to witness such communist exhibitions. To be sure, many devoted communists balked at this ultimate demand and their confessions had to be extorted from them in the well-known ruthless manner; but there were others who willingly complied, as a former Belgian Communist, Charles Plisnier, has attested.[32]

Everything else—blind obedience, humiliation and self-humiliation, the *sacrificium intellectus,* the renouncement of life's pleasures, of one's personal life, of life itself—all this has been asked and given before. The history of religions, churches and nations is full of examples. The peak of such self-denial up to our time was probably reached by the exalted prostration of Santa Teresa de Jesús: "He who is really humble must feel the desire to be despised, persecuted, and condemned without reason, even in serious matters. O Lord . . . give me the sincere desire to be despised by all creatures!" But this Christian self-abolition is fundamentally an act of self-identification with the *Crucifixus,* a magical and mystical union with Jesus Christ, and as such an inverse reassertion of self, resurrection of self in eternal life.

And indeed, even on this earth, the men and women who made such sacrifices were extolled as saints and heroes. Conversely, a Communist's surrender of his honor and dignity is consummate moral suicide. This plunge, not only into complete anonymity of martyrdom, but into the abyss of perennial defamation, is the extremity of annihilation, of eradication of personality.

CHAPTER FOUR

The Split from Within: I

SECOND CONSCIOUSNESS AND

FRACTIONIZED UNIVERSE

L'absurde c'est la raison lucide qui constate ses limites.

(The absurd is lucid reason stating its limits.)

CAMUS

IN THE LAST two chapters we were concerned with the splitting and disruption of the individual *from without*, as effected by the various evolutionary forces working toward collectivization and totalization of human beings. We shall now deal with certain modern developments that have arisen in the human psyche and in the human mind and which tend to disintegrate the human personality *from within*. Both these inner and outer processes were in many ways interconnected.

We saw how the Nazi terror in concentration camps attempted methodically to destroy the personality of its victims. Now among these victims there were a few people of particular moral strength, will power and intelligence who succeeded in developing a defense mechanism against such complete loss of personal identity. They

83

countered the Nazi disruption of personality with a split deliberately inflicted on themselves by themselves, with a *splitting of consciousness*. By detaching a hyper-conscious ego from their everyday consciousness, by holding fast to this hyper-ego in the most precarious situations, and establishing it as an observation post, they resisted that nightmare of unreality into which the weaker victims dissolved. They refused to shrink to mere objects of Nazi management; they wanted to remain subjects in some remote corner of their mind. They clung to *"cette idée fixe de rester quelqu'un de propre,"* that obsession to remain a distinct being, as Monique Nosley, an inmate of Ravensbrück, put it.

Among these rare people there were a few still rarer ones who not only were able to save themselves through this detachment of a higher consciousness, but who even could, under the most adverse conditions—undernourishment, lack of sleep, overwork and nerve-shattering experiences—train their memories so as to retain what they observed and put it down in reports after they had regained their freedom.

We owe such a revealing report to Dr. Bruno Bettelheim, a trained Viennese psychologist and a man of remarkable fortitude who, in his aforementioned study, described how he came to develop his defense mechanism: "During the first days in prison, and particularly during the first days in the camp, he [the writer] realized that he behaved differently from the way he used to. At first, he rationalized that these changes in behavior were only surface phenomena, the logical result of his peculiar situation. But soon he realized that what happened to him, for instance the split in his person into one who observes and one to whom things happen, could no longer be called normal but was a typical psychopathological phenomenon. So he asked himself: 'Am I going insane, or am I already insane?' . . . Moreover, he saw his fellow prisoners act in a most peculiar way, although he had every reason to assume that they, too, had been normal persons before being imprisoned. Now they suddenly appeared to be pathological liars, to be unable to restrain themselves, to be unable to make objective evaluations, etc. So another question arose, namely, 'How can I protect myself against becoming as they are?' The answer to both questions was comparatively simple: to find out what had happened in them and to me. . . . So I set out to find what changes had occurred and were occurring in the prisoners. By doing so, I realized that I had found a solution to my second problem: by occupying myself during my spare time with interesting problems, with interviewing my fellow prisoners, by pondering my findings for the hours without end during which I was forced to perform exhausting labor . . . I succeeded in killing the time in a way which seemed constructive. . . . As time went on, the enhancement of my self-respect due to my ability to continue to do meaningful work despite the contrary efforts of the Gestapo, became even more important than the pastime." [1] In such a way Bettelheim protected himself from disintegration of his personality.

A counterpart on the women's side is the equally courageous and self-controlled behavior of Germaine Tillion, to whom we owe the informative study in the book on Ravensbrück: *À la recherche de la verité*. She writes: *"Démonter mentalement, comprendre une mécanique (même qui vous écrase), envisager lucidement, et dans tous ses détails, une situation (même désespérée), c'est une puissante source de sang-froid, de sérénité et de force d'âme,"* [2] ("To defeat mentally, to understand a mechanism—even one that crushes you—to view with lucidity and in all its details a situation—even a desperate one—this is a powerful source of composure, serenity and mental strength.")

This splitting of consciousness which developed spontaneously in some of the concentration camp victims as a protective measure, this very behavior has been theoretically pondered and recommended by the German author Ernst Jünger in his brilliant essay *Über den Schmerz* (On Pain) which seems to me the most important or certainly the most momentous piece of work he has done. Jünger himself is a perfect representative of the attitude he explores and describes; his personality is no less revealing than his observations. He perpetuates and generalizes the situation and

the behavior of those self-observers, self-objectifiers in the concentration camps.

According to Jünger, our whole world condition calls for just
such an attitude. He analyzes this world condition, taking as its
model modern war which was his crucial experience, the core and
point of departure of his views. When Jünger became a soldier in
the First World War he had just completed high school and was
eighteen years old. He was then an extreme nationalist. Soon,
however, he came to realize war not so much as a national and
historic event that may be experienced emotionally or intellectually, but as a typical process of modern technology, as a revelation
of the new world power which is technology. He was no longer
interested in the abstract idea of war but rather in the concrete
phenomenon of the modern battle. He was an excellent officer and
led many actions with extraordinary presence of mind. This presence of mind went beyond the moment of action. He not only
kept his sang-froid and stoic poise throughout; he reached such a
degree of self-detachment as to scrutinize and note down his own
feelings and reactions in every phase of the battle. He still felt
something, he still reacted, but he detached his human sensorium
completely from his vantage post of observation. He established a
second center of perception, above the individual, human center.
While to Bettelheim and Germaine Tillion this detachment was
a temporary help, in Jünger it became a permanent psychic attitude with which he completely identified himself, which indeed
seemed to swallow up, to annul his own person.

Such an attitude corresponds to the perpetual presence of
danger which he finds looming in our world. The battle of the First
World War, which he described in several volumes with enthusiastic accuracy, was just a beginning and a pattern. Jünger was
chiefly concerned with the role of man in this modern battle, the
"battle of materiel" (*Materialschlacht*), as he called it. Men and
machines are on a par in this kind of battle; man is yoked to the
machine in a gigantic process that he can neither behold in its
entirety nor escape. Jünger regards this as symbolic of the whole

of modern existence. Behind the front and after the war, this process, according to him, develops into the total state, to the condition of "total mobilization" which forces all energies and activities of the people to serve one single purpose: the increase of state power. (These ideas were developed in the 1920's, before the Third Reich.) But to Jünger total mobilization is only an advanced stage of a phenomenon that manifests itself everywhere in modern life, even under a democratic constitution, in every factory, in every stadium, and even in modern amusement parks. Everywhere the human being is completely subject to the demands of a mechanized compound in which he as an individual is submerged. No matter where a human being is engaged, he marches in a column, he is a worker and at the same time a soldier. And in the face of this governing fact, it is immaterial whether this column is an empire, a classless society, or a football team. The empire is nothing but a world record; a world record is nothing but technical, purposeless will to power. "We understand the combination of organizational capacity and a complete color-blindness toward values, faith without content, and discipline without justification, a state of affairs in which technics and ethics are in a curious way synonymous." [3]

What Jünger describes is, apart from collectivization, a process of *formalization:* means swallowing ends, contents and meanings vanishing into technics, tactics and techniques. This formalization derives also from specialization, from the accumulation of life material and of modes of manipulation, gradually wasting away life itself; from the partitioning of all-round man into sectional functions. In all countries we encounter the technical type of man, the man who spends all his life with some technical work, some special technique which provides his whole support and satisfaction, without his ever asking to what end this work is done. In all countries there is the sportsman who, in fact, is the perfect representative, the perfect symbol of a completely formalized achievement, a performance for the sake of performing. Here the mere technique is one with the physical function, the body itself is pure technique. The Hellenic Olympic Games were aimed at developing the whole man, character and mind no less than physical excellence, the human form and not an athletic function. The contest was only a subordinate instrument serving this ritual aim. Today's sports performances serve people's vicarious enjoyment in the race or fight between functional skills, echoing their own daily functional competition.

Jünger professes an attitude which he calls "heroic realism," whereby the term "heroic" means much more than sacrifice in military action. Heroism comes to signify a general, comprehensive and entirely novel form of self-control and self-denial: not only denial of the individual in the self, but a last and resolute denial of the human being in the self, of the human part in man. We are reminded of Nietzsche's words: "Where are the barbarians of the twentieth century? They will be those capable of the greatest harshness against themselves, those who can guarantee the greatest duration of will power." [4]

In his essay *On Pain* Jünger attempts to demonstrate that in the great and cruel process of transformation which man is undergoing in our age the touchstone is pain and not value, pain which completely disregards all our values. "There is nothing," he says, "for which we are destined with greater certainty than pain"—the inevitable lot of every human being, most particularly in this vicious world in which we live today. Therefore a person can only maintain himself and prove himself worthy if he does not try to evade or push away pain but sustains it, faces it, and establishes distance from it; if he is able to place himself beyond the zone of pain, even of sensation, if he is able to treat that region of the self where he participates in pain, that is, the body, as an object.

Jünger points for exemplification to the Christian martyrs and ascetics, of whom a circular of the Church of Smyrna says: "in the hour of torture they were absent from their bodies." But what is crucial and what Jünger overlooks is the fact that these martyrs, while absent from their bodies, were present somewhere else, that they *had* a somewhere to be present, the fortress of values, the fortress of faith, which was unconquerable. Such a fortress of values no longer exists for most people today, except for devout Catholics or dedicated Communists or for those rare persons who succeed in developing and maintaining in their own lonely personalities an independent human criterion and a firm adherence to this criterion, adherence as a matter of human dignity.[5] The reports from concentration camps record unanimously that those who were able to survive mentally, those who were able to keep their personalities intact, were either Communists, devout Catholics, Jehovah's Witnesses, or members of the aristocracy. European nobility carried, physically ingrained in them, as it were, a traditional clan standard of conduct, a kind of disdainful subconscious discipline, which made them intrinsically invulnerable. Middle-class people, being just private individuals without any common ties or cause, were the first to break down and disintegrate.

Nor does such a fortress of values exist for Jünger himself; he explicitly states that today all ideas, institutions, leading persons are only substitutes for values which are not visible as yet. Nevertheless he demands, as a measure of self-preservation, indeed worthiness, the "detachment of life from itself, the objectification of self." His objectivity, his manner of pure statement does not derive from a personal, still emotionally flexible, still humanly sensitive consciousness as was the case with many unmethodical self-observers and psychologists since Montaigne. It derives from what he calls a *"second and coldest consciousness,"* a consciousness on another, even more detached plane, a consciousness beyond individual consciousness, as it were. This "second consciousness" into which he retires and from which he makes his observations obviously resides in the nought, in the nowhere. Since Jünger considers pain to be the supreme challenge and standard of our time which invalidates all values, he must by necessity see in the detachment from pain the prerequisite for self-maintenance. Hence the criterion of worthiness is transferred from value to pain, or rather to the measure of self-mortification of which a man is capable. But under present conditions such self-mortification again represents an extreme formalization, mechanization of the psychic process. In extreme situations, such as in concentration camps, and from a position of faith, it is very possible to mortify one's sensory being without eradicating human feeling altogether. But it is impossible to objectify, to mortify one's self habitually and from a position in a blank void, in a nowhere, without killing not only sensation or sentimentality but the psychic roots of sentiment altogether.[6]

The French existentialists developed a similar notion of a particularly detached consciousness. We shall observe it later in Sartre's *Nausée*. In his novel *L'âge de raison* we see young people striving in the most contorted ways to affirm their liberty through such aloofness. Camus, in his *Le mythe de Sisyphe,* asserts that in order to maintain one's reason—reason which is precisely what separates man from the world, from a universe deprived of illusions and enlightenment—in order to stand this absurdity, he needs *"une conscience perpétuelle, toujours renouvelée, toujours tendue . . . désespoir qui reste lucide, nuit polaire, veille de l'esprit. . . ."* ("perpetual consciousness, ever renewed, ever strained . . . despair remaining lucid, polar night, vigilance of the mind.") And, he says: *"Pour l'homme absurde il ne s'agit plus d'expliquer et de résoudre, mais d'éprouver et de décrir. Tout commence par l'indifference clairvoyante."* [7] ("For absurd man it no longer matters to explain and to resolve, but to experience and to describe. Everything starts with lucid indifference.")

THAT GHOSTLY second and coldest consciousness as conceived by Jünger is an impersonal position within the person. But Jünger indicates that such impersonal consciousness prevails also in many places of our contemporary public life, where it even *lacks any personal location.*

For a full clarification of this state of affairs we may recall what has been said at the end of the second chapter. There I mentioned the new phenomenon of *collective consciousness,* a consciousness present in institutionalized knowledge, be it scientific findings, searchings and applications, be it the various organizational and administrative institutions of our highly systematized social life. This corpus of institutionalized knowledge, I said, is beyond the grasp of individual consciousness; it is beyond personal location. Now the impersonal coldest consciousness that Jünger finds present in our public life is by no means identical with this collective consciousness, but it is an outgrowth of it, indeed, is made possible by it. The trans-personality of our institutional knowledge and of its technological embodiments is a prerequisite for the impersonality or rather non-personality of that anonymous coldest consciousness and for its peculiar relations to individual human beings. Collective consciousness, being itself depersonalized, objectified and objective to the extreme, turns every fact of life and of man which it handles into an object. As a result, much of what previously was left to personal vision and judgment is now taken over by functional rules; *values,* i.e., the inner directions through which a community guides the individual human being, come to be displaced by *standards,* i.e., norms for handling abstracted facts. In this manner, the relation of man to man is gradually supplanted by the relation of an objective unlocalizable criterion to an object.

What Jünger understands by his impersonal coldest consciouness prevailing in our contemporary social sphere is the depersonalizing effect of the ubiquitous collective consciousness. Thus a human life becomes a case that can be filed under certain categories. An official signing a document no longer makes his own evaluation but acts as an executor of a non-personal functional criterion. These non-personal criteria take hold even of our private, personal attitudes toward ourselves so that a person will view and experience his self through that completely non-personal criterion. So a person instead of immediately succumbing to his pain, instead of being unhappy, will at once scrutinize the cause of his frustrations objectively and in detached manner. Instead of using his personal judgment as derived from his own experiences, wisdom and values, instead of trying to resolve his situation independently in his unique fashion, including his pain, and in some way acknowledging the legitimacy of his suffering and unhappiness, he will analyze himself by means of pre-established psychological and sociological categories—he will manipulate himself as a psycho- or socio-clinical case. Thus he makes himself into an object visualized by an alien trans-personal eye.

In so deadening ourselves, distancing ourselves, we seem to protect ourselves. By analyzing our personal suffering through the anonymous criterion of functional systems, we certainly put ourselves outside the zone of pain. And whenever that cold trans-personal criterion is focused on the suffering of another human being, we also put ourselves outside the zone of *his* pain. Such objectification of life necessarily affects our attitude toward personal suffering and toward death. To a greater or lesser degree, sympathy gives way to a growing indifference, imagination gives way to abstract measuring.

All these effects become especially evident whenever and wherever the technical materializations of our institutional knowledge —machines and apparatuses—intervene in human relations. In many of today's sports contests, as Jünger also noted, the competition with an individual rival has turned into a competition between a functional skill and an abstract record, into a strict measuring procedure: "Neither the presence of the opponent nor a public is required. The decisive factor is the presence of the second consciousness which registers the achievement through the measuring tape, the stop watch, the electric current, or the camera lens." [8]

In photography we can best observe the coldest consciousness in action and the effects it produces. "It has," says Jünger, "a telescopic character. One senses clearly that all that happens is seen by an unfeeling and invulnerable eye. Photography retains with the same impassivity a bullet in its flight and a man who is being torn by an explosion. This now is our peculiar way—a very cruel way—of seeing things; and photography is just an instrument of this peculiarity of ours. . . . We have a queer tendency— difficult to describe—somehow to endow a live happening with the character of a laboratory preparation. Wherever an event occurs in our sphere, it is surrounded by camera objectives and microphones and lighted by the exploding flares of flashbulbs." [9]

THIS OMNIPRESENCE of non-personal, objective registering had a two-fold effect on human feeling and behavior. On the one hand it produced *a new insensibility*; it trained us, all of us, without our noticing it, to indifference, indeed, callousness. It greatly affected our attitude toward death. On the other hand it contributed its share—partly through photography again and its influence on human perception—to the creation of a *new sensibility,* a peripheral, a neural receptivity, as it were. This new sensibility arose as well from other origins which will be discussed in the next chapter. It enabled us to perceive details and nuances, to penetrate into levels of reality which heretofore were hidden from us due to our subjective attitude.

First of all, that impassible, invulnerable eye of the camera lens has seized upon the human beings who use it: reporters and newsreel men, film producers and directors, radio announcers, advertisers, and so forth; and the affectional deafness of these people which is professionally required and encouraged has spread to the audiences. Human susceptibility has shrunk to flashy nervous excitability, sentiment to sensationalism. We are constantly confronted with such a-humanity, and we have become thoroughly inured to it. In fact, this new callousness is an important prerequisite for modern atrocities and modern warfare.

In his book, *Escape from Freedom,* Erich Fromm characterized this state of affairs as follows: "The announcement of the bombing of a city and the death of hundreds of people is shamelessly followed or interrupted by an advertisement for soap or wine. The same speaker with the same suggestive, ingratiating and authoritative voice, which he has just used to impress you with the seriousness of the political situation, impresses now upon his audience the merits of the particular brand of soap, which pays for the news broadcast. Newsreels let pictures of torpedoed ships be followed by those of a fashion show . . . because of all this we cease to be genuinely related to what we hear . . . our emotions and our critical judgment become hampered, and eventually our attitude to what is going on in the world assumes a quality of flatness and indifference. In the name of 'freedom' life loses all structure; it is composed of many little pieces, each separate from the other and lacking any sense as a whole." [10]

The most ruinous influence in this respect issues from the popular picture magazines. *Life* magazine for instance—which in its editorials laments the shattering of family life and the increase of juvenile delinquency, and clamors for religion and Christianity—without the faintest awareness creates the very seeds of what it deplores. Not only does it regularly record with professional satisfaction and utter photo-technical nicety the crassest details of horror scenes, accidents, suicides and catastrophes; not only does it with its merciless camera flashes hunt out people in their most trying hours of dying, mourning or despair; but, beyond that, it advisedly intermingles these appalling pictures with displays or advertisements of sumptuous comforts and merry carousing.

Here we can find Chinese children dying of hunger alongside a display of the famous custom-made Brogan clothes for children costing around $120.00; Greek EAM girls on their knees holding posters with petitions for bread and freedom, and a few pages later Ibn Saud feasting with Standard Oil executives. Here we see vultures fattening on Indian corpses, horrible pictures of the hospital on Leyte and pictures of Nazi doctors working on human guinea pigs, while on the following pages we may find an elaborate picture story on a billionaire's club in Florida or a "house to swim in" in Palm Springs. We see turtles lying helplessly on their backs exposed to the sun on the beach, and the kindly maker of turtle soup charitably pouring a few drops of water into the mouths of the parched animals. We read the eulogy of that happily married couple, the expert divorce-spy and his wife, who, as *Life* tells us, are not in the least disturbed by the distasteful nature of their work, such as peeping through keyholes into people's private lives with a miniature camera. We see the starving Germans shortly after the war, followed immediately by the families of American occupation officers doing their shopping and, as *Life* assures us, having the time of their lives. In the same issue we see Grace Moore's body immediately after the airplane crash, and in the marvelous park of Al Capone's Florida estate his brother carrying beer to reporters at Al Capone's deathwatch. It is hardly possible to enumerate all the offenses against human sensibility and taste which these visual records contain.

In Germany in the 1920's, there existed a magazine called *Der Querschnitt* (Cross Section) which, in a more sophisticated manner, cultivated this thrill of harsh contrasts. Since then it has become a habitual practice and we hardly notice it any longer.

But how can we blame the people who make of this practice a profitable business? Their activity is legitimate, inasmuch as they present the actual state of affairs. As a matter of fact, if such things were done deliberately, with an overtone of shock and a definite aim to impress people with the clashing and calamitous contradictions of twentieth-century life, they could have constructive influence. But as it is, no one, neither the publishers nor the public, seems to realize the implications, and the wealth of facts is presented and absorbed helterskelter in a callous and casual way.

Indeed, *Life* magazine mirrors our life which itself has actually turned this way. We are hardly aware of the fact that much more happens today than in former ages. This is due, apart from population growth, to modern means of communication and to the intervention of mass media. These not only record and report every event occurring all over the globe but report it so quickly, so instantaneously, that through reactions and counterreactions, through perpetual chain reactions of happenings they initiate a real *mass production of events.* Other developments contributing to this effect were the multiplication of research and findings in the various specialized sciences and the now perpetual technological innovations. The result of all this is a crowding of events in the domain of our vision and consciousness, an oppressive closeness and overwhelming shiftiness of events, an excess of details and complexities in every single event—in short, what I would call an *overpopulation of the surfaces.* And so the sharpest contrasts and phenomenal discordancies, contrasts as sharp as the contrast between nature and machine, have become the normal fare of our daily life.

It is this general situation—the overpopulation of the surfaces and the violent contrasts it entails, as registered by the non-personal hyper-objective second consciousness—it is this situation that produced a new callousness, a new attitude toward death and suffering and at the same time greatly promoted the development of a new sensibility. While photography has accustomed us to its unfeeling perception, it has simultaneously trained us to observe a host of details, minutiae, shades of reality which we were unable to detect before. Through the sharpness and magnification of photographic techniques we have learned to see the textures of natural tissues and substances in their infinite design, the intricate network of living cells, the veins of leaves, and so forth; a butterfly wing unveils fantastic landscapes and a snow crystal the ultimate perfection of geometric architecture. Correspondences of structure have been revealed between the most different forms of existence and new spheres opened to our vision and to artistic endeavor. By uncovering all these, photography has often changed the whole aspect of a phenomenon. In the same way photography has also effected a fragmentation of phenomena and has taught us the charm, the infinite imaginary vistas of the fragment.

Impressionist painting has largely indulged in this fascination with segments cut out or cut off from their visual context. The arbitrary slicing of reality which the impartial lens accomplishes re-enforces a tendency of impressionism which arose also from the widening and deepening of artistic vision: the inclusion of light effects and color relationships. A human figure, an object, a natural composition of objects are at times partly cut off by the edge of the canvas. The concern of artistic visual conception has shifted its focus. A picture's coherence is no longer identical with the traditional organic coherence of objects or groupings in their wholeness, which our preconceived pragmatic conception of the world requires. An entirely new approach to composition took place. While up to the time of Constable, artists usually organized their picture in advance, even in the case of landscapes, that is to say, created their own composition and took only its elements from nature, the impressionists let their eyes survey nature itself and would arrest their gaze at a slice of reality where the natural motif coincided with their artistic conception, a process closely akin to the operation of the camera. Insofar as photography has been artistic, has been used under the humanly sensitized eye of artists— from Octavius Hill, Julia Cameron and Nadar in the beginning to Stieglitz, Steichen, Strand, Cartier-Bresson, Brassai, and others in our time—insofar it has deepened our perception and conception of nature and of man.

We are again confronted with a very complex and ambivalent process where positive, productive effects are deeply interrelated with disintegrating ones. Such ambivalence and all the changes this process brought with it in our way of seeing stand out most clearly when we study *the situation in the arts of our epoch.*

SHORTLY AFTER THE FIRST WORLD WAR, under the impact of its frightful, disillusioning experiences, a new artistic movement sprang up in Europe and began to prevail over expressionism, a movement which in Germany was termed *Neue Sachlichkeit* (New Factuality), or, as suggested by the art historian Franz Roh, "magic realism." The exuberant emotionalism and subjectivity of the expressionists abruptly turned into an exaggerated objectivity which, to superficial observers, looked like a return to realism. But it was by no means such a return. This new "realism" was very different from that which had been dethroned by the impressionist and expressionist movements. When we contemplate the paintings of the pre-impressionist era in Europe, all the different versions of realism since the Renaissance, from Dürer to Chardin, Leibl and Waldmüller, their sometimes lovingly accurate rendering of nature, their depiction, one would almost say their narration, of every little leaf in the tree, every blade of grass, every minute particular of a face or dress; when we compare this naïve, devout study of nature with the products of the new post-expressionist realism we become aware of the tremendous distance between the periods and of all that has happened in the meantime. In the neorealistic pictures of Otto Dix, Davringhausen, Carrà, Chirico, the early Beckmann, and so forth, we do have accuracy, an insistent, overstressed correctness; but what is new here is precisely this cruel, indeed vicious overstress of facts, this showing of objects in their inexorable suchness, in a glazed nakedness. The glossiness in which objects are sometimes dipped is sarcastic scorn; it exhales an inverted emotion, a silent bitterness hovering over the scene. We find the remnants of this manner of presentation in the surrealist pictures of Max Ernst, Tanguy, Dali and others, who render their monsters and disjointings with the same polished meticulosity. This realism has indeed an uncanny magic; it acts under the spell of unspelled experiences.

There are equivalents in the literature of the time. The style of the early Brecht shows the same attitude of pure statement carrying overtones of subdued revolt. Even in Kafka's mode of expression we find a similar quality of equable calm and preciseness of narration, sharply contrasting with the nightmarish things related and concealing an immense sadness. In all these works of art we still sense emotion, reversed and repressed as it may be.

All the elements of the human situation in the last decades: the new factuality with its unspoken emotion; the new attitude toward death and suffering and at the same time the new sensibility; a sense for the new language of the surfaces, their shiftiness and their fierce contrasts; all these we find expressed in the writing of Ernest Hemingway. Like other artists of the New Factuality, he was moved to his artistic innovations by the experience of the First World War and the climate it engendered in Europe. Out of this experience he created his peculiar prose style, a style perfectly geared to the new conditions and exerting a wide influence on Western writing. This influence was not entirely beneficial since such a method, when deprived of the artistic selectivity and imaginative drive of its originator, yields only a flat and extremely dull *sans-gêne*. Countless volumes are being filled with it.

What Hemingway discovered and conveyed in his new prose style is the symbolism of the inconspicuous, the *symbolism of the surfaces*. The "real thing" that he was seeking was, in his own words, "the sequence of motion and fact which made the emotion." His manner of presentation is related to that of the artists of Magic Realism, inasmuch as it is similarly characterized by a particularly strict, indeed strained detachment of the author from his story, and by a restrictive emphasis on the purely factual, on the bare statement of happenings or situations. Newspaper reports look sentimental in comparison. What distinguishes this style from naturalism is its lack of narrative elaboration, of the massive flesh of description, as well as the lack of outspoken social critique and explicit psychology. These are to be achieved by fact plus motion itself. The new style seldom reaches under the surface of daily events or situations; it says everything by showing just the surface alone, the seemingly irrelevant flow of trivial chatter and the incoherent flux of daily life, the "free association" of external facts. Surfaces are displayed without any reasoning, or even rational transitions; yet the trick is that what looks like aimless meandering turns out to be a concentration, a contraction. Factuality is handled so pointedly that it becomes symbolic; abruptness produces compression. Indeed, this peculiar factuality radiates an atmosphere which reflects the overstrained neutrality of the author—a neutrality that appears like an inversion of all the bitter experiences and disillusionments of the generation. The detachment and self-restraint of the author weighs upon the story like a tense aura, like a ghostly presence of fate. One never has that feeling with naturalistic works where everything is told neatly and elaborately.

In Hemingway's first book, a collection of short stories, *In Our Time* (1925), the brief reports forming transitions between the stories proper—notes on incidents in the war, at bullfights and executions—are pieces of a most lapidary and at the same time most dynamic factuality. It is most revealing to compare these pieces and the stories of the volume with the short stories of Stephen Crane. Crane's narrative style, in its conciseness and precision, went far beyond that of later naturalistic authors, such as Dreiser or Sinclair Lewis; he may be considered the initiator of modern epic prose in America.

In Stephen Crane's war tale, "The Upturned Face" (1900), two officers set out to bury their comrade under rifle fire, a situation which, one would think, should induce them to speed up their performance. But the reluctance to touch, even to look at the corpse, the respect, the awe they feel for the dead body is still stronger than the pressure of the rifle fire:

"What will we do now?" said the adjutant, troubled and excited.

"Bury him," said Timothy Lean.

The two officers looked down close to their toes where lay the body of their comrade. The face was chalk-blue; gleaming eyes stared at the sky. Over the two upright figures was a windy sound of bullets, and on the top of the hill Lean's prostrate company of Spitzbergen infantry was firing measured volleys.

"Don't you think it would be better—" began the adjutant. "We might leave him until tomorrow."

"No," said Lean. "I can't hold that post an hour longer. I've got to fall back, and we've got to bury old Bill." . . .

"Yes," he said, "we'd better see what he's got." He dropped to his knees, and his hands approached the body of the dead officer. But his hands wavered over the buttons of the tunic. The first button was brick-red with drying blood, and he did not seem to dare touch it.

"Go on," said the adjutant, hoarsely.

Lean stretched his wooden hand, and his fingers fumbled the blood-stained buttons. At last he rose with ghastly face. . . .

The adjutant said, "I suppose we should—we should say something. Do you know the service, Tim?"

"They don't read the service until the grave is filled in," said Lean, pressing his lips to an academic expression.

"Don't they?" said the adjutant, shocked that he had made the mistake. "Oh, well," he cried suddenly, "let us—let us say something —while he can hear us."

"All right," said Lean. "Do you know the service?"

"I can't remember a line of it," said the adjutant.

Lean was extremely dubious. "I can repeat two lines, but—"

"Well, do it," said the adjutant. "Go as far as you can. That's better than nothing. And the beasts have got our range exactly." . . .

The adjutant lowered his helmet to his knee. Lean, bareheaded, stood over the grave. The Rostina sharpshooters fired briskly.

"O Father, our friend has sunk into the deep waters of death, but his spirit has leaped toward Thee as the bubble arises from the lips of the drowning . . ."

The adjutant suddenly remembered a phrase in the back of the Spitzbergen burial service, and he exploited it with the triumphant manner of a man who has recalled everything, and can go on.

"O God, have mercy—"

"O God, have mercy—" said Lean.

"Mercy," repeated the adjutant, in quick failure.

"Mercy," said Lean. And then he was moved by some violence of feeling, for he turned upon his two men and tigerishly said, "Throw the dirt in."

The fire of the Rostina sharpshooters was accurate and continuous.

One of the aggrieved privates came forward with his shovel. He lifted his first shovel-load of earth, and for a moment of inexplicable hesitation it was held poised above this corpse, which from its chalk-blue face looked keenly out from the grave. Then the soldier emptied his shovel on—on the feet.

Timothy Lean felt as if tons had been swiftly lifted from off his forehead. He had felt that perhaps the private might empty the shovel on—on the face. . . .

Soon there was nothing to be seen but the chalk-blue face. Lean filled the shovel. "Good God," he cried to the adjutant. "Why didn't you turn him somehow when you put him in? This—" Then he began to stutter. . . .[11]

Compare with this the two following passages from Hemingway:

They shot the six cabinet ministers at half-past six in the morning against the wall of a hospital. There were pools of water in the courtyard. There were wet dead leaves on the paving of the courtyard. It rained hard. All the shutters of the hospital were nailed shut. One of the ministers was sick with typhoid. Two soldiers carried him downstairs and out into the rain. They tried to hold him up against the wall but he sat down in a puddle of water. The other five stood very quietly against the wall. Finally the officer told the soldiers it was no

good trying to make him stand up. When they fired the first volley he
was sitting down in the water with his head on his knees.

*   *   *

Nick sat against the wall of the church where they had dragged him
to be clear of machine-gun fire in the street. Both legs stuck out awk-
wardly. He had been hit in the spine. His face was sweaty and dirty.
The sun shone on his face. The day was very hot. Rinaldi, big backed,
his equipment sprawling, lay face downward against the wall. Nick
looked straight ahead brilliantly. The pink wall of the house opposite
had fallen out from the roof, and an iron bedstead hung twisted toward
the street. Two Austrian dead lay in the rubble in the shade of the
house. Up the street were other dead. Things were getting forward in
the town. It was going well. Stretcher bearers would be along any time
now. Nick turned his head and looked down at Rinaldi. "Senta
Rinaldo, senta. You and me we've made a separate peace." Rinaldi
lay still in the sun, breathing with difficulty. "We're not patriots." Nick
turned his head away, smiling sweatily. Rinaldi was a disappointing
audience.[12]

The crowding of experiences, the crowding of horrors in modern
war paralyzes sensibility, not to speak of the ancient respect toward
death. And the author senses this, of course, stresses it indeed by
exposing the grotesque contrasts, the jocular excessiveness of the
situation (the bedstead, the speech to the dying man). Throughout
his work Hemingway exhibits a peculiar relation to death; he presents the phenomenon in many forms, unsparingly, and yet seems
to be particularly drawn to it.

Even where he clings to the strictest factuality, however, Hemingway wants to produce emotion, that emotion of his which he
has concealed. This distinguishes him from Jünger who, in applying his rare sensibility, remains utterly detached and wants us
detached. It also distinguishes his attitude from that of certain
recent authors—Evelyn Waugh, Henry Green, Jean Stafford, Mary
McCarthy, Roald Dahl—who display an accomplished coldness
in their narrative. Some of them, when they tell a particularly odd
or shockingly cruel story, do it in a viciously insouciant way.
Earlier writers of gruesome stories—Poe, Villiers de l'Isle Adam,

Barbey d'Aurevilly, Gogol, E. T. A. Hoffmann, Maupassant—somehow belonged themselves in the monstrosity of their tales.

The Stephen Crane stories still retain the ordinary rational continuity of nineteenth-century narrative. Hemingway's short, explosive sentences convey an abrupt, sub-rationally connected sequence of happenings. Even in his first novel, *The Sun Also Rises,* we can observe how a random fluctuation of events can emanate symbolism. The novel shows the aimless doings of a group of young people after the war, their being pushed around by sensations and hidden anxieties, their mute despair amidst their pleasures, their vital exuberance issuing into nothing. All this centers in the terrible fate of Jake who has lost his manhood through an injury in the battle on the Tagliamento and thus is forever deprived of the consummation of his relation to the woman he loves. This personal doom assumes a symbolic character in that it spreads its poisoning effects among his whole circle, his surrounding world. And at the end a casual situation can be seen to embody the gist of the novel:

> Downstairs we came out through the first-floor diningroom to the street. A waiter went for a taxi. It was hot and bright. Up the street was a little square with trees and grass where there were taxis parked. A taxi came up the street, the waiter hanging out at the side. I tipped him and told the driver where to drive, and got in beside Brett. The driver started up the street. I settled back. Brett moved close to me. We sat close against each other. I put my arm around her and she rested against me comfortably. It was very hot and bright, and the houses looked sharply white. We turned out on to the Gran Via.
> "Oh, Jake," Brett said, "we could have had such a damn good time together."
> Ahead was a mounted policeman in khaki directing traffic. He raised his baton. The car slowed suddenly pressing Brett against me.
> "Yes," I said. "Isn't it pretty to think so?" [13]

The whole story is there in the last two pages, unsaid yet expressed: the heartrending story of Jake and Brett and the story of a whole generation—up to the Spanish Civil War.

Finally, in the Epilogue to *Death in the Afternoon* we have a

perfect example of what the new method of description is capable
of achieving by heaped and hurried contrasts. This piece seems
to represent just a hodgepodge of scenes and scenery, sayings and
doings, characters and destinies of people, all put in the conditional
so as to say: if all this had been told, it would have been Spain.
But in fact it is being told, and it gives us Spain, her panorama,
her atmosphere, her smell, intentionally presented in this manner:

It should have the smell of burnt powder and the smoke and the
flash and the noise of the traca going off through the green leaves of
the trees and it should have the taste of horchata, ice-cold horchata,
and the new-washed streets in the sun, and the melons and beads of
cool on the outside of the pitchers of beer; the storks on the houses
in Barco de Avila and wheeling in the sky and the red-mud color of
the ring; and at night dancing to the pipes and the drum with lights
through the green leaves and the portrait of Garibaldi framed in leaves.
It should, if it were enough of a book, have the forced smile of
Lagartito; it was once a real smile, and the unsuccessful matadors
swimming with the cheap whores out on the Manzanares along the
Pardo road; beggars can't be choosers, Louis said; playing ball on
the grass by the stream where the fairy marquis came out in his car
with the boxer; where we made the paellas, and walked home in the
dark with the cars coming fast along the road; and with electric lights
through the green leaves and the dew settling the dust, in the cool at
night. . . .[14]

Here the new sensibility is in full bloom, emerging from the
impact of the crowded surfaces, their kaleidoscopic, fleeting composition, their stirring contrasts. This enrapturing change, indeed
simultaneousness of sensations as shown in the visual flashes of
this passage, this is the very experience of our modern life.

The style of Gertrude Stein, young Hemingway's artistic tutor,
is related to Hemingway's mode of expression in some respects.
Yet while he conveys the inner life of his characters through an
objective rendering of the casual shuffle of daily events, through
"free association" of external facts, Gertrude Stein tells her sights
and insights most subjectively. She lets go, breaks through the flux
of surface happenings and even through syntactic coherence into

interior free association, indulging in her delight of idiomatic talk. Even where Hemingway uses stream-of-consciousness techniques, as in the feverish soliloquies of Harry in "The Snows of Kiliman-jaro," he hardly delves below the surface level—in contradistinc-tion to Faulkner who reaches deep into the darknesses and com-plexities of the psyche and with a grandiose linguistic recklessness mingles the various spheres and levels of human life.

THE SPECIFIC ANARCHY of our modern life, which results from an uncontrollable mass of events and impressions, has also affected the *style of modern poetry* everywhere in the Western world. In poetry, however, the momentum and expression of this condition extend into new, additional dimensions. The rapid sequence of abrupt and apparently discordant elements comprises many levels of reality, outer and inner levels, external manifestations as well as innermost tremors. This makes for an unlimited richness and com-plexity of interplay between the various elements, and implicitly brings about the often decried cryptic character of modern poetry.

Here the surfaces have cracked, as indeed they have in our very reality. Accordingly, the movement of the verse can no longer be that coherent flow in rational and syntactic order which marked all poetic diction up to the nineteenth century. Modern poetic diction moves in jumps, traverses phenomenal chasms and evokes inner contacts between diverse elements and spheres whose cor-respondences elude all rational evidence. Modern poetry is charac-terized by a terrific tempo which is a result of that inner telescop-ing, and by an outward incoherence which, in good poetry, is not actual incoherence but rather what I would call sub-coherence. Of course it is such sub-coherence only in the masterly, that means really controlled, creations of the true poet. Unfortunately, but nec-essarily, the new poetic style lends itself to an often whimsical use—and that is abuse—by epigones. While in former times epigones were more easily recognizable by the flatness of their mimicking the tone and manner of masters, today, conversely, their aping takes the form of outdoing; they distinguish themselves mostly by frantic leaps between things and aspects as discrepant as possible, without the control of an inner necessity.

The three founding fathers of modern poetry are Baudelaire, Gerard Manley Hopkins and Walt Whitman. Baudelaire, notably in his famous poem, *Correspondances,* revealed the experience of such inner contacts and correspondences as evinced by the modern poets.[15] He expressed the experience, yet did not drive it to a point where it would breed a new stylistic form. His peculiar role in the development of modern poetry becomes very clear when we juxtapose two complementary characterizations, one by André Gide and another by Rimbaud. Gide writes in a preface to his *Anthologie de la poésie Française:* "One did not notice at once the extraordinary innovation which Baudelaire brought into poetry. For a long time one condescended to see only the novelty of the subjects treated in the *Fleurs du Mal.* . . . But it was a revolution without precedent no longer to abandon oneself to the lyric flux, to resist the ease of 'inspiration,' not to relinquish oneself to rhetoric, not to drift along with words, images, and outdated conventions, but rather to treat the muse as an obstinate unruly one, one to be subjugated, instead of yielding to her with fettered intellect and captive critical sense; in short, requesting art to discipline poetry. Baudelaire, under the influence of Poe, and in contrast to his contemporaries, introduced into art consciousness and conscience, patience and determination." [16] And Rimbaud says in a letter to Paul Demeny (May 15, 1871): "The late romanticists have much of visionaries. . . . But since sighting the invisible and hearing the unheard is something quite different from apprehending the spirit of things dead, Baudelaire is the first great seer, king of poets, a veritable God. And yet he lived in a still too artistic milieu; and his much exalted form is trifling. The discoveries of realms unknown call for new forms." [17] Baudelaire, however, is an initiator in other respects as well, as we shall see later.

Gerard Manley Hopkins is an innovator not only through his use of "sprung rhythm" but through the whole nature of his verse of which sprung rhythm is just one element and which, his con-

scious artistry and theorizing notwithstanding, issued immediately
from the pressures of his passions and conflicts. As with scarcely
another poet, his theory and conscious working effort merge, coincide almost, with the spontaneity of his expression. In certain
respects, to be sure, his theoretical expositions are an *a posteriori*
justification of his practice, as when he looks for an ancestry to his
sprung rhythm in Latin and Greek and pre-Elizabethan verse and
in the choruses of "Samson Agonistes." Those specific metrical
irregularities which he claims as antecedents have a purely formal
character and are far from producing the explosive effects of his
own actual sprung rhythm. This sprung rhythm turns into something entirely different and novel through its combination, indeed,
unity with the other components of Hopkins' verse: alliteration,
repetition, interior rhyme, juxtaposition of stresses, variations of
consonance—which in conjunction with the sprung rhythm come
to act as dissonances—strange enjambments, complex and compressed words, archaisms and neologisms. All this, expressing as
it does the most violent inner conflicts, shocks and intellectually
sharpened emotions, produces that tempo, that jumping movement,
that unity and simultaneity of most discordant elements which are
the distinctive features of modern poetry:

Not, I'll not, carrion comfort, Despair, not feast on thee;
Not untwist—slack they may be—these last strands of man
In me ór, most weary, cry *I can no more*. I can;
Can something, hope, wish day come, not choose not to be.
But ah, but O thou terrible, why wouldst thou rude on me
Thy wring-world right foot rock? lay a lionlimb against me? scan
With darksome devouring eyes my bruisèd bones? and fan,
O in turns of tempest, me heaped there; me frantic to avoid thee
    and flee?

Why? That my chaff might fly; my grain lie, sheer and clear.
Nay in all that toil, that coil, since (seems) I kissed the rod,
Hand rather, my heart lo! lapped strength, stole joy, would laugh,
    chéer.
Cheer whom though? the hero whose heaven-handling flung me, fóot
    tród

Me? or me that fought him? O which one? is it each one? That night,
    that year
Of now done darkness I wretch lay wrestling with (my God!) my
    God.[18]

*   *   *

No worst, there is none. Pitched past pitch of grief,
More pangs will, schooled at forepangs, wilder wring.
Comforter, where, where is your comforting?
Mary, mother of us, where is your relief?
My cries heave, herds-long; huddle in a main, a chief
Woe, world-sorrow; on an age-old anvil wince and sing—
Then lull, then leave off. Fury had shrieked 'No ling-
ering! Let me be fell; force I must be brief.'

   O the mind, mind has mountains; cliffs of fall
Frightful, sheer, no-man-fathomed. Hold them cheap
May who ne'er hung there. Nor does long our small
Durance deal with that steep or deep. Here! creep,
Wretch, under a comfort serves in a whirlwind: all
Life death does end and each day dies with sleep.[19]

Hopkins' poetry, however, was published only in 1918, although
he died in 1889, and therefore it was late in exerting its influence.
For this reason Hopkins may be considered rather an anticipator
than an actual originator of the modern poetic mode of expression.
The real inaugurator was Walt Whitman whose *Leaves of Grass*
appeared in 1855 and was soon translated and widely read in
Europe. While Hopkins' style was the outcome of very personal,
singular coincidences, Whitman's dithyrambic commingling of di-
versities arose directly from the enrapturing experience of the
modern democratic *civitas,* from the sensing of the overwhelming
simultaneous omnipresence of all the disparate contents of our
civilization:

      Victory, union, faith, identity, time,
      The indissoluble compacts, riches, mystery,
      Eternal progress, the kosmos, and the modern reports.

This then is life[20]

and

One's-self I sing, a simple separate person,
Yet utter the word Democratic, the word En-Masse.

Of physiology from top to toe I sing, . . .
Of Life immense in passion, pulse, and power,
Cheerful, for freest action form'd under the laws divine.
The Modern Man I sing.[21]

This of course is a lesser poem by a great poet, but it shows
strikingly the characteristic quality from which a wide family of
modern poetic forms branches out. Even Ezra Pound, who actually
detested Whitman, could not help recognizing him as an ancestor:

It was you that broke the new wood,
Now is a time for carving.
We have one sap and one root—
Let there be commerce between us.[22]

THE STYLE CHARACTERISTICS of Whitman and Hopkins pervade
modern poetry in all Western countries. Sometimes it is Whitman,
sometimes Hopkins who seems more predominant. In most of the
prominent poets of our time our human situation manifests itself
through the new tempo, the jumping movement, the shrill, abrupt
contrasts between phenomena from most distant spheres and different levels of existence, from daily, slangy intercourse to innermost
intenseness. Densest visual concentration and sensual touch are
followed by sudden plunges from the visual into psychic depths,
or flights into the thinnest argumentative abstraction, stratospheric
abstraction, losing all sensory gravity. The crowding of events is
mirrored in a crowding of imagery, a general overcrowding of the
verse. Surface incoherence conceals inner sub-coherence.

We find new word combinations, lack of punctuation, the multifold tone-color, techniques of rhyme and alliteration as introduced

by Hopkins, mixing of languages, the strangest, wildest enjambments, sometimes to the point of absurdity (as for instance in Cummings), intended to stress the flow but in fact blurring or destroy-
ing the rhythmical, musical character of the poem.

All this expresses an overwhelming, often enrapturing feeling of
the simultaneity, the whirling co-existence of the disparate and
fragmentary multitude that populates our life and our consciousness: *all-embracement of discontinuity*. In some poets such feeling
led to a contraction, a spiritual transcendence of time.

The following selections from the work of some of the true poets
of our age, American, English, German, French, Spanish, will show
the stylistic relationships and common attributes of modern poetry
as described above.

Ezra Pound, a genuine and most influential poet, adds to the
diversity of contrasting matters and levels his specialties of slangy
vituperation, private esotericism, and promiscuous erudition. He
is also, as far as I know, the first to mingle different languages
and, inconsiderately, excessively to insert foreign quotations, names
of casual acquaintances, and so forth, in his context. In the midst
of his rarefied chaos blossom beautiful lines of tender emotion
and of exquisite, most delicately precise transparence.

> I sat on the Dogana's steps
> For the gondolas cost too much, that year,
> And there were not "those girls," there was one face,
> And the Buccentoro twenty yards off, howling "Stretti,"
> The lit cross-beams, that year, in the Morosini,
> And peacocks in Koré's house, or there may have been.
>   Gods float in the azure air,
> Bright gods and Tuscan, back before dew was shed.
> Light: and the first light, before ever dew was fallen.
> Panisks, and from the oak, dryas,
> And from the apple, maelid,
> Through all the wood, and the leaves are full of voices,
> A-whisper, and the clouds bowe over the lake,
> And there are gods upon them,
> And in the water, the almond-white swimmers,

The silvery water glazes the upturned nipple,
    As Poggio has remarked.
Green veins in the turquoise,
Or, the gray steps lead up under the cedars.[23]

* * *

For the seven lakes, and by no man these verses:
Rain; empty river; a voyage,
Fire from frozen cloud, heavy rain in the twilight
Under the cabin roof was one lantern.
The reeds are heavy; bent;
and the bamboos speak as if weeping. . . .

Behind hill the monk's bell
borne on the wind.
Sail passed here in April; may return in October
Boat fades in silver; slowly;
Sun blaze alone on the river.
Where wine flag catches the sunset
Sparse chimneys smoke in the cross light. . . .

Sun up; work
Sundown; to rest
dig well and drink of the water
dig field; eat of the grain
Imperial power is? and to us what is it?

The fourth; the dimension of stillness.
And the power over wild beasts.[24]

* * *

    slum owners,
usurers squeezing crab-lice, pandars to authority, . . .

the air without refuge of silence,
    the drift of lice, teething,
and above it the mouthing of orators,
    the arse-belching of preachers.
    And Invidia,
the corruptio, foetor, fungus,
liquid animals, melted ossifications,

slow rot, foetid combustion,
    chewed cigar-butts, without dignity, without tragedy,
. . . . .m Episcopus, waving a condom full of black-beetles,
monopolists, obstructors of knowledge.
    obstructors of distribution.[25]

The early T. S. Eliot was greatly influenced by Pound, but from the outset has been more disciplined. The same experience of a fractionized world seems to veer toward a spiritual conclusion which finds its accomplished expression in the great poems of his later periods. Here are some examples of the earlier stage:

His soul stretched tight across the skies
That fade behind a city block,
Or trampled by insistent feet
At four and five and six o'clock;
And short square fingers stuffing pipes,
And evening newspapers, and eyes
Assured of certain certainties,
The conscience of a blackened street
Impatient to assume the world.

I am moved by fancies that are curled
Around these images, and cling:
The notion of some infinitely gentle
Infinitely suffering thing.

Wipe your hand across your mouth, and laugh;
The worlds revolve like ancient women
Gathering fuel in vacant lots.[26]

*   *   *

Red river, red river,
Slow flow heat is silence
No will is still as a river
Still. Will heat move
Only through the mocking-bird
Heard once? Still hills
Wait. Gates wait. Purple trees,
White trees, wait, wait,
Delay, decay. Living, living,

Never moving. Ever moving
Iron thoughts came with me
And go with me:
Red river, river, river.[27]

*   *   *

Here the crow starves, here the patient stag
Breeds for the rifle. Between the soft moor
And the soft sky, scarcely room
To leap or soar. Substance crumbles, in the thin air
Moon cold or moon hot. The road winds in
Listlessness of ancient war
Languor of broken steel,
Clamour of confused wrong, apt
In silence. Memory is strong
Beyond the bone. Pride snapped,
Shadow of pride is long, in the long pass
No concurrence of bone.[28]

*   *   *

Unreal City
Under the brown fog of a winter noon
Mr. Eugenides, the Smyrna merchant
Unshaven, with a pocket full of currants
C.i.f. London: documents at sight,
Asked me in demotic French
To luncheon at the Cannon Street Hotel
Followed by a weekend at the Metropole.

At the violet hour, when the eyes and back
Turn upward from the desk, when the human engine waits
Like a taxi throbbing waiting,
I Tiresias, though blind, throbbing between two lives,
Old man with wrinkled female breasts, can see
At the violet hour, the evening hour that strives
Homeward, and brings the sailor home from sea,
The typist home at teatime, clears her breakfast, lights
Her stove, and lays out food in tins. . . .[29]

*   *   *

What is that sound high in the air
Murmur of maternal lamentation

Who are those hooded hordes swarming
Over endless plains, stumbling in cracked earth
Ringed by the flat horizon only
What is the city over the mountains
Cracks and reforms and bursts in the violet air
Falling towers
Jerusalem Athens Alexandria
Vienna London
Unreal [30]

The experience of simultaneity of the diverse is also present in
Auden's poetry. It is difficult to quote any single poem, for we
sense that experience throughout his work. Auden is the poet of
our modern city in its widest civilizational purport, of the vast,
accidental meeting place and crossroads it represents, with its multifarious aspects, avenues, transcendences: human, intellectual, social, political (I refer to poems like *The City, The Capital, The
Ship, The Labyrinth, New Years Letter, The Crossroads,* and so
forth). The crossroad stands out as his central symbol. He tries
to capture the friction of unlived lives, the frustrations, the whole
neurotic mess that settles in the lonesomeness of the metropolitan
cluster.

PETITION

Sir, no man's enemy, forgiving all
But will its negative inversion, be prodigal:
Send to us power and light, a sovereign touch
Curing the intolerable neural itch,
The exhaustion of weaning, the liar's quinsy,
And the distortions of ingrown virginity.
Prohibit sharply the rehearsed response
And gradually correct the coward's stance;
Cover in time with beams those in retreat
That, spotted, they turn though the reverse were great;
Publish each healer that in city lives
Or country houses at the end of drives;
Harrow the house of the dead; look shining at
New styles of architecture, a change of heart.[31]

Dylan Thomas, at the very opposite pole, was one among very few who was still able—and praised it like a blessing—to draw his vital power from the deep sources and resources of a distinct region and its unique nature, physical and human, from a restricted homeplace opening on the immensity of the sea. He sang the mythical and demonic transcendencies of this land Wales and these villages of his, men and beasts and common life and the province of his childhood. Yet in his songs, moving in strides, wave over wave of packed, compressed imagery, in this rendering of a "rumpus of shapes," we feel the same speed and abruptness, and at the same time comprehensiveness, which could only be infused by the atmosphere of our epoch. There are passages in his later poetry in which the cadences of both Whitman and Hopkins breathe through his very own rhapsodic diction; so in the marvelous "Author's Prologue" to the *Collected Poems:*

> Seaward the salmon, sucked sun slips,
> And the dumb swans drub blue
> My dabbed bay's dusk, as I hack
> This rumpus of shapes
> For you to know
> How I, a spinning man,
> Glory also this star, bird
> Roared, sea born, man torn, blood blest.
> Hark: I trumpet the place,
> From fish to jumping hill! Look:
> I build my bellowing ark
> To the best of my love
> As the flood begins,
> Out of the fountainhead
> Of fear, rage red, manalive,
> Molten and mountainous to stream
> Over the wound asleep
> Sheep white hollow farms
> To Wales in my arms. . . .[32]

I include only a touch of Marianne Moore and a "tinily" bit of Cummings from the many English and American poets who could still be presented within this context. In the poem quoted here, Marianne Moore gives an admirable description of the situation and predicament of the modern poet amidst the crowd of luxuriantly specialized sensations:

THOSE VARIOUS SCALPELS

those
various sounds consistently indistinct, like intermingled echoes
   struck from thin glasses successively at random—the
      inflection disguised: your hair, the tails of two
   fighting-cocks head to head in stone—like sculptured
         scimitars re-
      peating the curve of your ears in reverse order: your
        eyes, flowers of ice

and
snow sown by tearing winds on the cordage of disabled ships; your
      raised hand,
   an ambiguous signature: your cheeks, those rosettes
   of blood on the stone floors of French châteaux, with
   regard to which the guides are so affirmative—those re-
        grets
      of the retoucher on the contemporary stone: your
        other hand,

a
bundle of lances all alike, partly hid by emeralds from
      Persia
   and the fractional magnificence of Florentine
      goldwork—a collection of little objects—
   sapphires set with emeralds, and pearls with a moonstone,
      made fine
      with enamel in grey, yellow, and dragon-fly blue; a
      lemon, a

pear
and three bunches of grapes, tied with silver: your dress, a
      magnificent square
   cathedral tower of uniform
      and at the same time, diverse appearance—a

species of vertical vineyard rustling in the storm
   of conventional opinion. Are they weapons or scal-
      pels? Whetted

to
brilliance by the hard majesty of that sophistication which
     is su-
   perior to opportunity, these things are rich
     instruments with which to experiment; naturally. But
   why dissect destiny with instruments which
     are more highly specialized than the tissues of destiny
       itself?[33]

E. E. Cummings, finally, drives the new mode of poetic expression to the extreme, indeed, sometimes to the clownishly absurd.
He exploits to the full Ezra Pound's innovations. His work spans
a wide range, from the sweetest, most lyrical, most melodious and
enticing songs to sign-structures reminiscent of Dadaism and
Lettrism. Even in his less radical creations the telegrammatic tight-
ening and overloading of the verse, the exuberantly wanton play of
verbal and syntactical combinations and breaks, the hieroglyphic
juggling with punctuation and types—all these assume a teasingly
impeditive character, especially when applied to rapturous vistas
and ingenious insights most enchantingly formulated. Particular
devices—the use of opening and closing parentheses in reverse
order, or beginning and ending of poems in the middle of a sentence (unbeginnings and unendings as it were)—emphasize the
fragmentariness, the openness of his pieces toward all that roams
in the world. There is hardly another poet whose *oeuvre* would
show so well the conquests and disruptions of modern poetic
expression:

    light's lives lurch
            a once world quickly from rises

    army the gradual of unbeing (fro
    on stiffening greenly air and to ghosts go
    drift slippery hands tease slim float twitter faces)

only stand with me, love! against these its
until you are and until i am dreams

until comes vast dark until sink last things

(least all turns almost now; now almost swims
into a hair's width: into less? into

not)
       love, stand with me while silence sings

not into nothing and nothing into never
and never into (touch me! love) forever
—until is and shall be and was are night's

total exploding millionminded Who[34]

                *   *   *

      sunset)edges become swiftly
      corners(Besides
      which,i note how
      fatally toward

      twilight the a little
      tilted streets spill lazily
      multitudes out of final

      towers;captured:in
      the narrow light

     of

inverno)this
is the season of
crumbling & folding
hopes,hark;feet(fEEt
f-e-e-t-noWheregoingaLwaYs [35]

                *   *   *

luminous tendril of celestial wish

(whying diminutive bright deathlessness
to these my not themselves believing eyes
adventuring,enormous nowhere from)

querying affirmation;virginal

immediacy of precision:more
and perfectly more most ethereal
silence through twilight's mystery made flesh—

dreamslender exquisite white firstful flame

—new moon!as(by the miracle of your
sweet innocence refuted)clumsy some
dull cowardice called a world vanishes,

teach disappearing also me the keen
illimitable secret of begin[36]

SIMILAR TRAITS are easily recognizable in the poetic diction of the European continent. German lyric, even in its most stylistically advanced stages, is still tinged with romantic, dreamlike hues. I include pieces by three representative poets, Georg Heym, Georg Trakl, Gottfried Benn.

Georg Heym is the earliest among them, chronologically as well as stylistically. He died before the First World War in 1912, at the age of twenty-five. While skating, he fell through cracking ice and was drowned. Not only did he pre-sense his peculiar death: his poetry shows his magical attraction to water scenes, to death by water. He was also haunted by prophetic visions of an impending cataclysm, of burning cities, wars and apocalyptic ravages:

DIE NEBELSTÄDTE

Der Nebelstädte
Winzige Wintersonne
Leuchtet mir mitten ins gläserne Herz.
Das ist voll vertrockneter Blumen
Gleich einem gestorbenen Garten.

Wohl war im Frührot noch
Blutiger Wolken Krampf,
Und der sterbenden Städte
Schultern zuckten im Kampf.

Wir aber gingen von dannen
Und rissen uns auf mit ein Mal,
Dumpf scholl aus dem wilden Gestreite
Finsternis,—Unrat—siebenfarbiger Qual.

Doch niemand rühret das starre
Gestern noch mit der Hand,
Da der rostige Mond
Kollerte unter den Rand
In wolkiger Winde Geknarre.[37]

THE FOG CITIES

Foggy cities'
Tiny winter sun
Gleams right into my glassy heart.
Heart that is full of wilted flowers
Like a garden gone to its death.

In the early red was still
Throe of bloody clouds,
And the dying cities' shoulders
Twitched in struggle.

Yet we took leave
Took heart of a sudden,
Hollow from the wild scrimmage
Echoed darkness—filth—sevencolored pain.

Yet no one's hand the stark
Yesterday any more touches,
When the rusty moon
Toppled below the brink
In clouded winds' screak.

(*Translation by Hanna M. Loewy*)

Georg Trakl (1887-1914), an already oversensitive person,
was dragged into the war as a dispensary chemist. Having witnessed
its outer and inner ravages and the horrors of a typhus epidemic,
he went mad and poisoned himself in a military hospital in Poland.

Rationally inarticulate, this great poet speaks through deeply, intensely colored images which render somber, emotionally over-charged sceneries. Pictures and visions are incoherently juxtaposed, but just such strange combinations, interreflections of different spheres, convey a particularly intense feeling of real situations:

GEBURT

Gebirge: Schwärze, Schweigen und Schnee.
Rot vom Wald niedersteigt die Jagd;
O, die moosigen Blicke des Wilds.

Stille der Mutter; unter schwarzen Tannen
Öffnen sich die schlafenden Hände,
Wenn verfallen der kalte Mond erscheint.

O, die Geburt des Menschen. Nächtlich rauscht
Blaues Wasser im Felsengrund;
Seufzend erblickt sein Bild der gefallene Engel,

Erwacht ein Bleiches in dumpfer Stube.
Zwei Monde
Erglänzen die Augen der steinernen Greisin.

Weh, der Gebärenden Schrei. Mit schwarzem Flügel
Rührt die Knabenschläfe die Nacht,
Schnee, der leise aus purpurner Wolke sinkt.[38]

BIRTH

Mountains: blackness, silence and snow.
Red from the forest descends the hunt;
O, the mossy eyes of the deer.

Silence of the mother; under black firs
The sleeping hands unfold,
When in decay the chilly moon appears.

O, the birth of man. Nightly murmurs
Blue water in the depth of the rock;
Sighing the fallen angel espies his image,

There wakes a pallor in stuffy room.
Two moons
Light in the eyes of the stony old woman.

Pain, the birthgiver's scream. With black wing
Night brushes the temple of the boy,
Snow, that softly sinks from crimson cloud.

(*Translation by Hanna M. Loewy*)

FÖHN

Blinde Klage im Wind, mondene Wintertage,
Kindheit, leise verhallen die Schritte an schwarzer Hecke,
Langes Abendgeläut.
Leise kommt die weisse Nacht gezogen,

Verwandelt in purpurne Träume Schmerz und Plage
Des steinigen Lebens,
Dass nimmer der dornige Stachel ablasse vom verwesenden Leib.

Tief im Schlummer aufseufzt die bange Seele,

Tief der Wind in zerbrochenen Bäumen,
Und es schwankt die Klagegestalt
Der Mutter durch den einsamen Wald

Dieser schweigenden Trauer; Nächte,
Erfüllt von Tränen, feurigen Engeln.
Silbern zerschellt an kahler Mauer ein kindlich Gerippe.[39]

SOUTH WIND

Blind wail in the wind, moony winterdays,
Childhood, softly the footsteps die away at black hedge,
Long evening chimes.
In silent train the white night enters in,

Transforms into purple dreams pain and toil
Of stony life,
That never the thorny prick cease from the decaying body.

Deep in slumber outsighs the anxious soul,

Deep the wind in broken trees,
And there sways the wailing form
Of the mother through the lonely forest

Of this silent grief; nights,
Brimmed with tears, fiery angels.
Silverly shatters on bare wall a child's skeleton.

(Translation by Hanna M. Loewy)

Gottfried Benn (1886-1956) is less authentic, more intellec-
tualized. In his verse we find strong parallels to recent Anglo-
American poetry: speeding, telescoping, gathering as many and as
distant portions of reality into one visual unit. Characterizations
by quick touches are clothed at times in traditional stanzas, since
his emphasis was, in general, on strict artistic form which he considered the last mainstay of our crumbling world.

SEPTEMBER

Du, über den Zaun gebeugt mit Phlox
(vom Regenguss zerspalten,
seltsamen Wildgeruchs),
der gern auf Stoppeln geht,
zu alten Leuten tritt,
die Balsaminen pflücken,
Rauch auf Feldern
mit Lust und Trauer atmet—

aufsteigenden Gemäuers,
das noch sein Dach vor Schnee und Winter will,
kalklöschenden Gesellen
ein: "ach, vergebens" zuzurufen,
nur zögernd sich verhält—

gedrungen eher als hochgebaut,
auch unflätigen Kürbis nackt am Schuh,
fett und gesichtslos, dies Krötengewächs—

Ebenen-entstiegener,
Endmond aller Flammen,
aus Frucht- und Fieberschwellungen
abfallend, schon verdunkelten Gesichts—

Narr oder Täufer,
des Sommers Narr, Nachplapperer, Nachruf
oder der Gletscher Vorlied,
jedenfalls Nussknacker,
Schilfmäher,
Beschäftigter mit Binsenwahrheiten—

vor dir der Schnee,
Hochschweigen, unfruchtbar
die Unbesambarkeit der Weite:
da langt dein Arm hin,
doch über den Zaun gebeugt
die Kraut- und Käferdränge,
das Lebenwollende,
Spinnen und Feldmäuse—[40]

SEPTEMBER

You, bending over the fence with phlox
(cloven by down-poured rain,
with queer wild-gamish smell),
who love to walk on stubble,
approach old people
gathering touch-me-nots,
inbreathe with delight
and sadness spiralling field-smoke—

by mounting masonry,
still hoping for roof before snow and winter,
so hesitantly refrain
from calling to work-mates slaking lime
"Give up, it's all no good"—

thickset rather than tall,
with obscene pumpkin naked on boots,
fat and faceless, that toad-like growth—

outclimbed from plains,
all flames' outwaning moon,
from fruit- and fever-swellings
decaying, with already darkened face—

fool or baptist,
summer's fool, speech-mimic, obituary,
or the glacier's prelude,
nut-cracker anyway,
reed-mower,
busied with platitudes—

before you the snow,
high silence, the barren
unsowableness of distance:
so far your arm can reach,
but, bending over the fence,
the herb- and beetle-throngs,
the will to live—
spiders and fieldmice—

(*Translation by J. B. Leishman*)

Turning to France, we find milder and subtler forms of the same stylistic phenomena, the French language and temperament being by nature a smoothing and polishing medium, intrinsically rational and averse to incoherence. But, as will be seen in the following poems by three of the foremost poets of our age, Paul Éluard, Pierre Reverdy and René Char, the new mode of experience forces even this most graceful instrument into its service. Rimbaud, notably in his rather jocular *conneries,* was the first to revolutionize French language and verse and to impose on them the new poetic violences. All three, Éluard, Reverdy and Char, belonged to the Resistance. The impact of the horrors of our age resounds through their poetry.

PAUL ÉLUARD:

O rire végétal ouvrant une clairière
De gorges chantonnant interminablement

Mains où le sang s'est effacé
Où l'innocence est volontaire
Gaieté gagnée tendresse du bois mort
Chaleurs d'hiver pulpes séchées
Fraîcheurs d'été sortant des fleurs nouvelles
Constant amour multiplié tout nu

Rien à haïr et rien à pardonner
Aucun destin n'illustre notre front
Dans l'orage notre faiblesse
Est l'aiguille la plus sensible
Et la raison de l'orage
Image ô contact parfait
L'espace est notre milieu
Et le temps notre horizon

Quelques cailloux sur un sentier battu
De l'herbe comme un souvenir vague
Le ciel couvert et la nuit en avance
Quelques vitrines étrennant leurs lampes
Des trous la porte et la fenêtre ouvertes
Sur des gens qui sont enfermés. . . .

O vegetal laugh opening a clearing
Of throats humming interminably
Hands where blood is obliterated
Where innocence is voluntary
Gaiety won tenderness of dead wood
Heat of winter dried-out pulps
Coolness of summer springing from new flowers
Constant love multiplied all naked

Nothing to hate and nothing to pardon
No destiny shines on our forehead
In the tempest our frailty
Is the most sensitive needle
And the reason of the tempest
Image O perfect contact
Space is our center
And time our horizon

A few pebbles on a beaten pathway
Of grass like a vague memory
The sky cloudy night advancing
A few windows trying out their lamps
Of holes the door and window open
On men who are locked in. . . .

* * *

Je ne me méfie plus je suis un fils de femme
La vacance de l'homme et le temps bonifié
La réplique grandiloquente
Des étoiles minuscules

Et nous montons

Les derniers arguments du néant sont vaincus
Et le dernier bourdonnement
Des pas revenant sur eux-mêmes

Peu à peu se décomposent
Les alphabets ânonnés
De l'histoire et des morales
Et la syntaxe soumise
Des souvenirs enseignés

Et c'est très vite
La liberté conquise
La liberté feuille de mai
Chauffée à blanc
Et le feu aux nuages
Et le feu aux oiseaux
Et le feu dans les caves
Et les hommes dehors
Et les hommes partout
Tenant toute la place
Abattant les murailles

Se partageant le pain
Dévêtant le soleil
S'embrassant sur le front
Habillant les orages

Et s'embrassant les mains
Faisant fleurir charnel
Et le temps et l'espace. . . .[41]

I distrust myself no longer I am the son of woman
The vacancy of man and time made good
The grandiloquent reply
Of microscopic stars

And we go higher

The last arguments of nothingness are conquered
And the final buzzing
Of steps returning on themselves

Little by little are decomposed
The stammering alphabets
Of history of morals
And the submissive syntax
Of learnéd memories

And it's very quick
Liberty conquered
May-leaf liberty
Heated white
The fire in the clouds
The fire in the birds
The fire in the cellars
And the men outside
And the men everywhere
Holding all places
Breaking down the walls

Sharing the bread
Unveiling the sun
Kissing on the forehead
Dressing the tempests
Kissing hands
Making flesh flower
And time and space. . . .

(*Translations by Lloyd Alexander*)

PIERRE REVERDY:

CHEMIN DE PAS

Près du chemin ouvert
    Et du bois sous la neige
    La pointe qui soulève la nuit
La lampe veille
    Sur le visage blanc
    Les paupières baissées
    Sur le mur découvert
    Les volets refermés
Les ornières du sol se joignent
Le pont plus près
Les carrés tout autour
    Les formes
    Les objets

    Le mystère des portes
On franchit l'émotion qui barre le chemin
Et sans se retourner on va toujours plus loin
    La maison ne suit pas
    La maison nous regarde
    Entre deux arbres
      sa chevelure rouge
      et son front blanc
    Le silence s'attarde[42]

THE PATH

By the open path
    And the wood under snow
    The peak that lifts high the night
The lamp watches
    Over the white face
    The eyelids lowered
    Over the uncovered wall
    The re-closed shutters
The trails of the ground unite
The bridge closer
The squares all around
    The forms
    The objects

The mystery of doors
One crosses the emotion that bars the way
And without turning around one keeps going further
    The house does not follow
    The house looks at us
    Between two trees
       its red hair
       and its white brow
    The silence lingers

(Translation by Hanna M. Loewy)

LONGUE PORTÉE

Poissons dorés surpris dans les mailles du vent
   Catapultes de la lumière
Regains de soif lancés dans tous les coins
Détentes révolues des appétits déteints
Tout se mêle dans les remous des ondes prisonnières
La poitrine résonne comme un sol creux
Il y a des ombres sur le buvard de tes joues
Et des claquements de porcelaine bleue
Par-dessus tous les toits aux lames de violettes
Un rouge de valeur plus dense sans écho
Un sang plus étendu au flanc de la colline
Des oiseaux migrateurs sans orientation
Et tous ces hommes morts sans rime ni raison
Tant de coeurs desséchés
Sans plomb
Comme des feuilles[43]

FAR-REACHING

Golden fish caught in the meshes of the wind
   Catapults of the light
Resurges of thirst launched in all corners
Ultimate subsidence of faded appetites
Everything mixes in the rolling of captive waves
The heart resounds like a hollow ground
There are shadows on the blotter of your cheeks
And clatter of blue porcelain

Above all the violet-bladed roofs
A red more intense without resonance
A blood more outspread on the flank of the hill
Migrant birds without orientation
And all those humans dead without rhyme or reason
So many hearts dried up
Weightless
Like leaves

(Translation by E. K.)

RENÉ CHAR:

VICTOIRE ÉCLAIR

L'oiseau bêche la terre,
Le serpent sème,
La mort améliorée
Applaudit la récolte.

Pluton dans le ciel!

L'explosion en nous.
Là seulement dans moi.
Fol et sourd, comment pourrais-je l'être davantage?

Plus de second soi-même, de visage changeant, plus de saison pour la
flamme et de saison pour l'ombre!

Avec la lente neige descendent les lépreux.

Soudain l'amour, l'égal de la terreur,
D'une main jamais vue arrête l'incendie, redresse le soleil, reconstruit
l'Amie.

Rien n'annonçait une existence si forte.[44]

LIGHTNING VICTORY

The bird tills the soil,
The serpent sows,
Death, enriched,
Praises the harvest.

Pluto in the sky!

In ourselves the explosion.
There in myself only.
Mad and deaf, how could I be more so?

No more second self, nor changing face, no more season of flame and
season of shadow!

The lepers come down with the slow snow.

Suddenly love, the equal of terror,
With a hand I had never seen, puts an end to the fire, straightens the
sun, reshapes the beloved.

Nothing had heralded so strong an existence.

(*Translation by W. S. Merwin*)

The sensing of the co-existence, co-presence of most disparate
entities, that all-embracement of discontinuity, has in certain poets
become internalized; it has turned into a profound feeling of contraction not only of space but of time—a gathering of all times
and their contents, of our entire existence in one sublime moment,
a concentration which is almost equivalent to an abolition of time.
Such is the final and focal experience of T. S. Eliot whose concern
has come to be the "dreamcrossed twilight between birth and
dying"; "the place of solitude where three dreams cross"; the point
of "intersection of the timeless with time":

At the still point of the turning world. Neither flesh nor fleshless;
Neither from nor towards; at the still point, there the dance is,
But neither arrest nor movement. And do not call it fixity,
Where past and future are gathered. Neither movement from nor
  towards,
Neither ascent nor decline. Except for the point, the still point,
There would be no dance, and there is only the dance.

I can only say, *there* we have been: but I cannot say where.
And I cannot say, how long, for that is to place it in time.[45]

* * *

Words move, music moves
Only in time; but that which is only living
Can only die. Words, after speech, reach
Into the silence. Only by the form, the pattern,
Can words or music reach
The stillness, as a Chinese jar still
Moves perpetually in its stillness.
Not the stillness of the violin, while the note lasts,
Not that only, but the co-existence,
Or say that the end precedes the beginning,
And the end and the beginning were always there
Before the beginning and after the end.
And all is always now . . .[46]

* * *

Home is where one starts from. As we grow older
The world becomes stranger, the pattern more complicated
Of dead and living. Not the intense moment
Isolated, with no before and after,
But a lifetime burning in every moment
And not the lifetime of one man only
But of old stones that cannot be deciphered.
There is a time for the evening under starlight,
A time for the evening under lamplight
(The evening with the photograph album).
Love is most nearly itself
When here and now cease to matter.
Old men ought to be explorers
Here and there does not matter
We must be still and still moving
Into another intensity
For a further union, a deeper communion
Through the dark cold and the empty desolation,
The wave cry, the wind cry, the vast waters
Of the petrel and the porpoise. In my end is my beginning.[47]

This contraction of time, of all times, in the point of sheer existence is even more outspoken in the work of the exquisite Spanish poet, Jorge Guillén. In ever new versions this feeling recurs in his poetry: *"¡Oh presente sin fin, ahora eterno . . . !* ("Oh present without end, eternal now!"), *"¡Oh forma presente, suma realidad!"* ("Oh present figure, ultimate reality!") *". . . prodigioso colmo de la presencia.—¡Plenitud inmediata . . . Oh absoluto Presente!"* (". . . marvelous abundance of the presence. Immediate plenitude . . . Oh absolute Present!").

CIMA DE LA DELICIA

¡Cima de la delicia!
Todo en el aire es pájaro
Se cierne lo inmediato
Resuelto en lejanía.

¡Hueste de esbeltas fuerzas!
¡Qué alacridad de mozo
En el espacio airoso.
Henchido de presencia!

El mundo tiene cándida
Profundidad de espejo.
Las más claras distancias
Sueñan lo verdadero.

¡Dulzura de los años
Irreparables! ¡Bodas
Tardías con la historia
Que desamé a diario!

¡Más, todavía más!
Hacia el sol en volandas
La plenitud se escapa.
¡Ya sólo sé cantar! [46]

PEAK OF DELIGHT

Peak of delight!
All in the air is bird.
The immediate hovers
Resolving in distance.

Multitude of slender forces!
What dash of youth
In the graceful space,
Swelling with presence!

The world has the innocent
Deepness of a mirror.
The most limpid distances
Dream true things.

Sweetness of years that
Are irreparable! late weddings
With a story
I have ceased to love each day!

More, still more!
Towards the sun in flight
Plenitude escapes.
Only now can I sing!

(*Translation by Hanna M. Loewy*)

Indeed, so intensely is the present, the ripest presence of corporeal existence, felt that it reaches transcendence. Thus Guillén, starting from the fullest perception of nature, penetrates into new spheres, new levels of existence, an infinitely delicate, superlucid existence, existence seized, as it were, in a state of spiritual evaporation.

We have observed the emergence of a new sensibility—the reverse of a new insensibility—from the multifarious fragmentation of our modern universe and from the corresponding new way of seeing things which was taught us by the objective, non-personal eye inherent in our instruments and institutions. The experience of life as a simultaneity of the utterly diverse originated such a contraction of time as to produce a novel and most intense feeling of existence. And here we have reached a point where the development described in the previous pages fuses with a converging trend that has been under way for a much longer period. This trend is, in fact, the main evolutionary current that brought forth the new sensibility and finally drove it to its extreme in the existentialist experience where it breaks up the structure of human personality.

CHAPTER FIVE

The Split from Within: II

NEW SENSIBILITY, PSYCHOANALYSIS
AND EXISTENTIALIST EXPERIENCE

Le Poète se fait voyant par un long, immense et raisonné dérègle-
ment de tous les sens. Toutes les formes d'amour, de souffrance,
de folie; il cherche lui-même, il épuise en lui tous les poisons, pour
n'en garder que les quintessences. Ineffable torture où il a besoin
de toute la foi, de toute la force surhumaine, où il devient entre
tous le grand malade, le grand criminel, le grand maudit,—et le
suprême Savant!—Car il arrive à l'inconnu! Puisqu'il a cultivé son
âme, déjà riche, plus qu'aucun! Il arrive à l'inconnu, et quand,
affolé, il finirait par perdre l'intelligence de ses visions, il les a
vues! Qu'il crève dans son bondissement par les choses inouies et
innommables: viendront d'autres horribles travailleurs; ils com-
menceront par les horizons où l'autre s'est affaissé!

(The Poet makes himself a seer through a long, tremendous,
planned derangement of all his senses. All the forms of love, of
suffering, of madness; he himself seeks and in himself exhausts
all poisons, so as to keep only the quintessences. Ineffable torture
that takes all his faith, all his superhuman strength, that makes
him, among his fellowmen, the great Sick Man, the great Criminal, the great Accurséd—and the supreme Sage!—For he reaches

137

the unknown! Because he has cultivated his soul, rich already, more than anyone else! He reaches the unknown, and if, maddened in his pursuit, he should in the end lose all understanding of his visions, still he has seen them! Let him perish in his fling through things unheard-of and unnameable; other terrible toilers will come; they will start out from the horizons where he succumbed!)

RIMBAUD

IN THE PREVIOUS chapter I attempted to show how the peculiar conditions of our modern world, the crowding of events, the "overpopulation of the surfaces" with their dynamism and their violent contrasts, produced on the one hand a new human insensibility, indeed callousness, and, on the other hand, a new observational sensibility. But I indicated at once that this particular origin of the new sensibility is not the only one nor even the main one. It is just a late tributary of a broad and very complex stream of developments starting back in the eighteenth century and leading up to the existentialist experience which, in its special way, contributed to the shattering of the human personality. This chapter will be devoted to a brief survey of the main current.

Leaving aside those special determinants which we discussed in the last chapter, we may trace the development of the new sensibility to three evolutionary agents: 1—*a deep uneasiness, malaise,* which, from the eighteenth century on, kept stirring in the minds of people unceasingly and increasingly up to our present time; 2—*a steady growth of man's self-reflection and psychological introspection,* which started in the Renaissance and continued to spread in the form of unmethodical self-scrutinies entered upon by various personalities for various reasons, until, at the end of the nineteenth century, science seized on this free human activity, as on so many others, and turned it into systematic psychoanalysis; 3—*the autonomous proliferation of artistic techniques,* of modes of expression which, in turn, fostered an enhanced susceptibility of impression. These three agents interacted and concurred in the development of the new sensibility.

The *malaise* started as early as the eighteenth century as a weariness of civilization and reason, of overwrought civilization, and abused reason. It arose among a bored French aristocracy that had arrived at a stage of civilizational saturation, indeed corruption, as depicted in *Les Liaisons Dangereuses* by Choderlos de Laclos (1782). No book is more revealing of the mentality of French society under the *Ancien Régime*. We see here how the self-mastery of the human individual, a result of the ascendancy of Reason since the Renaissance, had degenerated in French society to a hybrid enjoyment of self, enjoyment of one's superiority over his own body and mind. The supreme value of this society was an exalted elegance—which is nothing else than a playfully easy control, not only of one's physical and intellectual gifts but of one's emotions as well. In the *Liaisons Dangereuses* we see the protagonists exhibit their artful badinage and scheming—scheming just for the sake of showing their frivolous skill and without the slightest regard for their victims. An indispensable part of their performance is the display of a cocky supremacy over their emotional life. They treat it the way a smart rider parades his well-trained, beautiful horse; never for a moment is emotion allowed to get out of hand, never is a pleasure, a *goût,* allowed to deviate into real feeling. Such abuse of rational control—the predominance of rule in every domain, the splendor of futile wit driven to the peak of self-negation and covering an inner erosion—was bound to collapse into utter lassitude, *ennui* in the full French sense of the word. *Ennui* does not express mere boredom, but the melancholy, the desolation that goes with it. The collapse can be observed in the correspondence of the Marquise du Deffand with Horace Walpole and the Duchesse de Choiseul. We are here at the source of French romanticism; we witness as it were its birth: *"J'admirais hier au soir,"* she writes to Horace Walpole (October 20, 1766), *"la nombreuse compagnie qui était chez moi; hommes et femmes me paraissaient des machines à ressort, qui allaient, venaient, parlaient, riaient sans penser, sans réfléchir, sans sentir . . . et moi j'étais abîmée dans les réflexions les plus noires; je pensais que j'avais passé ma vie dans les illusions; que je m'étais creusé moi-même tous les abîmes dans lesquels j'étais tombée . . . qu'enfin je n'avais parfaitement bien connu personne; que je n'en avais pas été connue non plus, et que peut-être je ne me connaissais pas moi-même. On désire un appui, on se laisse charmer par l'espérance de l'avoir trouvé; c'est un songe que les circonstances dissipent et qui font l'effet du réveil."* [1] ("Last night I admired the large company of people who were at my house; men and women appeared to me like machines working by springs, moving to and fro, talking, laughing, without thinking or feeling . . . and I myself, I was lost in the blackest meditations; I pondered over the fact that I had spent my life in illusions; that I had dug myself all the abysses into which I had fallen . . . that in the end I had really known nobody, and that I was not known by anybody either, and that maybe I do not even know myself. One longs for a support, one lets oneself be deluded by the hope to have found one; it is a dream which circumstances destroy having the effect of an awakening.") And on May 23, 1767, she writes: *"Ah, la raison, la raison! qu'est ce que c'est que la raison? quel pouvoir a-t-elle? . . . quel bien procure-t-elle? Elle triomphe des passions? Cela n'est pas vrai; et si elle arrêtait les mouvements de notre âme, elle serait cent fois plus contraire à notre bonheur que les passions ne peuvent l'être; ce serait vivre pour sentir le néant, et le néant—dont je fais grand cas—n'est bon que parce qu'on ne le sent pas."* [2] ("Ah, reason, reason! What is reason? What power does it have? . . . What good can it afford you? It controls passions? This is not true; and if it really were capable of checking the movements of your soul, it would be a hundred times more contrary to your happiness than the passions ever could be. It would mean living so as to sense nothingness, and nothingness, which means much to me, is good only inasmuch as we do not sense it.") Reading this correspondence we notice how the *ennui*, which she describes as *"la privation du sentiment avec la douleur de ne pouvoir s'en passer"* [3] ("loss of sentiment with the painful feeling not to be able to do without it"), stimulates psychological analysis and self-scrutiny.

Even earlier, in 1731, two French authors, Marivaux, in his *Vie de Marianne,* and particularly the Abbé Prévost in *Manon Lescaut,* had emphasized the irresistible force of passion. While all this happened within the pale of French court society, a vigorous revolt against civilization and rationalism arose from without. Between 1761 and 1770 Jean-Jacques Rousseau, the founding father of continental romanticism, published his *Nouvelle Héloise* and his *Confessions,* the keynote of which, needless to recall, is the embittered championing of the rights of passion and sentiment as against the supremacy of reason, and the call to revert from corrupt civilization to the purity and sincerity of nature. The liberating influence of Rousseau—in concurrence with that of English realism and sentimentalism—was enormous. In Germany Goethe's *Werther* (1774) broke the path for the pre-romantic Storm and Stress movement that passed over into German romanticism. In France, where the resistance of traditional classicism and rationalism was much harder to overcome, the corresponding trend, stimulated by Mme. de Staël's transmission of German romantic ideas, made its appearance at the beginning of the nineteenth century with Châteaubriand's *René* (1805), Sénancour's *Oberman* (1804), and Benjamin Constant's *Adolphe* (1805). The movement broadened into predominance in the works of Victor Hugo, George Sand, Alfred de Musset and Alfred de Vigny, and others, while at the same time the trend spread over most of the European countries.

All this is well known and restated only to set the background for various developments pertinent to our study. Decisive among these, kindling all others, is the growth of *malaise.* We see it stirring in the Marquise du Deffand as a revolt against French aristocratic society, as disgust with the sophisticated levity and futility of all its gossipy doings and dealings. What is important to note is that she already senses a shudder of nothingness rising from beneath these glittering surfaces. We are reminded of a beautiful image in Maxim Gorki's novel, *Foma Gordeev* (1899): "A man is gliding down a river in a boat. . . . The boat may be a good boat, but, beneath, the water is deep. . . . The boat is solid . . . but as soon as the man begins to feel the dark depth beneath, no boat will save him."[4] Such a feeling seems to have brushed Mme. du Deffand, if only as a passing shudder.

In Goethe's *Werther* the outburst of *Weltschmerz*, of desolation and forsakenness of the sentient, sensitive individual was already directed against bourgeois society, against its humdrum dreariness, unfeelingness and rationality. Such was the whole mood of the German pre-romantic and romantic movements. While Rousseau broadened and generalized the target of his aversion, fighting civilization as a whole and rationalism as a principle that had dominated the scene for about three centuries, it was most specifically bourgeois society which, during the nineteenth century, remained and increasingly became the archenemy of the sensitive personality. It was the specifically bourgeois civilization with all its implications and accessories which kept rousing and spreading the *malaise*. In fact, the growth of the *malaise* is proportional to the growth of our technological and industrial civilization. It gradually ceased to be confined to the artists, the outcasts of bourgeois civilization; it began to take hold of the unconscious and finally even the consciousness of the carriers of this civilization themselves.

An increase of psychological scrutiny is noticeable ever since Marivaux's *Marianne* which, characteristically, was a favorite book of Stendhal. Such self-searching became closely linked with the *malaise* and dissatisfaction with reason. We observe this in Mme. du Deffand, in Rousseau's *Confessions,* in German and especially in French romanticism. Everywhere this deep, inmost uneasiness stimulates self-analysis and introspection; and, in turn, the progression and elaboration of this introspection, together with the emphasis on sentiment and passion as against the obtuseness of the environment, develops a new sensibility. I merely point out two crucial figures who show these connections most clearly: Sénancour and Stendhal.

Sénancour's *Oberman* is, to my mind (apart from Stendhal's and Balzac's epic works which defy classification), the most important novel of French romanticism and would certainly deserve closer study. Although it lacks the sweep of genius which we feel in its German prototype, *Werther,* it goes in its scope beyond *Werther* and far beyond all epic prose of French romanticism. Actually, the book is not a novel but a sequence of confessional meditations expressed in letters to an unspecified friend; it has no plot and no end. The main concern of this man Oberman is the search for himself, for his character, his real existence, that is, for something permanent in him, who feels himself to be just a succession of fleeting mental states and impressions. The main task is, *"de nous maintenir semblables à nous-même"* [5] ("to maintain ourselves identical with ourselves"). He exerts and trains his sensibility on various scenes which he visits while traveling; he deeply enjoys and appreciates nature and people and the little pleasures of life, but he does not find the haven: himself. He has lost religion, but he does not trust reason either; lacking a firm, persistent core in himself, he is forlorn, without orientation in the maze of his world, *"cette nature inconcevable qui, contenant toutes choses semble pourtant ne pas contenir ce que cherchent mes désirs."* [6] (This incomprehensible world, which, although containing everything, does not seem to contain what my desires seek.") *"Pourquoi la terre est-elle ainsi désenchantée à mes yeux? Je ne connais point la satiété, je trouve par-tout le vide."* [7] ("Why does the world appear so disenchanted to me? I do not find satiation, but the void everywhere.") His experiments with the moral effects of select physical conditions, stimulants of various kinds, his symbolistic sentience of colors and odors, anticipate Baudelairian experiences, and there are passages in the book that read like Gide[8] or Sartre. After he had left his hometown and his social position to seek his self elsewhere, he writes: *"Dans ce jour, le premier où je sentis tout le néant qui m'environne . . . dans la plus grande anxiété*

*où j'eusse jamais été, j'ai joui pour la première fois de la con-
science de mon être . . . forcé d'être quelque chose, je fus enfin
moi-même . . ."* [9] And finally: *"C'est dans l'indépendence des
choses, comme dans le silence des passions, que l'ont peut étudier
son être."* [10] ("On that day, the first when I felt that complete
nothingness that surrounds me . . . in the worst anxiety I had
ever experienced, I enjoyed for the first time the consciousness
of my being . . . forced to be something, I was myself at last
. . . It is in the independence of things, and in the stillness of
passions, that we can best study our being.")

Stendhal was a romanticist by his predilection for heroic adventure and the glamorous dynamism of the Napoleonic era, as
well as by his hatred for the rising middle class. In him, too, a
deep disillusionment and revolt against bourgeois society engendered poignant psychological observation, passionate but at
the same time coldly factual, self-detached and yet self-enjoying.
And again we see arising from this state of mind a rarefied and
very modern sensibility which he used for his pleasure, for the
hedonistic "egotism" into which he withdrew. We recall the famous
episode when he watched the burning of Moscow. He called it
"le plus bel incendie du monde" ("the most beautiful conflagration
in the world"), *"mais il aurait fallu être seul ou entouré de gens
d'esprit pour en jouir"* ("but one should have been alone, or in the
company of intellectually sensitive people to really enjoy it").

THE HISTORY of the identification of *malaise* as a *mal du siècle*
has been delineated by Prof. Armand Hoog in his erudite study,
Who Invented the 'Mal du Siècle'? [11] Mr. Hoog traces the "vocabu-
lary" of the phenomenon to the beginning of the nineteenth
century, and the phenomenon itself, rightly, to the middle of the
eighteenth century, thereby correcting the prevailing opinion that
it was Alfred de Musset or Châteaubriand who invented the disease. The *malaise*, however, was not invented by anybody; it grew,
as I tried to show, out of a social and intellectual situation. Nor
did it stop with Baudelaire, in whom Mr. Hoog wants to see its

last representative. The *mal du siècle*, therefore, is not just, as Mr. Hoog has it, a *mal de deux siècles*; it is, so far, a *mal de trois siècles,* since it was only after Baudelaire that it became actually virulent. I leave aside the fact that in France proper Flaubert's *Éducation Sentimentale* was published after Baudelaire's death in 1874, and that his *Bouvard et Pécuchet* was written in his last years, around 1880. I leave aside personalities like Rimbaud, Lautréamont, Laforgue, Villiers de l'Isle Adam, Mallarmé, to name just the most prominent figures among a multitude who form the bridge to the *hommes absurdes et révoltés* of our own age, and in all of whom we can observe the symptoms of the same psychic disease. The *mal du siècle* passed over without interruption into the condition of the *fin de siècle* which was identified with decadence and morbid gloom. At that time, Sar Péladan published his multi-volume panorama of the *Décadence Latine.*

But all these are minor incidents when we look at the European picture at large: the rise, within the German orbit, of Nietzsche, Burckhardt, Stefan George; in Scandinavia, of Ibsen, Strindberg, Hamsun; in Russia, of Dostoievsky and Tolstoy. None of these men stood for their countries alone. What else did these great authors express, most of them with the help of a newly developed psychological perception, but the deep unrest, uneasiness and alarm at the effects of our modern middle-class civilization: the increasing hollowness and precariousness of conventional values, the derangement of human relations? What else did they voice but the rumbling of revolutionary forces, of a whole underground level of reality that burst into the open in the various crises of the twentieth century? In our century that uneasiness spread to the European population at large, so that the inner conditions of people since the First World War came to resemble that psychic situation which a century before was described by Sénancour's Oberman: loss of religion and, with it, the firm personal foundation of values, of an understandable cosmic order and hierarchy of beings; loss of a person's established outer and inner status; and, in the wake of the First World War, a dwindling of belief in the power of reason; finally, as a result of all this, the loss of orientation in the maze of the modern world, the loss of meaning, of inner security, the feeling of forsakenness, anxiety and alienation.

A good barometer of our present *malaise* is the enormous success of such books as *Peace of Mind, Peace of the Soul, How to Stop Worrying, The Art of Real Happiness, Guide to Confident Living,* and so forth.

Up to the end of the nineteenth century, the *malaise* had been fostered primarily by discontent with rationalism, middle-class mentality and civilization as a whole. With the advent of Nietzsche, a new motive came to the fore: anti-historicism. The crumbling of the belief in progress and evolution, in fact, the overgrowth of scholarly historicism itself brought about a devaluation of history, an all-out "anti-passatism," to use the futuristic term.

The futurist movement which sprang up in Italy even before the First World War—it was no accident that it arose in Italy where the remnants and traditions of the past weigh so heavily on the present—is particularly interesting to us here, for it was a foreboding of both fascism and existentialism. At the time when the first Futurist Manifesto appeared, dated February 20, 1909, it was considered to be just another sensational eccentricity of some intellectual fools. Hardly anybody would have guessed that what was proclaimed then would be the reality of some fifteen or twenty years later. In this astonishing document we read the following: "The furious sweep of folly snatched us from ourselves and chased us over the ways, precipitous and deep as the beds of torrents, and we, like young lions, were bent on pursuing death. And yet, we did not have an ideal lover, who would lift up even to the clouds his sublime figure, nor a cruel queen, to whom we should offer our bodies . . . [we had] nothing to wish to die, but the desire to liberate ourselves from our too oppressive boldness. We issued from wisdom as from a horrible husk. Let us give ourselves to the unknown, though not through desperation, but only to brim up the deep wells of the absurd. . . . We will extol aggressive, feverish insomnia, the double-quick step, the somersault, the box on the ear, fisticuffs. We declare that the splendor of the world has been enriched by a new beauty: the beauty of speed. . . . Burn the libraries, break the courses of the canals in order to inundate the museums; demolish, demolish the venerated cities! . . ." (*"Date fuoco agli scaffali delle biblioteche! Sviate il corso dei canali, per inondare i musei! Demolite, demolite le città venerate!"*).[12]

Now when we skim off the rhetorical foam of these utterances, there remain some most important symptoms to be noted, most important with regard to what was to follow. To be sure, we easily recognize in these manifestoes the traces of Nietzsche's barbarism, of Baudelairian satanism and epatism. But the question of values, even of a transvaluation of values, is not raised any longer. It is an eruption of superforces, a Storm and Stress, such as had stirred the youth of many periods before. Its new feature, however, is its aimlessness. "Nothing to wish to die, but the desire to liberate ourselves from our too oppressive boldness." They fought, of course, against bourgeois civilization, against paralyzing rationality, its critical arguments and historical ballast, against the sciences, the museums, the books. They wanted to smash not only the institutions, but also all their forms of expression, the artistic structures, the linguistic syntax: *"Bisogna orchestrare le immagini secondo un maximum di disordine."* [13] ("We must orchestrate pictures and imagery with the aim at a maximum of disorder.") The movement, as is well known, passed over later into Dadaism and surrealism; the last stage is Lettrism, founded in 1945, which even wants to break up the structure of the word. But in spite of the futurists' professed hatred for rationalism and science, technology, the very product of both, was glorified. Not, of course, for its usefulness, but solely for its stimulant effects, for the roaring grandeur of the big machines, their mastery over the material world, indeed over man himself, for the benumbing tempo that stirs the feeling of life, for the anti-sentimentality, anti-humanity which technology implies. The futurists extolled technology in the funniest way—with romantic exuberance; they actually reveled in

factuality. And, what is most important to note, these naïve cyber-
neticists already conceived and advocated the mechanical displace-
ment and disjunction of the human individual: *"Noi prepariamo
la creazione dell' uomo meccanico dalle parti cambiabili."* [14] ("We
prepare the creation of mechanical man, a type of man with inter-
changeable parts.")

The incentive for this youth is no specific idea whatever, and
by no means the "beauty" of *l'art pour l'art* or of aestheticists
like D'Annunzio. On the contrary, out of sheer defiance the futurists cultivate the ugly. What they are after is the pure vacuum,
the "unknown," the "absurd." Here, the unknown still carries a
positive connotation as with Baudelaire:

> *O Mort, vieux capitaine, il est temps! levons l'ancre!* . . .
> *Verse-nous ton poison pour qu'il nous réconforte!*
> *Nous voulons, tant ce feu nous brûle le cerveau,*
> *Plonger au fond du gouffre, Enfer ou Ciel, qu'importe?*
> *Au fond de l'Inconnu pour trouver du* nouveau!

> Oh Death, old captain, it is time! Let us raise anchor! . . .
> Pour us your poison that it may comfort us!
> We want, so does this fire burn our mind,
> To plunge to the bottom of the abyss, be it Hell or Heaven,
> To the bottom of the Unknown to find *something new!*

Later, after the war, the accent changes. In André Breton's Second
Surrealist Manifesto, as well as in the pronouncements of the
existentialists, notably Camus, absurd man, answering an absurd
world, issues from sheer despair.

THE ARTIST, the intellectual, being by nature the first and foremost
to pre-sense, and suffer from, the effects of modern society, was,
since Rousseau, in ever-increasing opposition to society; and this
opposition developed into a fateful rift. The conflict began in
Germany, where the intellectual was homeless, without social
status since the Renaissance. It is patently expressed in Goethe's
Werther and *Tasso*; and the cult of genius, the *Geniekult* of the

Storm and Stress movement, the laments and the destinies of Schiller, Hölderlin, and Kleist accentuate the isolation of the artist. Novels and stories dealing with artists and art, which started flourishing among the German romanticists—Friedrich Schlegel, Novalis, E.T.A. Hoffmann, and so forth—are another symptom of this situation. In the Western countries, the same opposition took the form of dandyism, aestheticism, epatism—challenging the bourgeois—and it ended up with the artist's withdrawal to the ivory tower, the *l'art pour l'art.*

From the end of the nineteenth century on, with the rapid expansion of industrial and technological civilization, the problem of the artist's communication with his audience became increasingly urgent and the rift deepened. In proportion, as society grew collectivistic, the artist, the intellectual, became more and more individualistic: his very isolation turned him into a hypertrophical individual, into an outpost of individual man. This worked like a vicious circle in the relation between artist and society. His alienation, driving him into *l'art pour l'art,* induced the artist to concentrate exclusively on the search for new techniques and modes of expression fit to render the ever more intricate totality of our world and of our life experience. This greatly developed his sensibility and forced him into transcendence and abstraction and ever-growing symbolic complexity.[15] This, in turn, increased his alienation. The situation became such that the variance between the artist and his audience was no longer a mere distance within the same pale, caused by the artist's sublimation of common human experience and language, as has been the case ever since Shakespeare. It has become a difference in kind: the artist and the public hardly share the same language any longer, and it needs a real effort on the part of the audience, it needs the help of education and interpretation, to bridge this gap. Never before has the mediatory task of criticism assumed such importance as in our time; never before did the poet himself feel compelled to annotate his poems. The result of such alienation was that artists who were longing for an immediate contact with the people became themselves suspicious of art, of its social role and significance. Art itself became a problem for them.

Ibsen in *When We Dead Awaken* (1899) brands the artist as the one who misses life, fails in life, betrays life. In Arthur Schnitzler's *Lebendige Stunden* (*Hours Alive,* 1901), an author whose mother committed suicide to free him for his work is told by a friend: "What is all your scribbling, and even supposing that you were the greatest genius, what is it compared to such an hour, such a living hour, when your mother was sitting in that armchair here, and talked to us—or was silent—but was present, here and now, was alive, alive!" Chekhov was full of doubts whether literature had any meaning and function in the society of his time. Thomas Mann's whole work deals, from diverse angles, with the estrangement of the artist and the shadowy character that modern society has cast upon the function of art. His *Doctor Faustus* tells the tragic story of modern art, which, through its very faithfulness to the traditional task of all true art—the expression of the innermost state of the human being—is carried away into realms desperately divorced from living humanity. Hermann Broch, in his novel, *Der Tod des Vergil* (*The Death of Vergil*), has his poet, in the hours of his death, reject his (and all) art outright because the cult of artistic beauty and perfection prevented him from fulfilling the basic human calling: humble service to man.

As indicated above, the exclusive concentration on artistic perfection, resulting from the artist's withdrawal into *l'art pour l'art,* greatly furthered the development of new modes of artistic expression and, by implication, the new sensibility. In studying this development, it is hardly possible to separate the subject of artistic presentation from the method of its treatment or to disentangle the interdependent changes of both. The "how" of expression affects the "what," and the "what" reflectively impels the "how." A new expression, be it the multi-meaning hint of the early symbolists or the pursuit of utmost precision, such new *ex*pression evokes or creates new *im*pressions, through associations or elaboration of the phenomenon to be rendered; and the effort to seize new *im*pressions with perfect precision in turn engenders new modes of expression. In this manner, the new techniques foster the flowering of the new sensibility. Just as the growing *malaise* was intrinsically connected with self-analysis and psychological introspection, the developing artistic techniques yield new psychological insights.

The crucial achievement of the new exploratory techniques and the new sensibility that sprang from them was the *conquest of new reality*, a reaching into new levels of reality.

This is, of course, what all Western art, true art, has been doing in every stage of our cultural evolution. Only in our era, however, has it become so conspicuously evident because of the particularly rapid and fundamental changes that occurred in our ways of viewing our world. To understand clearly the nature of these recent developments, we must bear in mind this specific function of art. There is one aspect which seems to me omitted, or not sufficiently expressed in the otherwise brilliant study of Erich Auerbach, *Mimesis*, the very topic of which is the transformation of the treatment of reality during the ages. True art is not "mimesis," imitation; it is, and has to be, an act of conquest, the discovery of a new sphere of human consciousness, and thereby of new reality. It lifts into the light of our consciousness a state of affairs, a layer of existence, that was dormant in the depth of our unconscious, that was buried under obsolete forms, conventions, habits of thought and experience. And by showing this latent reality, by making it visible to us, open to our grasp, the work of art actually *creates* this new reality as a new sphere of our conscious life. There is no true art without this exploratory quality, without this frontier venture to make conscious the pre-conscious, to express what has never been expressed before and what heretofore had seemed inexpressible. It is from the accumulating changes in the condition of our life, the hidden, unavowed changes in our life experience, that true art arises; and it is, in turn, the unveiling of this hidden reality, the delivery of a latent reality, which is the achievement of true art. By this means, art imperceptibly transforms our life and our human condition.

Thus, the transformations going on in the arts are implicitly a transformation of what we call reality. We have to give up the notion that reality is something absolutely stable. Until the beginning of our century people had been trained, largely by the teachings of modern science, to rely completely on the world of our senses. The substratum of our common sensory experience was regarded as the ultimate reference of objective existence, that is, of reality. The very word "evidence" means "clearness to vision." Meanwhile science again—our basic science, physics—has informed us that this substratum is neither reliable nor stable. A stone, a rock, which to our everyday experience appears as the paragon of solidity and durability, revealed itself to be a delusion of our senses; underneath its appearance nothing but motion and change is going on. The concept of the "element," in its original sense as something irreducible and ultimately immutable, has ceased to exist. Indeed, it has been shown that, on the lowest, sub-atomic level, our instrumental observation affects the observable itself. Our sensuomorphism then, or to put it more adequately, our aesthetomorphism, seems to be just a last residue of anthropomorphism.

The first conclusion to be drawn from these experiences is the invalidation of our worn "isms" which made life so easy for certain critics and historians of the arts. And it is most particularly our concept of "realism" that has become problematic. We have to be very precise about this. It has become clear to us that reality is something very relative, something that depends on the capacity of our perception, on the degree of power, sharpness and rarity of perception. It has become clear to us that the "reality" of the sixteenth, eighteenth, and twentieth centuries is by no means the same reality. Actual reality seems to be just the last frontier to which our perceptive capacity has progressed. Seen in this aspect, "realism," in the old conventional sense of the word, is not valid realism at all; it is—rendering as it does crude reality, the reality of our sheer surface experience—a very shallow and obsolete realism.

Thus, the transformation that occurred in the domain of letters, although it happened quite independently, is in a striking way related to the disclosure of a new subsensory sphere of reality in physics. It is, as we shall see presently, almost inseparably connected with the delving into new transpersonal depths of the psyche, with psychoanalysis, or depth-psychology. Likewise, it corresponds to the developments in the visual arts. If we compare portraits by Clouet, Titian or Holbein with those by van Gogh, Kokoschka or Picasso, we see the whole process at a glance. In the works of the sixteenth-century artists, the last attainable truth of physical appearance coincides with actual everyday reality, with the "resemblance" recognizable by all. Here, the most "life-like" presentation of an individual is identical with the artistic investigation of sensory appearance as such. In a portrait by Kokoschka or Picasso, on the other hand, we are struck by the immense contrast between the everyday appearance of the person portrayed and the psychic, even psychological depth of the portrait, which has been carried into a metaphysical sphere. The individual is condensed, as well as heightened, to a psychic attitude, a spiritual type, a trans-individual, abstractly structural form. And it will be useful to remember the great transformation that took place in the visual arts since the nineteenth century: the development from the conceptual, social, realism of Millet and from the actual naturalism of Courbet to pleinairism and impressionism; the gradual disintegration of the concrete object, first through the dissolving effect of light in Monet's painting, through the quasi-scientific "divisions" of the neo-impressionists, through the pursuit of structural form by Cézanne, van Gogh and the cubists, to Picasso's experiments in structure; and, as a final result, modern abstract painting and the surrealists, rendering their visionary life in all its "paranoiac" flux, with explicit reference to Freud's free association. It will be useful to bear this great process in mind as another parallel to what we are going to contemplate now.

IN THE PREVIOUS CHAPTER I dealt with Baudelaire only in a very specific aspect: as an initiator of a new dimension of modern poetry by detecting subtle new contacts between distant phenomenal spheres. But, as I indicated at once, it is not his poem *Correspondances* alone which makes him an ancestor of our new perceptional experience. Another poem of his is just as crucial and initiatory in a different respect, and this is the poem *Une Charogne* ("A Carrion"). Baudelaire is widely regarded as an aesthete, exalting beauty above all other concerns of life, as a dandy, an *épateur,* a challenger of the bourgeois. But the roots of his attitude, human and artistic, lie much deeper. He sought and practiced what he called *"une franchise absolue,"* an absolute candor, sincerity, in relation to the facts of life. And by virtue of this attitude he—and some of his followers[16]—pushed the inquiry into reality much farther, much deeper than the pronounced realists. It was the symbolists who, by their extreme and unsparing penetration into the foundations of reality, effected the decisive transformation of reality. While the declared realists described just the reality of social developments and environments, deliberately emphasizing the hideous and gloomy aspects of modern society, the symbolists set out to scrutinize the very texture of existence. They focused their attention on the minutest phenomena and particulars, and in so doing they did not shrink from envisaging the most repulsive matters. *Les Fleurs du Mal* is full of the subtlest depictions of senility, defects, anxieties, decay. But the poem *Une Charogne* marks an epoch: the beginning of a new transcendence of the existing, a transcendence of sensory reality which is radically different from all former transcendence, from both Christian and romantic transcendence. It is not a transcendence upward into the sphere of the supranatural and spiritual. It is a transcendence downward, inward, into an "inner beyond," the sub-existential. This transcendence arose, not from an elevation into incorporeal, celestial or chimerical spheres, but from the thorough and unrestricted pursuit, pursuit to the end, of the very corporeal, from a piercing analysis of the texture of sensory appearance, of the texture of existence itself. Cézanne knew Baudelaire's *Charogne* by heart and saw in it a confirmation of his own efforts. Rilke wrote in a letter to his wife Clara on October 19th, 1907: "The whole development toward factual, fully objective presentation which we now are inclined to recognize in Cézanne could not have set in without this poem; first it had to be there in its mercilessness. First, artistic vision had to bring itself to seeing even in the frightful and apparently repulsive an existing thing that is just as valid and real as any other being." We see how this new approach implies a penetration beyond surface appearance, into a layer of existence transcending decay and putrescence:

UNE CHAROGNE

Rappelez-vous l'objet que nous vîmes, mon âme,
* Ce beau matin d'été si doux:*
Au détour d'un sentier une charogne infâme
* Sur un lit semé de cailloux,*

Les jambes en l'air, comme une femme lubrique,
* Brûlante et suant les poisons,*
Ouvrait d'une façon nonchalante et cynique
* Son ventre plein d'exhalaisons.*

Le soleil rayonnait sur cette pourriture,
* Comme afin de la cuire à point,*
Et de rendre au centuple à la grande Nature
* Tout ce qu'ensemble elle avait joint;*

Et le ciel regardait la carcasse superbe
* Comme une fleur s'épanouir.*
La puanteur était si forte, que sur l'herbe
* Vous crûtes vous évanouir.*

Les mouches bourdonnaient sur ce ventre putride,
* D'où sortaient de noirs bataillons*
De larves, qui coulaient comme un épais liquide
* Le long de ces vivants haillons.*

Tout cela descendait, montait comme une vague,
  Ou s'élançait en pétillant;
On eût dit que le corps, enflé d'un souffle vague,
  Vivait en se multipliant.

Et ce monde rendait une étrange musique,
  Comme l'eau courante et le vent,
Ou le grain qu'un vanneur d'un mouvement rhythmique
  Agite et tourne dans son van.

Les formes s'effaçaient et n'étaient plus qu'un rêve,
  Une ébauche lente à venir,
Sur la toile oubliée, et que l'artiste achève
  Seulement par le souvenir.

Derrière les rochers une chienne inquiète
  Nous regardait d'un oeil faché,
Épiant le moment de reprendre au squelette
  Le morceau qu'elle avait lâché.

—Et pourtant vous serez semblable à cette ordure,
  A cette horrible infection,
Étoile de mes yeux, soleil de ma nature,
  Vous, mon ange et ma passion!

Oui! telle vous serez, ô la reine des grâces,
  Après les derniers sacrements,
Quand vous irez, sous l'herbe et les floraisons grasses,
  Moisir parmi les ossements.

Alors, ô ma beauté! dites à la vermine
  Qui vous mangera de baisers,
Que j'ai gardé la forme et l'essence divine
  De mes amours décomposés!

A CARRION

Can you recall, my dear, that lovely day,
  To what our footpath led?
How, as it turned, a hideous carrion lay
  On a dry torrent's bed:

Legs, like some female wanton's, in the air,
  Burning and sweating pest,
With cynical indifference it laid bare
  Its pullulating breast.

The sun was blazing down as though it meant
  To cook with fondest care
And give great Nature back at cent per cent
  All she'd united there.

And the sky watched that carcass uncompeer'd
  Like a great flower expand.
The stench was so terrific that you feared
  You'd faint there out of hand.

Flies buzzed above that belly's putridness,
  Whence issued from their beds
Black grubs that flowed like some thick liquidness
  Along those living shreds.

And all this, like a wave, advanced, retired,
  Or darted sparklingly;
It seemed the body, by some breath inspired,
  Lived reproductively.

The whole emitted a strange harmony
  Like wind's or water's sound,
Or like the grain a winnower rhythmically
  Keeps shaking round and round.

Into a shadowy dream all shape retreated,
  A sketch come gradually
On some forgotten canvas, and completed
  Only from memory.

Behind the rocks a restless bitch stayed on,
  With aggravated look,
Bent on retrieving from the skeleton
  The morsel it forsook

—One day, though, you'll be like that loathsomeness,
  That thing without a name,

You, the bright centre of my consciousness,
    My angel and my flame.

That's what you'll be, whom all the graces tend,
    When, the last rites conferred,
Under the grass and rank growths you descend
    To rot with the interred.

Then, O my beauty, tell the worm which thence-
    -forth eats you with its kiss
I've kept the form and heavenly quintessence
    Of my corrupted bliss.

(Translation by J. B. Leishman)

This new sensibility grew richer and rarer still with the second great founding father of the French symbolist movement, Stéphane Mallarmé, who, in fact, is a crucial figure in regard to the genesis not only of modern poetry, but of the modern form of expression in general. No Proust, no Joyce, no Virginia Woolf, no Sartre is conceivable without Mallarmé. To be sure, in his theory he wanted poetry to do away with all fetters of definite content and precise meaning of words. The words should, through their evocative sound and friction alone, release the bouquet of infinite associations and potential connotations of which they are imaginatively replete; just as the fragment opens up an infinity of possible completions. The attempt, however, to practice this theory led Mallarmé, as he himself recognized, into an *impasse*, a dead end; the poet who was able really to approximate this fulfillment was Joyce in *Finnegans Wake*. What Mallarmé himself actually accomplished in his poetry was something else.

Mallarmé is the first poet in whom the spiritual faculties appear to be extending into the very senses, indeed, into the nerves, a characteristic which later developed to the extreme in Rilke and Virginia Woolf. The sensorium itself seems to operate in a spiritually analytical manner. Impression and expression mutually generate each other: a most delicate sensory receptivity fosters a new, one would think unlimitedly diversifying, precision of expression, and expression in turn—the word, with its "aura" of associations—inspires a more and more penetrating perception of phenomena, a mental microscopy, as it were. And thereby something even more important happens: in Mallarmé's poems for the first time minute details, fragments, slightest stirrings and sensations are brought into the focus of attention and treated not as derivative from the human being, not as parts of a coherent world of man, but as something separate and independent, something in their own right. Here, in the functioning of this new penetrating sensibility, we find the first traces of a disjunction of the organic, disjunction of the sensorially coherent being, of the person and of the object.

Compare Baudelaire's poem *Correspondances*, which already spiritualizes sensory experiences, with Mallarmé's *Autre éventail de Mademoiselle Mallarmé* and *Une dentelle s'abolit . . .* and the crucial turn will be evident:

CORRESPONDANCES

> *La Nature est un temple où de vivants piliers*
> *Laissent parfois sortir de confuses paroles;*
> *L'homme y passe à travers des forêts de symboles*
> *Qui l'observent avec des regards familiers.*
>
> *Comme de longs échos qui de loin se confondent*
> *Dans une ténébreuse et profonde unité,*
> *Vaste comme la nuit et comme la clarté,*
> *Les parfums, les couleurs et les sons se répondent.*
>
> *Il est des parfums frais comme des chairs d'enfants,*
> *Doux comme les hautbois, verts comme les prairies,*
> *—Et d'autres, corrompus, riches et triomphants,*
>
> *Ayant l'expansion des choses infinies,*
> *Comme l'ambre, le musc, le benjoin et l'encens,*
> *Qui chantent les transports de l'esprit es des sens.*

CORRESPONDENCES

Nature is a temple where living pillars
At times give out obscure utterances;
There man moves through forests of symbols
Watching him with knowledge in their look.

Like long echoes fusing from afar
In a somber and profound union,
Vast as the night and as lucent light,
Perfumes, colors and sounds correspond.

There are perfumes fresh as children's bodies,
Sweet as the oboes, green as the prairies,
—And others, rank, rich and triumphant,

Having the boundless expanse of infinite things,
Like amber, musk, benzoin and incense,
That sing the ecstasies of the spirit and the senses.

(*Translation by E. K.*)

AUTRE ÉVENTAIL DE MADEMOISELLE MALLARMÉ

*O rêveuse, pour que je plonge
Au pur délice sans chemin,
Sache, par un subtil mensonge,
Garder mon aile dans ta main.*

*Une fraîcheur de crépuscule
Te vient à chaque battement
Dont le coup prisonnier recule
L'horizon délicatement.*

*Vertige! voici que frissonne
L'espace comme un grand baiser
Qui, fou de naître pour personne,
Ne peut jaillir ni s'apaiser.*

*Sens-tu le paradis farouche
Ainsi qu'un rire enseveli
Se couler du coin de ta bouche
Au fond de l'unanime pli!*

Le sceptre des rivages roses
Stagnants sur les soirs d'or, ce l'est,
Ce blanc vol fermé que tu poses
Contre le feu d'un bracelet.

ANOTHER FAN OF MADEMOISELLE MALLARMÉ

Oh dreamer, that I may plunge
Into the pure delight of no trail,
Know, through a subtle lie,
To keep my wing in your hand.

A fresh whiff of dusk
Comes upon you with each flutter
Whose captive beat tenderly
Distances the horizon.

Frenzy! there thrills
The space like a great kiss
Which, mad to exist for no one,
Can not bloom out nor be stilled.

Do you feel that wild bliss
Like a buried laughter
Rippling from the corner of your mouth
Deep into the concordant fold!

Scepter of the rosy shores
Stagnant above the golden evenings,
That is it, this closed white flight
Which you place against the fire of a bracelet.

(*Translation by Hanna M. Loewy*)

UNE DENTELLE S'ABOLIT . . .

Une dentelle s'abolit
Dans le doute du Jeu suprême
A n'entr'ouvrir comme un blasphème
Qu'absence éternelle de lit.

Cet unanime blanc conflit
D'une guirlande avec la même,
Enfui contre la vitre blême
Flotte plus qu'il n'ensevelit.

Mais, chez qui du rêve se dore
Tristement dort une mandore
Au creux néant musicien

Telle que vers quelque fenêtre
Selon nul ventre que le sien,
Filial on aurait pu naître.

A LACE CURTAIN IS WEARING OUT . . .

A lace curtain is wearing out
In the doubt of the supreme Game
Exposing like a blasphemy
Nothing but the eternal absence of bed.

This harmonious white conflict
Of a curtain with a curtain,
Fleeing against the pallid glass
Flutters more than covers up.

But, who goldens himself with dream
There sadly sleeps a mandolin
With its hollow musicianly void

Such that towards some window
Out of no womb but its,
One might have been born a son.

(*Translation by E. K.*)

In Baudelaire's poem the spiritualized relationships between sensory phenomena still play within a coherent universe; in fact, what the poem renders is a newly discovered coherence of the universe. In the center is still man who "moves through forests of symbols," and the almost untraceable, ethereal extensions and emanations of things are shown issuing from man's spiritualized sensorium;

indeed, they are one with man's rarefied experience. The human sphere is extended but not pierced. In Mallarmé's *Autre éventail* the fan is in the center of the poem, and the human being moving the fan is just an occasion, an accidental agent or medium in the relationship between this delicate object and infinite space. In the poem *Une dentelle s'abolit . . .* the human connection is even more marginal. The lace curtain and the mandolin point only distantly, hypothetically, toward the human, toward the birth of the artist.[17]

The same fundamental shift of focus and emphasis is apparent in Rilke's poetry. Rilke explicitly conceived of the poet as the "mouthpiece of objects," *"der Mund der Dinge."* For instance:

> *Atmen, du unsichtbares Gedicht!*
> *Immerfort um das eigne*
> *Sein rein eingetauschter Weltraum. Gegengewicht,*
> *in dem ich mich rhythmisch ereigne.*

> *Einzige Welle, deren*
> *allmähliches Meer ich bin;*
> *sparsamstes du von allen möglichen Meeren,—*
> *Raumgewinn.*

> *Wie viele von diesen Stellen der Räume waren schon*
> *innen in mir. Manche Winde*
> *sind wie mein Sohn.*

> *Erkennst du mich, Luft, du, voll noch einst meiniger Orte?*
> *Du, einmal glatte Rinde,*
> *Rundung und Blatt meiner Worte.*

> Breathing, you invisible poem!
> World-space constantly in pure
> interchange with our own being. Counterpoise,
> wherein I rhythmically happen.

> Solitary wave,
> whose gradual sea I am;
> most sparing you of all possible seas,—
> winning of space.

How many of these places in space have already been
within me. Many a wind
is like a son to me.

Do you know me, you air, still full of places once mine?
You onetime smooth rind,
rondure and leaf of my words.[18]

(*Translation by M. D. Herter Norton*)

Here it is breathing, "world-space constantly in pure interchange
with our own being," which dominates the poem; breathing not
as an organic, vital function of man, but as a quasi-independent
atmospheric to and fro in a wave "whose gradual sea I am,"
"wherein I rhythmically happen."

THIS EVOLUTIONARY PROCESS continued through ever deeper analytical advances into the underground zone of the human psyche
and an ever more acute scrutiny of the texture of human experience. We may distinguish three different stages of this penetration
of the psychic depths. The *first step* reached into the depth of the
personal unconscious and started dissolving the unity and coherence of the psyche into various levels and into a complexity of
complexes, drives, and associative memories. Freudian psychoanalysis divided the psyche into *id, ego* and *superego,* that is, roughly
speaking, into a broad objective foundation of the uncontrolled unconscious and a rather narrow subjective crest of self-controlling
consciousness. Thus, paradoxically, by establishing the unconscious
as the major part of the human psyche, yet subjecting it to
conscious inquiry and making it more and more graspable to
consciousness, psychoanalysis has actually extended consciousness itself.

Psychoanalysis, however, made its initial appearance in literature. It is no accident that the stream-of-consciousness technique
was introduced by the symbolist Édouard Dujardin in his novel,
Les lauriers sont coupés (1887). Another symbolist, Jules Laforgue, who died in 1887, declared, partly under the influence of

Eduard von Hartmann's *Philosophie des Unbewussten,* that "The unconscious is a sphere which will open up for us the primitive woods of life." Herman Melville was well aware of two distinct spheres in the human mind and the dynamic relations between them. From the many instances in his work I quote one, a passage from *Billy Budd* (written between 1888 and 1891): "Though the man's even temper and discreet bearing would seem to intimate a mind peculiarly subject to the law of reason, not the less in his heart he would seem to riot in complete exemption from that law having apparently little to do with reason further than to employ it as an ambidexter implement for effecting the irrational." At the same time, and even earlier, Dostoievsky and Tolstoy began to delve into the unconscious without identifying it explicitly. It would need a special study to describe in detail the various ways in which Dostoievsky anticipated psychoanalysis. He described inhibition, repression and the "death-drive," he explored the symbolic quality of the dream. In *Notes from the Underground* (the literal translation would be "The room below the floor"), written in 1864, this "underground" is meant neither as an actual locality nor as a social layer, but as a psychic sphere: the place of the unconscious, where drives and passions rage. Tolstoy, in his great story, *The Death of Ivan Ilyich* (1884), has a dish of dried plums unleash a whole chain of memories from the unconscious, long before Marcel Proust dipped the *petites madeleines* into his tea and into his past. In this famous passage of *À la recherche du temps perdu* Proust describes the psychoanalytic process in a classic way: "*Un plaisir délicieux m'avait envahi, isolé, sans la notion de sa cause . . . et je sens tressaillir en moi quelque chose qui se déplace, voudrait s'élever, quelque chose qu'on aurait désancré, à une grande profondeur; je ne sais ce que c'est, mais cela monte lentement; j'éprouve la résistance et j'entends la rumeur des distances traversées.—Certes, ce qui palpite ainsi au fond de moi, ce doit être l'image, le souvenir visuel, qui, lié à cette saveur, tente de la suivre jusqu'à moi . . . Arrivera-t-il jusqu'à la surface de ma claire conscience, ce souvenir, l'instant ancien que l'attraction d'un*

*instant identique est venue de si loin solliciter, émouvoir, soulever
tout au fond de moi?"* ("A delicious pleasure had invaded me, an
isolated sensation, without a notion of its cause . . . and I feel
quivering in me something that displaces itself, that wants to rise
up, as if it had been unanchored at a great depth; I don't know
what it is, but it is mounting slowly; I sense the resistance and I
hear the rumbling of great distances traversed.—Surely, what thus
palpitates in my depth must be the image, the visual memory,
which, linked to this taste, tries to follow it towards me. . . .
Will it ever arrive at the surface of my clear consciousness, this
memory, this ancient instant which the magic of an identical instant
has come to claim from so far away, to stir, to lift up, from the
ultimate depth of my being?") Indeed, Proust, most probably
before knowing Freud, planned his series *À la recherche du temps
perdu* as a "sequence of novels of the unconscious." [19]

Psychoanalysis furthered the development of new narrative
techniques such as the stream of consciousness, free association,
and the interior monologue. These three terms, which criticism
frequently uses in a rather indiscriminate manner, should be clearly
kept apart since they represent distinctly different modes of expression. The three techniques have only this in common: happenings are viewed from within the experiencing person, with the lens
of inner perspective. The stream-of-consciousness technique, so
called after a theory which William James developed at about the
same time (1890) as Dujardin already practiced it, puts to use the
experience of continuity, the dynamic nature of our consciousness;
it reflects the promiscuous stream of events, immediately but
consciously lived. Perfect examples, apart from Dujardin, are
Arthur Schnitzler's *Leutnant Gustl* (1900) and Dorothy Richard-
son's series of novels, which appeared much later (1915 onward)
and can in no way be regarded as an innovation. Free association,
deriving from Freud's theory and therapeutic method, includes
the flow of the unconscious and presents the loose stream of associations as they pass through the mind when we relax its rational
control; for instance the flow of thoughts, emotions, memories of

Mrs. Marion Tweedy Bloom at the end of Joyce's *Ulysses*. The interior monologue is more complicated. It comprises stream of consciousness and sometimes even free association, but extends beyond both into guided contemplation. While occasionally drawing on the contents of the unconscious, it pursues an independent course of self-clarification. As far as I know, the first story written (in 1900) as interior monologue is *Der Tod Georgs* (*The Death of George*) by the Austrian poet Richard Beer-Hofmann. Other versions of the interior monologue are Virginia Woolf's *Mrs. Dalloway,* Hermann Broch's *Der Tod des Vergil* (*The Death of Virgil*), and the beautiful ending of Faulkner's *Wild Palms.*

These new techniques effected something most important: they have broken through the bottom of our consciousness—on which the psyche had hitherto rested with confidence—and have likewise cracked the supposedly solid foundation of chronological time. A new time began to germinate within time, the time of inner experience within the time of outer happenings. This new kind of time has no definite limits—the depths into which it expands are practically infinite. It cannot be measured by means of chronological time. As we all know, a dream of a few minutes may span or encompass long stretches of our life; and once we become attentive to the full contents of our continuous inner experience, a dimension is added which escapes all logical and chronological sequence. With this feeling of the boundlessness of experience there emerges a peculiar anxiety, or dizziness, a feeling—as Virginia Woolf's Clarissa puts it—"that it is very, very dangerous to live even one day."

In *Orlando* the same temporal boundlessness of experience is shown in inverse perspective: here Virginia Woolf presents the synchronization of different lifetimes, indeed, historical ages, in a given personal moment. "The true length of a person's life, whatever the *Dictionary of National Biography* may say, is always a matter of dispute. For it is a difficult business—this time-keeping; nothing more quickly disorders it than contact with any of the arts. . . ." And, correspondingly, while many times may be con-

centrated, telescoped, in one personal moment, the rapidly succeeding impressions of a short piece of what is called the present
may tear apart the identical presence of a person: "After twenty
minutes the body and mind were like scraps of torn paper tumbling
from a sack and, indeed, the process of motoring fast out of London so much resembles the chopping up small of identity which
precedes unconsciousness and perhaps death itself that it is an
open question in what sense Orlando can be said to have existed
at the present moment." [20]

Reaching down into the individual, or personal, unconscious
was only the first step; the next went farther down into what C. G.
Jung called the *collective unconscious* and what I have preferred
to call the *generic unconscious,* the sphere of archetypal recurrences.
Joyce's *Ulysses* and *Finnegans Wake,* in one of their many aspects,
and Thomas Mann's Joseph tetralogy may serve as literary
examples.

And there is a third push that reached even deeper, into the
unfathomable zone of existence proper. This is what may be called
the *existentialist experience,* which is again connected with psychological search, indeed, with psychotherapy. In Europe, and particularly in Switzerland, a psychoanalytic group is practicing what
they call *Existenz-analyse,* existential analysis.

THE EXISTENTIALIST EXPERIENCE must be clearly distinguished
from existentialist philosophy, which will—in the last chapter—concern us only inasmuch as it derives from the existentialist experience
certain conclusions which are supposed to indicate a way out of
our human crisis. Existentialist philosophy, although in various
ways related to the existentialist experience, is partly a result of
purely theoretical currents. It goes back to Søren Kierkegaard [21]
whose existentialism originated in an immediate metaphysical,
religious experience. Apart from the Kierkegaardian ancestry,
existentialist philosophy carries Nietzschean elements and, in its
German version, it is primarily an outgrowth of the phenomenol-
ogy of the Austrian philosopher Edmund Husserl; insofar it

represents the final stage of the long and complex development of epistemological thinking started by Kant. In Sartre's philosophy, most specifically, the speculative prefigurations of Fichte, Schelling and Hegel are noticeable.

We have observed the antecedents of the existentialist experience in the rise of the new sensibility and its disintegration of the organic. As a full-grown phenomenon this experience appeared only since the beginning of our own century in personalities from various parts of Europe.

The existentialist experience is an individual, even extremely subjective, experience, and, curiously enough, at the same time an abstract experience. It is an abstract experience although it starts with physical sensations, and, in fact, reaches down to the very bottom of physical existence. It is an isolated experience, and the existentialists do what they can to keep it isolated, to posit it as an isolated fact, to establish it as the core, the focal point, the point of departure of their experience of the world. It is, however, important mainly as an experience, not as the nucleus of a philosophy. It is important mainly insofar as it is a symptom of the present condition of man.

It does not matter so much how many or how few individuals have had such an experience, but that such things have actually been felt by men, by different men at different times in different places, this is what makes it a momentous and frightening phenomenon. The existentialist experience may be seen as the accumulation, the concentration, indeed the quasi-physical climax of all the intellectual and moral crises of the past generations, and most especially of the crisis of the individual.

Now what is this experience? Let us trace its different phases. I first quote a passage from Rilke's *Aufzeichnungen des Malte Laurids Brigge* (1906-1909), published in English under the title *Journal of My Other Self:* "Have I said it before? I am learning to see. . . . For one thing, it has never occurred to me before how many different faces there are. There are quantities of people, but there are even more faces, for each person has several. There are some who wear the same face for years: naturally it wears out; it gets dirty; it splits and folds; it stretches, like gloves one has worn on a journey. These are thrifty, simple folk; they do not change their face; they never even have it cleaned. . . . There are others who change their faces in uncannily rapid succession, and wear them out. At first they think they have enough to last them forever; but they have scarcely reached forty when, behold, they have come to the last of them. This naturally leads to tragedy. They are not accustomed to being frugal with faces. Their last is worn through in a week, has holes in it, and in many places is as thin as paper; and then gradually the lining—the no-face—comes through, and they go about with that. . . . But the woman, the woman: she had completely sunk into herself, her head in her hands. It was at the corner of the rue Notre-Dame-des-Champs. I began to walk softly as soon as I saw her. When poor people are reflecting they should not be disturbed. . . . The street was too empty; its emptiness was bored with itself; it caught my step from under my feet and clattered about with it hither and yon, as with a wooden clog. The woman took fright and was torn too quickly out of herself, too violently, so that her face remained in her two hands. I could see it lying in them, its hollow form. It cost me an indescribable effort to keep my eyes on these hands and not to look at what had been torn out of them. I shuddered to see a face thus from the inside, but I was still more afraid of the naked, flayed head without a face."[22]

In this piece one can clearly observe the splitting of surface reality; how the indiscreet, all too imaginative look disintegrates the organic figuration and texture of surface reality, and how, under its animistic vivification, parts and segments assume an independent, swarming life. This happens as if under a compulsion, and the man who looks seems himself to be just an instrument, or victim, of this irresistible seeing. "I still defend myself," he says, ". . . I should so gladly stay among the significances that have become dear to me; and if something must . . . change, I should like at least to be allowed to live among dogs, who possess a world akin to our own and the same things. . . . For a while yet I can write all this down and say it. But there will come a day when my hand will be distant from me, and when I bid it write, it will write words I do not mean. The day of that other interpretation will dawn, when no word will properly follow another, and all meanings will dissolve like clouds, and fall down like rain. . . . But this time I shall be written. *I am the impression that will transform itself.*" [23]

Here is the second stage of the existentialist experience as described by the Austrian poet Hugo von Hofmannsthal in his *Ein Brief,* an imaginary letter of Lord Chandos to Francis Bacon (written in 1901) and in his *Briefe eines Zurückgekehrten* (Letters of a Man who Returned, 1907).

In the *Letter of Lord Chandos* the writer explains to his illustrious friend the reasons why he finds it forever impossible to complete the philosophical treatise he had planned, or even to put down any coherent piece of writing: ". . . it might appear a well-designed plan of divine Providence that my mind should fall from such a state of inflated arrogance into this extreme of despondency and feebleness which is now the permanent condition of my inner self. Such religious ideas, however, have no power over me: they belong to the cobwebs through which my thoughts dart out into the void, while the thoughts of so many others are caught there and come to rest. To me the mysteries of faith have been condensed into a lofty allegory which arches itself over the fields of my life like a radiant rainbow, ever remote, ever prepared to recede should it occur to me to rush toward it and wrap myself into the folds of its mantle.—But, my dear friend, worldly ideas also evade me in a like manner. How shall I try to describe to you these strange spiritual torments, this rebounding of the fruit-branches above my outstretched hands, this recession of the murmuring stream from my thirsting lips?—My case, in short, is this: I have lost completely the ability to think or to speak of anything coherently. —At first I grew by degrees incapable of discussing a loftier or more general subject in terms of which everyone, fluently and without hesitation, is wont to avail himself. I experienced an inexplicable distaste for so much as uttering the words 'spirit,' 'soul,' or 'body.' I found it impossible to express an opinion on the affairs at Court, the events in Parliament, or whatever you wish. This was not motivated by any form of personal deference (for you know that my candour borders on imprudence), but because the abstract terms of which the tongue must avail itself as a matter of course in order to voice a judgment—these terms crumbled in my mouth like mouldy fungi. Thus, one day, while reprimanding my four-year-old daughter . . . for a childish lie of which she had been guilty and demonstrating to her the necessity of always being truthful, the ideas streaming into my mind suddenly took on such iridescent colouring, so flowed over into one another, that I reeled off the sentence as best I could, as if suddenly overcome by illness. Actually, I did feel myself growing pale, and with a violent pressure on my forehead I left the child to herself, slammed the door behind me, and began to recover to some extent only after a brief gallop over the lonely pasture.—Gradually, however, these attacks of anguish spread like a corroding rust. Even in familiar and humdrum conversation all the opinions which are generally expressed with ease and sleep-walking assurance became so doubtful that I had to cease altogether taking part in such talk. It filled me with an inexplicable anger, which I could conceal only with effort, to hear such things as: This affair has turned out well or ill for this or that person; Sheriff N. is a bad, Parson T. a good man; Farmer M. is to be pitied, his sons are wasters; . . . . All this seemed as indemonstrable, as mendacious and hollow as could be. My mind compelled me to view all things occurring in such conversations from an uncanny closeness. As once, through a magnifying glass, I had seen a piece of skin on my little finger look like a field full of holes and furrows, so I now perceived human beings and their actions. I no longer succeed in comprehending them with the simplifying eye of habit. For me everything disintegrated into parts, those parts again into parts; no longer would anything let itself be encompassed by one idea. Single words floated round me; they congealed into eyes which stared at me and into which I was forced to stare back—whirlpools which gave me vertigo and, reeling incessantly, led into the void." [24]

But this uncanny decomposition of the universe does not stop at terms and concepts. In the fourth of the five *Letters of the Man Who Returned,* the letter "On Colors," the decomposition creeps into the sensory perception of objects and phenomena, which in their simple, ineffable presence had still been to "Lord Chandos" sources of saving "revelations." To be sure, even to "the man who returned" the objects in the paintings of van Gogh finally seem once more to re-emerge from the abyss of non-being into the wordless language of colors—"a language loftier than sounds" because it "springs immediately out of mute presence"; but he knew "that each of these objects, these creatures, had been born out of a terrifying doubt, and that they by their sheer existence covered up forever the ghastly abyss of yawning nothingness." The corroding experience could not be annulled, the experience which "I could no longer tear out of myself." Of this experience, he says himself: "It is no spleen . . . it is more than an observation, it is a feeling, a component of all feelings, a feeling of existence."

Here is the account of his experience: "Certainly I have passed through no good time. This has only become clear to me through a certain little experience I had three days ago . . . I felt myself sicken from inward out, but it was not my body, I know my body too well. It was the crisis of an inner ill-being, whose earlier manifestations had been as imperceptible as might be . . . just small, nonsensical waves of listlessness were these earlier touches, without significance, absurdities, almost momentary vacillations of thought, or of feeling—but, to be sure, something entirely new in me. And this I believe, trivial as these things are, I never have sensed anything of the kind, except in these few months, since I again tread European soil. . . . Sometimes it came in the morning in these German hotel rooms, so that the jug and the washbasin, or a corner of the room with its table and the clothes rack, appeared so wholly and utterly non-real, despite their indescribable vulgarity so utterly non-real, ghostly as it were and at the same time provisional, hovering, one might say, temporarily replacing the real jug . . . the jug . . . was, one could say, a spectre. From its appearance there went forth a slight disturbing dizziness, but not a physical one. Then I would walk to the window and experience the very same sensation with three or four cabs, which stood waiting at the curb. They were spectres of cabs. To look at them produced an almost imperceptible flashing of nausea: it was like a momentary swinging over the groundless, the eternal void. . . . Or a few trees also, these meagre but carefully tended few trees, which they have standing here and there on their squares between the asphalt, protected by fences. I would look at them, and I knew that they reminded me of trees—were not trees—and at the same time something shivered through me, something that severed my being like a breeze, such an indescribable whiff of the eternal Nought, the eternal Nowhere, a breath not of death but of Non-Life, indescribable. Then it happened on the train, more and more often . . . in the most ordinary light, at three in the afternoon, or whenever: little town left or right of the track, a village or factory, or the whole landscape, hills, fields, apple trees, scattered houses, all in all; they assumed a countenance, a peculiar, ambiguous mien, so full of inner uncertainty, vicious unreality. . . . My dear friend, I have spent three and a half months of my life in a cage, which had no other view than an empty pen with half-dried buffalo manure piled man-high where a sick buffalo cow dragged herself about . . . and yet, in the pen, in the yellow-grey heap of dung and the dying yellow-grey beast, when I looked out at that, and when I think about it—there was still life there, the same life that is also in me. But in that world, into which I look from the train window, there is something—I have never shuddered before death, but before that, which is there, before such Non-Life, my whole being shudders. But this is certainly nothing more than a kind of evil eye that I sometimes have, a subtle poisoning, an infection, creeping and concealed, such an infection as seems to lie in wait in the European air, for one returning from afar. . . . That my malady was of a European nature, of this I became aware . . .

at the very moment in which I understood that it had now spread to my inner being, that I now, I myself, my inner life, lay under this evil eye. . . . Through a thousand confused and simultaneous feelings and half-feelings, my consciousness dragged itself along, in nausea and disgust. . . ." [25]

"IN NAUSEA AND DISGUST"—here we are on the verge of the final stage of the existentialist experience, as described in Jean-Paul Sartre's novel, *La Nausée,* the very plot of which is the story of the crumbling of sensory reality. It is a dramatic story, full of suspense, full of tragic comedy. On the factual level nothing whatsoever happens. We watch a most inconspicuous personality moving through his ordinary day, on the very surface of daily life. But in the midst of this normality something happens indeed, something very consequential: the surface breaks, it gives in. The phenomena of everyday life assume a somewhat grotesque appearance. They wrinkle and disintegrate, they crack; and man, like the company of Korah in the Bible, falls into a bottomless abyss.

What we witness here is a metaphysical drama: it is—on the level of personal, indeed, sensory experience—the self-abolition, the self-reversal, the self-defeat of positivism. It is the transcendence of positivism. The phenomena of daily life are seen so meticulously, so sharply, so nakedly, they become so much themselves, so purely themselves and nothing else, nothing more than their most physical, factual, existential self, that, under this most intense, most concentrated sensory scrutiny, they dissolve, they pulverize. What grew out of our modern empirical value-free science, out of the anonymous precision of isolated details exposed through photography and microscopy, as well as through the equivalent perspectives in the arts—this increasing factuality ends in a vicious circle. Our positivistic everyday life has literally pursued itself to the absurd. With a *salto mortale* it turns into transcendence and the strictest, most exact, most accurate objectivity lands in the most singular subjectiveness.

Indeed, the actual subject of Sartre's strange novel is the transcendence of positivism, a transcendence downward, so to speak, into a region *au dessous de toute explication,* below all explanation, into the wholly inexpressible, unspeakable, unnameable, into the feeling of sheer existentiality. It is the story of the gradual decomposition of the substance of our phenomenal world. First of all, decomposition of all abstraction and rational explanation, of all general terms and concepts; and then the decomposition of objects and their qualities, of the images of objects, and of human perception; decomposition of time, of memory, of history, of ego-sensation, or ego-perception; decomposition of all coherence altogether, decomposition down to the most singular, the most single, the most momentary, the extreme present, down to the dissolution into the nought, indeed, if it is possible to put it this way, to the dissolution *of* the nought, the nothing *itself.* For the nothing, too, is seen as something deriving from existence, it is post-existential; it presupposes man, who thinks it, who conceives it; it is a thought of man, therefore an abstraction, therefore non-existent. What ultimately remains, the only thing left, is existence itself, something inexpressible, indescribable. Some silly accident and incident without substance, in which the apparent beings find themselves caught involuntarily as it were, without being able to get rid of it, a supernumerary remainder of eternity, a *saleté,* a horror and disgust.

Now let us see how all this comes to pass in the novel. The report starts out from the point of view of a most scrupulous objectivity. The writer of this diarylike report is a man without any extraordinary or unusual qualities, an ordinary, commonplace man, living in easy circumstances. He is engaged in historical studies. He wants to write the biography of some minor personage of the eighteenth century, and for that purpose he has settled down in a little provincial town where the library possesses the pertinent material. Now this man has had a disquieting experience and, in order to clarify this experience to himself, he proposes to record whatever happens to him, down to the most insignificant details of his daily life. In doing this, he wants to be as exact, as objective as possible. In fact, what he sets about to do, is the model of a scientific study: "Not the slightest nuances must escape my attention, none of all those tiny little facts, even if they look like nothing at all; and above all they have to be classified. I must say how I see this table, the street, the people on the street, my pack of tobacco, because it is exactly this that has changed. I must most accurately determine the extent and the nature of this change." He takes a position, an observation post of the utmost detachment from his self and from the objects he wants to investigate, in order to discover whether this change has taken place in himself or in the objects. What he wants to achieve is precisely that second, coldest consciousness, that objectification of life, that Jünger also has in mind.

Of one thing he pretends to be sure: that he is not crazy; and in this he, or rather his inventor, Sartre, is probably right. To be sure his psychic condition has some resemblance to what psychiatrists call "alienation." However, it is a kind of philosophical alienation, and it is too much in the line of general developments, of the boundless growth of artistic sensibility, to be considered a mere individual abnormity.

Antoine Roquentin, the man in the little French town, experiences the crumbling of his world in a twofold manner: he first experiences what Hofmannsthal's Lord Chandos tries to express— the invalidation of rational terms and arguments; and afterward, what the man in Hofmannsthal's piece "On Colors" relates—that peculiar failing of objects and sensory phenomena.

First of all, in trying to clarify and explain the somewhat problematic eighteenth-century figure whom he chose as the subject of his historical study, in trying to grasp the motives and acts of this man with utmost scholarly precision, Roquentin gets confused in his arguments and experiences a disintegration of the means of rational understanding. Not only do the motives of his hero appear to him more and more complex, but he comes to feel a strange incapacity to make them comprehensible to the reader. "I begin to believe," he says, "that one can never prove anything. My hypotheses are honest, and they are based on the facts; but I feel so strongly that they issue from me, that they are simply a way of unifying my findings. In a slow, lazy, and morose manner the facts comply with the order I want to give them; but this order remains quite external to them. I have the impression of doing a work of pure imagination." This belief is confirmed when he watches the activities of a little employee, whom he regularly meets in the library, a man whom he calls the "autodidact," and who is the caricature of a scholar. He studies whatever he can get hold of, reads all items of the catalogue in alphabetical order, and takes whatever he reads equally seriously: all theories and ideologies are for him equally valid. He is a supporter of all the great liberal ideals of the nineteenth century, a believer in progress, a philanthropist, a humanist. All this helps to discredit ideologies-as-such in Roquentin's mind. Ideas and ideologies become utterly unreal to him; they cease to exist. Nothing else exists but the single object, the single fact. "Objects," he says, "are just what they appear to be; behind them there is nothing." This, however, is only the preliminary setting for Roquentin's other experience, *the* experience: the single object also disintegrates.

The experience starts in a quite inconspicuous manner. Roquentin's report reads almost literally like the one of Hofmannsthal: "Something has happened to me . . . it came in the way of an illness . . . it has settled down gradually, slyly; I felt a little bit funny, a little bit embarrassed, that's all. And now it begins to grow and unfold."

But there is a difference: Hofmannsthal's experience arises from a vision, a visual impression. Roquentin's or Sartre's experience starts lower down, in the sphere of touch. It starts when Roquentin picks up a wet, slippery pebble, and from there it spreads to the other senses. From the outset, it is more physical, more in the body, more intense. It goes to the very roots of existence: "In my hands, for instance, there is something new, a certain way to grasp my pipe or my fork. Or better the fork has a new way to let itself be grasped, I don't know. Just now, when I came home and entered my room, I stopped short because I felt something cold in my hand that retained my attention through a kind of personality. I opened my hand, I looked: I simply held the latch of my door in my hand. . . ."

A kind of uncontrollable exposure to the environment takes hold of him, as with one who has stayed up all night, or who has lived too lonely for a long time, or who has undergone some psychic shock: the world of phenomena changes. It assumes a feverish, oversharp, exaggerated appearance. Things break out of their context, become all too present, all too momentary; they come too close, indiscreetly close; they seem to touch you, to fall out on your senses. They entangle the senses, cling to the senses, deprive them of their freedom. They become ever more real, over-real to the degree of surreality, improbability, and in this way seem to disclose their apparitional, illusionary character. And the senses, accordingly, react with nausea and disgust.

Here is just one example of the funny, almost teasing way in which the phenomena irritate Roquentin's senses. He sits in a little restaurant and cannot help watching the manager behind the bar. The man is coatless and his suspenders are of a faded mauve, which hardly shows against the blue of his shirt. These suspenders almost merge into the blue; they seem to obliterate themselves; but, as Roquentin puts it, it is a "false humility." "They irritate me," Roquentin says, "by their sheepish stubbornness—as if on their way to becoming purple they had suddenly stopped, but without giving up their intention to become purple. One is tempted to tell them: 'Now go on, become purple, and let's not talk about it any more.' But no, they stay in suspense, they persist in their unfinished effort."

From here on, there unfolds the whole drama of the phenomenal crumbling of Roquentin's world. First, objects lose their names. Roquentin sits on a bench in a streetcar: "This thing, on which I sit . . . is called a bench . . . I murmur bench, like an incantation, an exorcism. But the word remains on my lips, it refuses to put itself on the object." But by losing its name, the object also loses its coherence, its character, its objectness. The object disintegrates, its parts fall asunder or, better, they assume existences of their own and enter new, separate combinations. A man sits opposite Roquentin in the streetcar: "This man there, half sitting, half lying on the bench. . . . The whole right half of his body has slumped, the right arm sticks to his body, the right part hardly lives, it lives painfully, with great economy, as if it were paralyzed. But on his whole left side, there is a little parasite existence that proliferates: the arm has begun to tremble, it lifts itself up, and the hand at the end is stiff. But then the hand also has started to tremble, and when it arrives at the head, a finger stretches and starts scratching the hairy leather of the head, with its nail. A kind of voluptuous grimace has come to settle down on the right side of the mouth, and the left side has remained dead. The windows tremble, the arm trembles, the nail scratches, scratches, the mouth smiles under the fixed eyes, and the man tolerates, without being aware of it, that little existence that inflates his right side, that has borrowed his right arm and his right cheek in order to realize itself." [26]

Roquentin steps out of the streetcar and enters the Jardin Publique. And here, in the park, the last breakthrough occurs, in that objects, deprived of their names, give up their borderlines, their singleness, their individuality. "The diversity of things, their individuality, was nothing but appearance, a varnish. This varnish had melted away, and what was left were soft, bare, disorderly masses, monstrous and obscene in their frightful nudity. All things were gently, tenderly abandoning themselves to existence, like those slack women who let themselves go and plunge into laughter, saying in a liquid voice: 'It's good to laugh;' they exhibited themselves to one another, they made each other abject confidences of their existence. . . . We were a lot of existents, ill at ease, embarrassed by our selves; we did not have the slightest reason for being there, not one of us, and each existent, confused and vaguely troubled, felt that it was superfluous in relation to the rest. Superfluity: that was the only relationship I could establish between these trees, these iron gates, these pebbles. . . ."

Now all quality, action, movement of life—all this parts with its organic substance and structure, becomes isolated, establishes itself as a separate existence: "The tips of the branches swarmed with existences, with existences that regenerated incessantly, and were never born." And then, getting down to the extreme bareness of existence, all these existences merge with existence as such, that common predicament of all and everything, that "*pâte même des choses*," that "paste of things."

"This root, with its color, its shape, its frozen motion, was . . . beneath all explanation. Each of its qualities escaped from it a little, flowed outside of it, becoming half solidified, almost a thing. . . . That black there, against my foot, did not seem to be black but rather the confused effort to imagine black by someone who had never seen it . . . someone who had imagined an ambiguous state of being, beyond color. It resembled a color—but also . . . a bruise, or also a secretion, an oozing—and something else, a smell, for instance; it melted into the smell of wet earth, of warm wet wood, into the black smell spread over this sinewy wood, like a coat of varnish, into the savor of sweet, chewed fiber. I did not simply *see* that black; seeing is an abstract invention, a polished idea, something neat, an idea of man. But that black there, that sickly and amorphous presence, overran by far the sense of sight, smell, and taste; and this profusion turned into a muddle, and in the end it was nothing, because it was too much."

Time dissolves, since movement too appears to be an existence in itself: there is no continuity, no past, no future, since it would presuppose a substratum of continuity; everything is merely now, an ever-new and vanishing, merging present.

And finally, under the impact of all this tumult of amorphous existence, of constant suddenness, something happens like a revelation, like a mystical union, because the ego too gives in; the thinking, perceiving ego merges with the phenomenal mass of external existence. It is a mystical union, but by no means a mystical act. It is rather the opposite: a mystical giving in, a mystical breakdown. It is the last union of perception with the phenomena perceived, of the subject with the absolute. But it is a union that is not achieved through transport and ecstasy, through an effort of most intense concentration, as was the case with mystical movements of all times, but through *"nausée,"* through disgust. The absolute is not the supreme idea, not a supreme comprehensive meaning; it is the most dejected absurdity. Roquentin's painstakingly objective scientific search to understand the nature of his experience, this empirical scrutiny, has turned into the most abstract mysticism.

THIS EXISTENTIALIST EXPERIENCE, a psychic condition which could be called *schizaesthesia,* is, like the schizophrenia we discussed before, a totally new phenomenon. To be sure, such things have always been felt in certain physiological circumstances. Puberty, fever, long insomnia, extreme stress, the influence of drugs,[27] can produce states of personal and temporary alienation. Only in our time, however, in our human situation, and out of the sharpened sensitivity, spirituality, intelligence of our senses, could this peculiar alienation evolve as a meta-physiological experience, an experience of general import and philosophical concern. I do not know of any document relating such a consciously sustained and far-reaching existential experience before the beginning of our century, whereas since 1900 it has been expressed by more authors than could be quoted here, before and independent of explicit existentialism. It was in order to demonstrate the symptomatic character of this phenomenon that I found it necessary to trace its history, to examine how it gradually formed through the concurrence of the three related agents: the growth of cultural *malaise,* the development of psychological introspection and the subtilization of artistic techniques.

Again, as in the case of science and technology, we are confronted with an ambivalent development. The luxuriant growth of the new sensibility has brought forth the most admirable artistic creations which have enriched and deepened not only our life experience but the reality of our life itself. Yet the splendor of all these accomplishments should not blind us to the fact that they also carry a formidable danger. The arts, as well as science and technology, have enormously extended man's reach; but in the course of and through this very extension, they threaten to tear away the basis from which they sprang. They are about to destroy the human personality.

CHAPTER SIX

Man Without Values

Turning and turning in the widening gyre
The falcon cannot hear the falconer;
Things fall apart; the centre cannot hold;
Mere anarchy is loosed upon the world,
The blood-dimmed tide is loosed, and everywhere
The ceremony of innocence is drowned;
The best lack all conviction, while the worst
Are full of passionate intensity.

YEATS

IN THE FOUR previous chapters I attempted to show the situation of the individual in our time and the various forces that tend to disrupt him from without and from within. I surveyed the different forms of collectivization and totalization of human beings which split the individual *from without* into a functional and a human part, and showed how the functional part keeps growing through the rising power of the collectives, while the human part shrinks in importance and effectiveness. We observed a corresponding movement evolving *from within* the human psyche and the human mind, which, partly as a consequence of the outer situation, partly in opposition to it, worked toward a fragmentation of the human being and of his experience. We saw how the scientification and technicalization of our world and of our life brought about that impersonal collective consciousness inherent in our institutions and techniques, tending to objectify all human relations and make man and all his outer and inner manifestations an object of impassible scrutiny and analysis. We saw how this technical, impersonal approach and the overcrowding of the surfaces of our world, with its new violent incongruities and contrasts, produced a new *human insensibility* and at the same time fostered *observational sensibility,* a sensibility which had originally arisen from a revolt against middle-class civilization and its rationalistic, commercial and mechanistic spirit. Cultural uneasiness and discontent, a growing alienation of the intellectual and particularly of the artist from his society drove the artist into *l'art pour l'art* and, through the exclusive concentration on artistic techniques, into the development of an ever more rarefied sensibility. In concurrence with increasingly acute psychological and scientific analysis, this sensibility wound up in decomposing the organic object and the organic person, indeed, the underlying texture of our feeling of existence. In the scientific and practical, as well as in the artistic sphere we observed the same process, an immense and glorious expansion of man's scope and, at the same time, a bursting, a disruption, a sweeping away of the very basis of his existence: the human personality.

This, then, is the situation and the network of correlations which I wanted to demonstrate in this study. Our task appears to be to counterbalance the perilous effects of otherwise irresistible and unpreventable developments. We are in a state of transition from an individual form of existence to a supra-individual form of existence, the character of which is still in the dark. But whatever this new supra-individual form of existence may be, *it should not be a mere collective, but a new comprehensive community, a human community.* However, before making an attempt to answer the question of how this could be achieved, we have to consider the problem of *values,* which is closely connected with this question.

In the course of the present book I have repeatedly pointed to the fact that the human communities have been shattered and displaced by the ever more powerful collectives, and that these external groups, through their overemphasis on the functional, collective part in the person, have reduced the individually human part. But by acting against the human part in man, the collective influences inclusively destroy the roots from which human communities can grow. Thus, the collectives have not only tended to efface community from without but, through their predominance in the individual, they have indirectly worked against human community from within. I have talked in Chapter Two of the alienation among human beings and the lack of immediacy in human contacts which is due to the fact that people relate to each other more and more with the functional part of the self, i.e., the socially legitimate self, and neglect or suppress communication between the human, actually individual centers in man. The attempt to re-establish on a higher level a true community of men requires as its crucial prerequisite that people relate to each other again with their human rather than with their functional part; it requires immediacy between man and man.

The feeling of human community, the habit of living together and working together with humans as humans, this is—at least under everyday urban conditions—on the point of dissolving and being replaced by functional, operational solidarities. It is rarely your neighbor who is closest to you; it is the co-worker, and intimacy is based on his capacity as a co-worker. The sphere in which the average person lives is the sectional network of his job with all its narrow operational patterns and standards. To the degree that humanity has become practically and technically one, it has in an unprecedented proportion grown humanly disjoined.

To be sure, a perfected human community, be it that of a people or of mankind, has never yet materialized. No actual accomplished social democracy, no united humanity has ever been achieved. Yet through the influence of religion and tradition—both mythical and normative projections of initial human communities—a certain inner coherence, a vital feeling of human community *did* prevail among human beings, a common stock of attitudes, of likes and dislikes, of yes and no with regard to the facts of life, an intrinsic community of what we call *values*. There existed values, human values which, in an affirmative or prohibitive manner, determined human behavior and which were strongly effective in everyday life.

WHAT ARE VALUES? A value, I would say, is a fundamental significance which man attaches to matters of his life and through which he orients himself in his conduct. I say *fundamental* significance; this is essential. It means a significance which has a certain degree of *permanence,* and which is or claims to be *valid for a human community;* which has formed and emerged from some stratum deeper than just the individual human being. Kant's famous categorical imperative expresses this: "Act in a way that the maxim of thy will could always be valid as a principle of general legislation." Values have another indispensable characteristic: a value involves a *choice,* it *calls for a choice.* An old Indian adage says: "The world has been created for the sake of choice and for him who makes a choice." And in the Biblical story of Adam man becomes veritably man by making a choice.

The combination of these two features, *fundamental purport* and *choice,* distinguishes a value from the kind of significance that attaches to a mere sensation or to a practical means. A sensation also bears a certain positive or negative coloring, but this coloring may be just personal and temporary; it may change with a person's mood or whim. You may like an automobile or a dress today, and tomorrow a new automobile may be produced, not only more operative but more pleasing, if only because of its novelty and thrill; a new dress may appear on the market which attracts you more or reflects a shift of your temper and makes the old one look dull and faded. And as your feeling for the object changes, the significance of the object changes.

The same obtains with respect to a purpose. A person, an object, a certain attitude may be useful to somebody for attaining some end. When the person or the object ceases to be useful it loses its significance. All such personal or temporary significance we would not call value. Certainly, even in the personal domain there exists a kind of significance which has permanence. You love a person not just for the advantage or pleasure you may derive from him, not for any generally "good qualities"—in fact, one mostly loves women rather for their bad than for their good qualities—you love a person because of that profound, constitutional relationship, that spark of mutual response and inspiration that can never be properly explained. You love and are loved because, as it is said, you are "meant for each other." Indeed there are no general categories of quality by means of which we may express why we love a man or a woman. When Montaigne was asked to tell his reasons for his exceptional relationship to a friend he gave an unsurpassable answer: *"Parce que c'était lui, et parce que c'était moi"* ("Because it was he and because it was I"). So even the supreme significance which a human being we love assumes for us cannot be considered a value since it is so intrinsically, inexpressibly personal.

On the other hand there are objects that have common significance for *all* human beings, such as food, clothing, shelter and so forth, objects answering elementary needs and urges. What distinguishes the meaning of such objects from a value is the fact that as such they do not carry a choice. When we are starving or freezing, any food or clothing will satisfy us; we have no choice. Only when it comes to passing judgment as to whether an object is good or bad, beautiful or ugly, only when it comes to choosing and when the judgment and choice are based on a fairly general, categorical and, to some extent, permanent notion, a more than strictly personal and temporary notion, only then can this significance be called a value.

A value, however, should not be considered as a separate, isolated entity. Every single value forms part of some coherent system of valuation. It belongs within a consistent view of life, an organic concept and style of life of a human community. Any genuine community, primitive or advanced, the ancient Greek, the Roman, the Chinese, the Hindu, the Islamic, the Jewish, the Christian community—every one of them carries a specific concept of life and of man and, implicitly, a specific system of values. Such a system of values is just a rationalization, a sublimation and pragmatic elaboration of a primary view of life; it derives from a peculiar fundamental attitude which a community has developed toward its outer and inner world. And since there is evidence that the most mature and most influential civilizations—the Chinese, Hindu, Hellenistic, Judaeo-Christian—although having evolved distinctly and independently, have converged into some fairly common lines of conduct (no matter how specifically expressed) we may assume that a certain basic trend of valuation is inherent in the human form, that certain values are constitutional in man and come to the fore in his highest cultural stages.

It was *religion* and *tradition* which originally created and cultivated values. They not only cultivated them, they taught people atmospherically, climatically as it were, but also explicitly, how to apply values, how to strive after qualities and attitudes whose significance is valid beyond sensations and personal ends. They fostered a capacity for subtle distinction, a keen sense continually concerned with the elaboration and differentiation of values. Such a creative sense of value-distinction we see at work in the old religious leaders, the Chinese and Hindu sages, Buddha, the Jewish prophets and Jesus, the Talmudic and Hasidic masters, in the dialogues of Plato and the meditations of the Stoics, in poets and thinkers from Dante and the mystics to Pascal and Vauvenargues. All of them show a passionate care for values, a sensitivity to values, indeed a relish in values and valuation. None of this can be found any longer in our kind of society, except as a private luxury. How indeed could such an active sense of values maintain itself in the turmoil of a modern working day, under the constant pressure of collective demands? All that is left us instead are the academic value theories, mere descriptions or abstract analyses of the perplexities of modern existence, far remote from actual life.

What I mean by sensitivity to values and working on values may be illustrated by a few examples. I begin with two Chinese stories. The first is taken from the book that in Chinese literature goes

under the name of *Lië Tzu* (*Master Lië*), and is an intermediary
between the basic concept of Lao Tzu's Tao Te King (sixth century
B.C.) and the synthesis of all Taoistic teachings ascribed to Chuang
Tzu (fourth century B.C.). The second story is taken from Chuang
Tzu.

Tzu-Hia asked Kung, the Master [that is, Kung Fu Tzu, Confucius,
sixth century B.C.]: "What kind of man is Yaen-Hui?"
The Master said: "He surpasses me in love."
"And how about Tzu-Gung?" Tzu-Hia proceeded.
The Master answered: "He excels me in sagacity."
"And what do you think of Tzu-Lu?"
The Master answered: "He outdoes me in intrepidity."
"And Tzu-Tchang?"
The Master said: "He outshines me in dignity."
Tzu-Hia rose from his seat and said: "But, Master, how does it hap-
pen that the four of them are so particularly devoted to you?"
The Master said: "Keep your seat. I will explain it to you.
Yaen-Hui knows how to love, but he does not know how to resist
the one he loves. Tzu-Gung is very acute, but he is unable to agree
with others. Tzu-Lu is very bold, but he lacks caution and cannot
restrain himself. Tzu-Tchang is extremely dignified, but he is incapable
of associating with others. If you take all these excellent qualities of
the four together and want me to accept them in exchange for my
own personality, I would not do it. This is the reason why they are
devoted to me and nobody else."

* * *

When Yang Tzu went to the Sung State, he passed a night at an
inn.
The innkeeper had two concubines, one beautiful, the other ugly.
The latter he loved; the former he hated.
Yang Tzu asked how this was: whereupon one of the inn servants
said, "The beautiful one is so conscious of her beauty that one does
not think her beautiful. The ugly one is so conscious of her ugliness
that one does not think her ugly."
"Note this, my disciples!" cried Yang Tzu. "Be virtuous, but without being consciously so; and wherever you go, you will be loved."[1]

Turning to the Judaeo-Christian tradition, we find the same
subtle value distinction in regard to the various situations of daily

life. I quote a little-known story of Jesus, as related and commented upon by Oscar Cullmann in his book, *Christ and Time*. "How much each word of Jesus is to be understood, not as a law, but in its concrete application, is shown by that profound word concerning the Sabbath, which unfortunately is preserved only in the Western text and therefore is lacking in most modern translations, although it is certainly genuine:

"As Jesus saw a man working on the Sabbath, he said to him: 'Man, if you know what you are doing, you are blessed. If you do not know, you are cursed and a transgressor of the law'." (Luke 6:5 in the manuscript D).

If the man concerned works only out of indifference to the Sabbath, that is, if he considers that which Jesus has elsewhere said concerning the Sabbath to be simply a 'general' law, then he is accursed in his working on the Sabbath. . . . Only if he knows what he is doing, that is, if he can support it from the concrete situation, is he blessed in his working on the Sabbath." "Precisely this," Cullmann states, "is also the position of Paul concerning the ethical question. . . . The working of the Holy Spirit shows itself chiefly in the 'testing' ($\delta o \kappa \iota \mu \acute{a} \zeta \epsilon \iota \nu$), that is, in the *capacity of forming the correct Christian ethical judgment at each given moment. . . . This 'testing' is the key of all New Testament ethics. Thus Paul writes in Rom.12:2: 'Be ye transformed by the renewing of your mind, in order that you may attain . . . the capacity to distinguish what God's will is.' Likewise Phil.1:9f.: 'This I pray, that your love may grow more and more in knowledge and in all sensitiveness for . . . the testing and determining, of that which is necessary.' " [2]

The following Islamic story was told to me by a Turkish friend:

A stranger passing by a Moslem who was studying the Koran stopped and asked him:
"What are you reading?"
"I am reading the Koran," said the Moslem, "a sacred book."
"What is it about?" the stranger asked.

"It is about God," the Moslem replied.

"Who is God?" asked the stranger.

"God," said the Moslem, "is the Lord of the World."

"The Lord of the World?" the stranger wondered. "But where is he? Where does he reside? Where is he to be seen? I only believe to exist what I can see with my eyes."

Whereupon the Moslem rose from his seat, held the open book up to the stranger at a great distance and told him to read.

"How can I read this when you hold the book at such a distance?" the stranger shouted. "This is too far, I cannot see anything."

The Moslem approached and now held the book so close before him that it touched his nose.

"Can you read now?"

"But how should I be able to read when the book is so near? Again I cannot make out anything."

"So you see," said the Moslem, "just as far and as near as that is God."

I conclude this little selection with two Jewish stories showing the manner in which values were taught and followed to their vital implications and applications by the masters of the mystical sect of the Hasidim. This movement, which evolved in Eastern Europe in the eighteenth century, carried on the old intuitional, anti-formalistic tradition of the prophets and the Kabbalah and was, in the form of a reformation, a true resurgence of the spirit of original Christianity. It was as much opposed to the ritualism of Talmudic orthodoxy as to the partisans of rationalistic enlightenment.

When Levi Yitzhak became rav in Berditchev, he made an agreement with the leaders of the congregation that they were not to ask him to their meetings unless they intended to discuss the introduction of a new usage or a new procedure. One day they asked him to come to a meeting. Immediately after greeting them, he asked: "What is the new procedure you wish to establish?"

They answered: "From now on we do not want the poor to beg at the threshold. We want to put up a box and all the well-to-do people are to put money into it, each according to his means, and these funds shall be used to provide for the needy."

When the rabbi heard this, he said: "My brothers, did I not beg you not to call me away from my studies and summon me to a meeting for the sake of an old usage or an old procedure?"

The leaders were astonished and protested. "But master, the procedure under discussion today *is* new!"

"You are mistaken," he cried. "It is age-old! It is an old, old procedure that dates back to Sodom and Gomorrah. Do you remember what is told about the girl from Sodom, who gave a beggar a piece of bread? How they took her and stripped her and smeared her naked body with honey, and exposed her for bees to devour because of the great crime she had committed! Who knows—perhaps they too had a community box into which the well-to-do dropped their alms in order not to be forced to face their poor brothers eye to eye." [3]

*   *   *

One day the rabbi of Zans was standing at the window and looking out into the street. Seeing a passer-by, he knocked on the pane and signed to the man to come into the house. When the stranger entered the room, Rabbi Hayyim asked him: "Tell me, if you found a purse full of ducats, would you return it to its owner?"

"Rabbi," said the man, "if I knew the owner I should return the purse without a moment's delay."

"You are a fool," said the rabbi of Zans. Then he resumed his position at the window, called another passer-by, and put the same question to him. "I'm not so foolish as all that," said this man. "I am not such a fool as to give up a purse full of money that comes my way!"

"You're a bad lot," said the rabbi of Zans, and called in a third man. He replied: "Rabbi, how can I know on what rung I shall be when I find the purse, or whether I shall succeed in fending off the Evil Urge? Perhaps it will get the better of me, and I shall appropriate what belongs to another. But perhaps God, blessed be He, will help me fight it, and in that case I shall return what I have found to its rightful owner." "Those are good words!" cried the zaddik. "You are a true sage!" [4]

The stories told here come from the most diverse ethnic and historical climates and from very different concepts of life. And yet they have something essential in common: whatever qualities or attitudes of man or of God they deal with—God in this case stands for everything spiritual, suprasensual—values do not appear as fixed, external impositions, as mere commandments or obligations. They are embedded in life, indeed, in the life of the universe; they form part of life, grow out of life. This gives them their freshness and vital seriousness. Here we can hardly make out whether values are the very blossoms and fruits of life or the guiding principles that bring life to fruition. In fact, they are both at the same time; they are lasting and yet in perpetual flux. What we would call morality is wisdom, empirical knowledge of reality, and it was searched for as eagerly, as attentively as we are searching today for the technically useful facts of nature. Values, in that genuinely religious stage of man, were what made life worth living, and in the manner in which their quintessence was explored we feel the savoring of a precious good.

We could characterize the distance between those ages and ours by a dictum of another Chinese sage, Meng Tzu (Mencius, fourth century B.C.):

"He who gets up at cockcrow and thinks of nothing except doing the good is a fellow of the holy Shun. He who gets up at cockcrow and thinks of nothing except his profit is a fellow of the brigand Chih. Do you want to know the difference between the holy Shun and the brigand Chih? It consists of nothing else than of the difference between the good and the profitable." [5]

This dictum certainly touches on a focal, an initial point of the fundamental change that has taken place in regard to human values. The more people's consciousness has been beset by the "profitable," by the merely practically useful and advantageous, the more human values have been crowded out of real life into topics of Sunday sermons and ceremonial addresses. But the fact is that matters are no longer as simple as they were in the times of Mencius. Let us consider the chain of determinants of that fundamental change, point by point.

THERE IS, first of all, *secularization*, a process which is, I think, irrevocable and irreversible in spite of recent revivals of religious currents. Long periods of rationalism and empiricism have pushed the divine farther and farther back behind ever-growing scientific, technological and economic material, behind the manifold orders of intermediary causations and evolutionary processes. Indeed, the divine has been shoved beyond and into the very rear of one huge single process of continuous creation which, starting from a dynamic "expanding" universe of gaseous stars and nuclear transformations, proceeds through natural selection of living forms to a thoroughly explored social evolution of man. We no longer live our days in nearness to the divine; we do not sense its permanent presence in every form of nature as the ancients did, or medieval man amidst his dogmatic cosmos. The divine has been banished into a far-removed sphere of vagueness and silence. Such silence and absence of God have been bitterly felt by various modern minds, such as Rilke and Simone Weil, who were only too disposed to listen and to respond to the voice of the divine.

The thorough invalidation of personality in our time, the growing habit of thinking in terms of collective and technical motivations, the quantification of criteria and, last but not least, the overwhelming temporality of our life—all these are bound to weaken religious bonds. To be sure, the religious urge persists in many people, but it is blocked or misled by prevailing currents. Personal God addresses Himself to the personal soul, to the individual who is supposed to have a fair amount of freedom to decide on his conduct, his inner conduct at least. But the constant pressures and collective encumbrances of personal choice which a person feels in his social and economic situation must imperceptibly, unconsciously devitalize the concept of a personal God. Transpersonal, transhuman forces of an entirely different order have displaced the personal guidance of God.

In times when the course of daily events was visibly dependent on decisions of individuals—monarchs, statesmen, single entrepre-

neurs—and when personal influences could be countered by personal responses, in such a world the rule of a supreme personal
Lord suggested itself naturally to the mind; it corresponded to
people's daily experience. The behavior of secular rulers could
be evaluated in terms of the values of a transmundane authority.
The first disturbance of such genuinely religious relationship was
effected by Luther who legitimized through religious doctrine the
rule of thoroughly secular authorities, be they as they may, and,
in fact, identified the will of God with the will of the princes in
their capacity as God's rods of correction. When the individual
is supposed to submit unconditionally to the will of the secular
powers as instruments or substitutes of the supreme power, then
the will of God is stripped of its actual influence on earth. Another
form of such invalidation of God's perpetual control was the Calvin-
istic emphasis on predestination, the intention of which with
regard to the individual was to be established by secular means:
success in worldly affairs was made a proof of divine election.

The demiurgic quality, the creative immediacy of God has
been fatefully affected by the interception of an almost gapless
line of creative evolution as evidenced by the findings of modern
science. The Catholic Church, through the various enunciations
of Pope Pius XII, is inclined to see in the newly revealed fluidity
of the universe a confirmation of God's creation of the world.[6] The
instability of matter, the replacement of laws of nature by mere
statistical laws and of strict causation by contingency, would imply,
so it is argued, an initiating act of God. But even if this argument
were more consistent than it is—in the domain of organic evolution the Church has become entangled in hopeless contradictions[7]
—the most conclusive rational argument would prove to be of
little effect in the face of the daily demonstration of the dwindling
of absolutes and of the practical effectiveness of scientific laws,
restricted as they may be. In spite of their fundamental limitations, such laws continue to be valid and to be sought for in the
domain and dimensions of our human existence, and their technical applications are overwhelmingly present everywhere. In point

of fact, the deistic, Newtonian view, according to which the ever-lasting laws of nature were pre-established laws of God, seems less harmful to true faith in God than the present relativization and objectification of these laws.

The religious *sacrificium intellectus* which in early Christian times was a manifestation of enthusiastic, mystical fervor has assumed a new character in our day, the character of an escape or a drug. Thus, unless a person takes the position of Augustine, according to which this earthly world is doomed from its beginning so that a true citizen of the Kingdom of God cannot but leave it to its senseless doom and live in it as a stranger and exile—that is to say, if he considers intramundane values at all—he cannot expect true guidance from a personal God. God is either total or He is not at all. He is either felt to be penetrating our world and controlling every incident of our life, or He loses His serious actuality altogether. It is impossible to imagine Him in some remote cosmic anteroom, leaving the evolutionary, empirically rational, technical processes to follow their own independent course. Nor can He be conceived of as acting through a thoroughly mechanized world in which man has become more and more subject to the rule of his own creations. Even chastisement by means of such subjection would have a meaning only if a person were free to live in a different way. Therefore, values which are seriously valid here and now no longer issue from a divine personal Lord. In order to be effective, they would have to be derived from and supported by secular criteria. Secular criteria furnishing current guidance are the only possible source of values to live by today.

WHERE DO WE FIND these secular criteria? Our present life is guided by *science,* which means an *increasing prevalence of determinism.* This is the second powerful agent contributing to the crumbling of the world of values. Values, as we have seen, call for choice; and choice is possible only when there is a certain degree of *free will.* But fairly everything that modern science has taught us points in the direction of determinism. Nor could this

be otherwise since science, by principle and implication, is searching for laws of nature. Countless discoveries and resulting theories
have undermined the validity of free determination. Experimental
psychology with its expanding research in perception and the
operation of the brain; genetics, physiology, endocrinology with
their concern for constitutional conditions, muscular and glandu-
lar processes; behaviorism, cybernetics, psychoanalysis, sociological study of environmental influences—all these imply a
restriction of free will, an objective determination of human behavior. Seen from the point of view of modern science, all our
acts and thoughts seem to be completely conditioned by inner and
outer circumstances, and in a way this assumption of modern
science is probably correct. What we feel to be free choice may
be the result of hidden urges, conditions or pressures. When I
decide to take a walk or to work, when I am susceptible to this
or that opinion, when I am angered or gay, full of energy or in a
low state of mind, I am never aware of the complex combination
of circumstances that induced me to a particular attitude. I am
defined by my heredity and the coalescence of my genes; I have
been brought up in this or that tradition and environment; I have
been schooled by a certain educational spirit, have undergone
certain distinct experiences, known such and such persons who
have attracted or shocked me and whom I unconsciously connect
with specific trends or views. All such conditions and many more
are constantly conjoining to influence and compel me not only
to act, but to choose the way I do.

This seems to justify a new fatalism. But, fortunately, science
with all its most legitimate statements does not present the complete picture. Choice exists: our most elementary, we may say
our immediate existential experience, tells us that both in thought
and action we are making decisions, and that means that we are
free. The mere process of thinking implies that we are seeking
what is right and true and rejecting what is wrong. We may para-
phrase the famous Cartesian axiom by saying: *Cogito, ergo volo.*

Certainly, truth is not something stable and absolute. It is always in flux and, by necessity, relative. Since we are incapable of grasping the totality of our world, what is true for us rests on primary assumptions which, at best, are furnished by a restricted range of evidence, by facts selected collectively or individually in specific perspectives, thus taken out of their context and perpetual flux. These initial assumptions have proven to be dependent not only on a specific stage and reach of human knowledge but also on specific ideologies, styles of thinking, and on emotional dispositions and impulses.

While we are thus conditioned in our thoughts and acts and while our feeling of freedom may be deceptive, the feeling in itself is alive and, like all living things, is acting and reacting. The feeling of freedom is not a hollow mechanism moving on a wholly predetermined track; its vital energy surges from the incommensurable sources of life and is in constant process of creation, capable of influencing events and conditions and of changing given directions. Our subjective feeling of freedom with the energies and potentialities it expresses is an agent in the shaping of events. To conclude from scientific findings that we are just mechanically pushed automata and that our stakes are inevitably set by objective necessities or contingencies would mean the elimination of essential factors which are in the play, which count in the play.

Thus, free will appears to be included, built in, in a system of interdetermination, which is infinite in its creative possibilities. One could say that in man determination assumes the character of free will, determination uses free will, as it were. And while it may be true that determination pervades everything we think and do and while in retrospect all developments and happenings may prove to be dependent on definite objective conditions, not the least of which being the amount of vitality a person is endowed with, our freedom of will which is active and effective at any given moment is not invalidated by this. The problem of free will is nothing else than a specific form of the problem of life proper.

Just like the biological dilemma existing between mechanism and vitalism, the problem of free will seems to invite the application of Niels Bohr's principle of complementarity. This principle is based on the experience that the very same system of reality shows different features and effects which appear to be incompatible, indeed, mutually exclusive as to describability. Therefore the full nature of such a system of reality may be grasped only by considering the conflicting features together, by seeing them as complementary.

The same principle may be applied to that age-old controversy between the materialistic and the idealistic school of historical theory: whether historical events are, according to Marx, completely determined by social and economic conditions, or whether, as the German historian Leopold von Ranke maintains, they are shaped by the will of men, by ideas and by the initiative of great personalities. Here, within a broader framework, the same dichotomy confronts us that manifests itself in the life of an individual. In history, that is, in the life of ethnic groups, free will, conscious choosing and acting, is represented by outstanding personalities. Those we call great men may be regarded as personified spearheads of objective developments, loci of convergence, where long-ripened, latent conditions come to light in the thought and action of a single human being. In fact, personalities may be considered historically prominent only insofar as they raise a situation or conclusion which had evolved extrinsically and had not been recognized before into personal consciousness and will, insofar as they enact the disposition and unconscious tendencies of their people or of humanity.

Just as the individual in making full use of his reason and free will is nevertheless determined by the influences of his heredity and his environment, so the course of history often seems to be the outcome of the ideas and resolutions of leading men who, however, are conditioned by distinct national traditions and by a particular social and epochal climate and whose very deeds and explorations are directed by developments far beyond their individual scope. And yet these deeds and explorations are their very own achievements.

REGARDING THE GENERAL HUMAN SITUATION we may, therefore, assume that free will and individual initiative are just as real as objective determination. Yet in our present concrete situation the deterministic and objectifying instruction of science is overpowering, and this instruction is manifestly corroborated by the social condition in which the individual finds himself today. His freedom of choice is imperiled in a particular way. Freedom of choice depends on a certain amount of free space around us, on a certain range of decision in which we may exert our will. This range of decision has increasingly shrunk in proportion as the scope of events and action has extended beyond the individual domain, as the pivot of determination has moved from the individual to the collective, from the subjective to the objective sphere.

It is needless to repeat what I have tried to demonstrate from different angles throughout this book: the closing in of collective pressure on the individual, the irresistible influence of impersonal, functional forces reducing the range of choice, the elbow room of the individual, and the individual's loss of orientation in an overextended, overcrowded and overcomplex world. Such manifold restriction of the individual's choice is the third and foremost determinant of the invalidation of human values.

Finally, there is a fourth factor that needs to be recalled as particularly important in this connection: *the effects of analysis, both scientific and artistic,* the penetrating scrutiny of our human situation which I discussed at great length in the previous chapter. Such analysis is, of course, a consequence of the real situation; it is the recognition, the conscious establishment of reality. Psychoanalysis in its various forms has blurred the borderlines between the normal and the abnormal; in fact, it has abolished the notion of integral normality. We have learned that there is no such thing as a completely normal person, but that every one of us carries a disposition toward some type of potential neurosis or psychosis.

The psychiatrist Ernst Kretschmer was the first of a number of succeeding medical theorists to distinguish personalities according to the type of mental disease toward which they might be predisposed. Similarly, the leading writers of our age have demonstrated the precariousness of norms. Values are no longer clear-cut and immune for them. They are, as it were, infected with each other: good and evil blend and merge. The Faustus motif, being most appropriate to such exposition, has recently been used by three eminent writers: by Thomas Mann in his *Doctor Faustus*, by Valéry in *Mon Faust*, and by Sartre in *Le Diable et le bon dieu*. Every one of them in his own peculiar manner has arrived at the same result.

Thomas Mann has illustrated the blending of values by the predicament of the modern artist, of spiritual man in our age. He has shown us that God and the devil dwell in the same body, that they are susceptible to exchanging their significance and that in our modern circumstances it is the purest, the most chaste mind who, by pursuing his impeccable sublimation, is committed to alienation from his fellow men, to sin. In Valéry's existentialist farce the devil is antiquated, an anachronism; he freezes out of existence in the glacial mountain air of the absolutely single, lonely man, the "*Solitaire*," who has surpassed him by far. For Faust, "*Il n'est ni chaud ni froid . . . il n'y a ni haut, ni bas*," and, "*Il y a énormément de rien dans le Tout. . . .*" ("There is neither hot nor cold . . . there is no high, nor low. . . . And there is an enormous amount of nothing in the All.") In Sartre's beautiful play, Götz, his Faustus, after first having gone through a stage of doing evil and later, having tried to do only good for men, finds out that, "*Les hommes d'aujourd'hui naissent criminels, il faut que je revendique ma part de leurs crimes si je veux ma part de leur amour et de leurs vertus . . . sur cette terre et dans ce temps, le Bien et le Mauvais sont inséparables: j'accepte d'être mauvais pour devenir bon*." ("The men of today are born criminals, I must accept my part of their crimes if I want to have my part of their love and of their virtues . . . on this earth and in this time, the

Good and the Bad are inseparable: I consent to be bad in order
to become good.") An extreme case, oddly revealing in regard to
our context, is the figure and the writing of Jean Genet, the thief,
"Saint Genet," who aspires to a peculiar sort of sanctity through
his self-willed status of criminal outlaw, this status representing
the deepest degree of moral solitude, hence of asceticism; not,
though, in the sense of Dostoievsky to whom crime is the catharsis,
the catalyst of Christian sublimation, but only as an instrument of
his entirely un-Christian, desolate exceptionality. Genet's sanctity
is, as Sartre rightly remarks, a *descente,* it is, in fact, a parallel
to the existentialist downward transcendence.

WHAT IS THE RESULT of all this? It is not just a devaluation of
specific values, nor a mere invalidation of a world of values; it
is a *dwindling of the faculty of valuation altogether;* it is a *devaluation of valuation as such.*

Albert Camus has given us, in his story, *L'Étranger* (*The
Stranger*), the paradigm of a man without values, a man completely
devoid of the faculty of valuation. He describes a small employee
who, without suffering and without joy, without imagination or
expectation, drifts along, or lets himself be driven along by the
currents of daily life. To all the sensations or challenges he encounters he reacts with a naïve, almost innocent candor which is
the result of extreme indifference. Again, it is a case of alienation
—hence the title of the book. But in Camus' book this alienation
is not brought about by a stirring experience consciously pursued
to a metaphysiological end as in Sartre's *Nausée;* it is a constitutional alienation stemming from a person's complete lack of
relatedness to other human beings, to anything at all. In this
model case which Camus presents, the hero's alienation stands
out so sharply because of his imperturbable sincerity, his genuine
disregard of all conventional decorum to which most people surrender out of sheer laziness and cowardice, out of reluctance to
take the trouble to resist. Owing to his total lack of relatedness,
Camus' Stranger has no trouble in resisting. He puts his mother

in a home for aged people because they both feel bored with each
other and because there she finds more contact with people of her
age. Her death is just a natural happening to him and does not
strike him in any particular way. At the wake and the funeral he
does not feel anything but heat, fatigue, boredom, a desire to
smoke, and he does not take much trouble to conceal his feelings.
In the afternoon he has a swim with his girl and in the evening he
goes to the movies to see something funny. When the girl asks
him whether he would marry her, he answers, "Why not?" for
he does not see any reason against it. But when she goes on and
asks him whether he loves her, he says with the same unimpres-
sionable candor that he does not think so. Through his indifferent
compliance he gets into the company of a gangster and unwittingly
becomes entangled in all sorts of evil feuds and brawls and finally,
through the automatic course of events and the effects of a little
too much wine and the Algerian sun, he is driven to the point
of murdering somebody with whom he has nothing to do whatever. This, too, and what happens to him later as a consequence
of his act he accepts without any deep concern or emotion. In
the hearings and before the court he tells what happened in a
dry and factual way, refuses to admit feelings he did not have,
although this could improve his situation. It is not positive honesty
that prompts him to do this. Out of sheer impassivity he lets
things happen the way they do. He is, to be sure, a little annoyed
by the inconveniences of the jail; but he has no feelings of guilt or
defiance. To him everything is just what it is: arid, meaningless,
inarticulate happening. To the court, the prosecutor, the jury, to
his defense counsel, to the prison chaplain who comes to comfort
him—to all these people he seems a sheer monster, which in a
way he actually is, but not in fact for their conventional reasons:
not because he falls short of their ideas of a loving son, a repentant
or at least shaken criminal, a Christian sinner. He is a monster
because he represents the extreme exponent, the caricature of
the absurd normality of our world, of a meaningless, valueless,
value-free world in which everything has become pure happening,

pure phenomenon again, as of nature, but of a nature that has lost its innocence. He resembles a type of youth which Jünger has characterized by that "complete color-blindness toward values," a youth for whom "technics and ethics are in a curious way synonymous."

At the end, after the death sentence, there finally occurs an outburst of human feeling in the man, directed against the chaplain and the comfort of religion. Here Camus seems to substitute himself for the figure he has created in order to reveal the meaning of the story—much as Chaplin did at the end of his beautiful film, *Monsieur Verdoux,* slipping into the character and elucidating his situation, one deeply related to that of Camus' Stranger. Camus interprets his man-without-values the existentialist way: "The chaplain," says the Stranger, "was so certain of everything, wasn't he? And yet, none of his certainties was worth one strand of a woman's hair. . . . It might look as if my hands were empty. But actually I was sure of myself, sure about everything, far surer than he, sure about my present life and about that death to come. That, no doubt, was all I had. But at least that certainty was something I could get my teeth into—just as it had got its teeth into me . . . I had acted thus and not otherwise. I had done this and I had not done that. . . . Nothing, nothing had the least importance, and I knew quite well why. . . . From the bottom of my future all through that absurd life I have been leading some somber, persistent breeze had been blowing toward me from the years that had not yet come. And on its way, that breeze had nullified, invalidated, leveled out all that was offered me in the years I lived, which were in no way more real than those of my future. . . ."

And after that catharsis in the death cell there is even a kind of happy end: "As if that great outburst had purged me of all evil, [so the Stranger notes], as if it had emptied me of all hope, so, in the face of this night, gazing up at the dark sky spangled with its signs and stars, for the first time, the first, I laid my heart open to the benign indifference of the universe. To feel it so like myself, so fraternal, after all, made me realize that I had been happy and that I was happy still." [8]

L'ÉTRANGER is a parable presenting a neat conceptual type such as hardly ever occurs in reality. How does the devaluation of valuation manifest itself in the life of our epoch? What are its effects on our civilization?

One unmistakable symptom is our *lack of a definite style of life*.

To be sure, there still exist national tastes and predilections. Italians are still viewing and tasting life very differently from the French, the British, the Americans; every one of the various peoples of the earth has its specific preferences, its traditional likes and dislikes. But when we look back to former ages, we become aware of momentous changes. Ever since the rise of the Christian era a supra-national mode of life has been forming and what we call the Romanesque, the Gothic, the Renaissance, the baroque, the rococo, all these "styles" are such epochal modes and aspects of life, consecutive versions of a generally European or Western attitude. Although these epochal modes of life, coinciding as they did with specific national hegemonies, bore the traits of the nations predominant at their time—the Renaissance, for instance, made Italian, the baroque, Spanish, the rococo, French characteristics prevalent—they were nevertheless supra-national and extended their sway all over Europe and her colonies.

Such modes of life, expressing themselves in every detail of human attitudes and manners, moral as well as aesthetic, political as well as private, were of course very complex. They mirrored the dynamic tensions of their time; tensions between divergent trends, tensions between different generations always coexist in one and the same epoch. In the late Middle Ages, for instance, Christianity was generally predominant and was interpreted in widely varying ways by the militant knights and the guild-controlled cities, by the papal hierarchy, the mendicant orders, the heretic sects. The baroque reflects the fanatic rigidity and exaltation of the religious struggles no less than the overabundant ostentation of rival secular monarchies. And yet there existed a common ground on which these variations moved, there existed a language beneath all languages by which people communicated, by which even opponents understood each other: the language of values. And every turn of an era was, in fact, a conflict of values, a struggle between new and old values.

These modes of life and their changes developed spontaneously, unconsciously, out of the changing conditions and experiences of an inwardly coherent human community. Within it, national and religious currents mingled and crossed: humanism, for example, related back to a common Romanic family tradition originating in pagan times, while Protestantism carried an old Germanic repugnance against Rome. Although such value conflicts evolved between subliminal tendencies of national and religious communities, they were consciously fought out by the intellectuals of the epoch. The intellectuals, to be sure, were ahead of the people and paved the way for the great transformations; but in their advances they were sustained by an anonymous support, sustained even by the counterweight of resisting tradition; they found a common frame of reference in the general mode of life of the period.

In our day the life of people all over the world is, for the first time, on the point of following an immediately universal pattern and not, as in former periods, pursuing a distinct mode of life which had originated in and expanded from a particular human attitude. The present forms of living as generated all over the globe by Western civilization are not a genuine style of life; they are *abstract standards* imposed by objectively tested experiences, by scientific and technological precepts, by industrial production and baseless, commercially devised fashions. What determines the conduct of people today is, in a rapidly diminishing degree, tastes and preferences, but more and more the inexorable factual and practical necessities of collective work and the collective facilities it produces.

This radical change of affairs has deeply affected the status of the intellectual. He is no longer, as in previous ages, exponent and at the same time shaper of a dominant "style," of the value-currents of a community. Intellectual life has assumed a character substantially alien to that of people's actual lives; it moves along quite autonomously. Science, to be sure, is still closely connected with the life of people through its practical applications. It is through these alone, demonstrating as they do the effectiveness of its methods, that science exerts its authority over people and not, by any means, through inner directions. Modern science is inherently value-free; it requires and fosters the exclusion of values.

Among the arts, only architecture maintains close contact with social life owing to its synthesis of art and technology; it has always expressed an epochal form by means of practical use. In modern architecture, indeed, and in architecture alone, the general trend of our age, the bare factuality, the technical and collective character of modern life has found a valid stylistic expression.

In the other arts, however, in those concerned with the inner condition of man, the true artist lacks a consistent frame of reference, a solid mainstay, through support or opposition, of a naturally grown and effective values system. His is a remote and lonely endeavor; hence his overstrained and delicate balance, his inner insecurity, his multifold experimentation. What he faces is not an established system of values to be perfected, advanced or changed as it inhered, for instance, in the worlds of Dante, Cervantes or Shakespeare, but a chaotic wilderness in which he has to create his own order. The material of his structures, the reality from which he starts is not transmitted to him in a coherent shape which could only be provided by an intrinsic style of life. He has to start from scratch, that is to say, he has to create the premise of values, a coherent picture of his world. He has first to establish the inner state of affairs before he can begin to search for values. This is why the emphasis of the true artist today is on sheer description rather than on valuation, on groping his way through the thicket of our age toward a focal point from which an orientation may be achieved. This is why, in the course of their analyses, important authors such as André Gide, Valéry and Thomas Mann have come to recognize the commingling of "good" and "bad"; why complaints are heard ever so often that our great writers destroy values rather than establish them, that no guidance can be derived from their work. The artists of our age are condemned to extreme personal peculiarity. Hypertrophic individuals that they are, lacking a general style of life to which to refer, they create so many personal styles. If there is anything to be found that Picasso, Klee, Utrillo, Rouault, Chagall, Mondrian, Chirico, Miró, or Gide, Joyce, Kafka, Musil, Thomas Mann, Faulkner, have in common, it is not a general mode of life and system of values from which they took off, but is rather the chaotic, deeply disturbed condition of their world material and, correspondingly, certain new experiences and techniques, or trends of technique, developed in the attempt to cope with it. While in former ages one comprehensive style of life passed over into another and linked the artistic generations to each other, today it is the purely artistic, "aesthetic" element, the mode of perception and description, that is taken over and pushed further by successive artistic generations. Indeed, the material substance of experience comes to coincide more and more with the mode of experience and technique of expression.

This is not to deny that these artists most sincerely strive for contact with the people of their age. Their remoteness is not of their own choosing; it is forced upon them by tragic circumstances. In some of them a social critique implying valuation is strongly expressed, as in existentialist prose, French resistance poetry, Picasso's *Guernica* and *Massacre in Korea*. Indeed, in such Picasso pictures and in the work of Ben Shahn the impact of social situations, carrying strong value emotions, expresses itself not merely in the motif and in the violent intensity of its treatment, as in Goya's *Desastres de la Guerra,* or in Daumier's satires, but, more intrinsically and immediately, in the very style of these paintings, their pictorial form, their compositional and color symbolism.

Our lack of definite valuation has, on the other hand, enabled us to appreciate the most diverse styles of life of all times and places in their own right, to come nearer than ever before to grasping the genuine character of foreign cultures. In this we were, of course, greatly helped by the neutral, scientific attitude of scholarly research, by its stupendous new discoveries and explorations.[9] Our concept of classical antiquity is no longer that of Italian humanism, of baroque bucolics, of Racine's tragedies, or even of Napoleonic *Empire,* all of which bear the distinct imprint of their respective eras and nations. Today the Orient is no longer naïvely adapted to the taste of a Western society as was the China of French rococo. We are free to see things as they really are.

A SECOND SYMPTOM of the devaluation of valuation, related to the first one, is *a change in our attitude toward crime and moral offense.*

Until the nineteenth century, Christianity, still fundamentally unshaken—broken by reform and secularized by enlightenment though it was—involved a generally unquestioned validity of its moral principles.

This does not imply, of course, that in those times people were leading immaculate lives. They were far from it and politics in particular has always been a somewhat dirty job. But, apart from colonial and frontier situations in which the old Christian exclusion of infidels from common humanity, a residue of the ancient concept of barbarism, still persisted long after Las Casas and Francisco Vitoria,[10] apart from these situations, a criminal knew himself to be a criminal and acknowledged himself as a criminal because an intrinsically established order made crime an actual crime, not merely something conventionally punishable by law. As Julien Benda in his book, *La Trahison des Clercs* (*The Betrayal of the Intellectuals*), rightly put it: "Formerly, leaders of States practiced realism, but did not honor it; Louis XI, Charles the Fifth of Spain, Richelieu, Louis XIV, did not claim that their actions were moral. . . . With them morality was violated, but moral notions remained intact; *and that is why, in spite of all their violence, they did not disturb civilization.* . . . Up till our own times men had only received two sorts of teaching in what concerns the relations between politics and morality. One was Plato's, and it said: 'Morality decides politics'; the other was Machiavelli's and it said: 'Politics have nothing to do with morality.' Today they receive a third. M. Maurras [the leader of the French Royalists] teaches: 'Politics decide morality.' However, the real departure is not that this doctrine should be put before them, but that they should accept it. Callicles [the Sophist] asserted that force is the only morality; but the thinking world despised him. . . . Machiavelli was covered with insults by most of the moralists of his time. . . ." [11]

The watchword of the French royalists became the declared maxim of the Nazi state: "Right and lawful is what is useful to the state." With the official adoption of this maxim, which not only legitimized but enforced all the atrocities of the Third Reich, something decisive happened. To be sure, it had been brewing for a long time, and the open proclamation of such a rule by a supreme collective was only the final conclusion of subtler processes which had been under way in many countries of the world. Everywhere the old values had degenerated into hollow conventions; while they were still preached and outwardly recognized, they became snowed under in reality by the new economic and social developments. This moral situation had been exposed by thinkers and writers of the nineteenth century, but not before the Third Reich had the abolishment of the Christian values been explicitly professed and exploited by a government.

A direct consequence of the new trend of affairs was a *widespread political vitiation of jurisdiction,* which weighs more heavily in an age that has accustomed the minds of people to civil liberties and to the concept of equality before the law. In the last decades more decent people in many countries have been jailed, mingled with criminals, put to death officially by sentence or otherwise than ever in the periods of feudal regimes; and all this has been done in the name of the people. Certainly the feudal rulers were reckless enough in the exercise of their prerogatives, but the powerless people were not involved in their behavior. What the rulers did was clearly their own responsibility. In our time, however, even dictatorial regimes could not help but pay a certain tribute to the principles of democracy, if only through demagogy, with the result that they made every citizen a voluntary or involuntary accomplice of their acts. Whatever crime they committed, the people as a whole was supposed to authorize it by fake elections or by tacit consent. And the retroactive effect on people's minds of this common responsibility for outright criminal or unscrupulous acts on the part of their government should not be underestimated. Every citizen in such a situation is put under a moral stress which only strong personalities can withstand. The average person will try to evade the unbearable dilemmas by suppressing his qualms or, what is worse, by taking things lightly and persuading himself to approve.

Under the influence of collective pressures, in the shove and shift of a hurried life, people have acquired a new levity in regard to criminality, inured as they are by the daily consumption of Hollywood horror films, murder and mystery stories with which radio and television, magazines and paperback books stimulate their leisure hours. Crime has come to arouse the kind of tickled interest people take in sports contests: the criminal tries to get away with it, the law tries to get him; the thrill increases with the stakes and, of course, when caught, the criminal has to pay. This apparently is all there is to it. People see gangsters rising to a social status more rapidly than before. Careers that have become less and less attainable by legitimate means are achieved by breaking out of the legal frame. The reports of the Kefauver Committee have shown the infiltration of our society by crime, the blurred borderlines between regular, indeed official, and illegal operations. Gangsters, like all other elements in our age, have come to organize collectively, to form big syndicates. When they have reaped their money, they no longer attempt to incorporate individually with respectable society; they seem to have developed into a social class of their own. Remaining what they are, active criminals, they invest their money in industry, sponsor inventions, influence politics and retire to their millionaire estates where they enjoy unencumbered peace of mind.

Criminality went with the times; it has reached the stage of big enterprise, and investments are considerable. What John Gay and Bertolt Brecht had conceived in their *Beggar's Opera* and *Three Penny Opera* as a colossal farce has been almost surpassed by reality. *Murder, Inc.* and its better-screened successor associations were vast "combinations" with divided administrative functions and an extensive staff. Their "income was derived from a multitude of rackets—liquor distribution through dummy corporations, gambling, syndicated prostitution, muscling in on legitimate business, control of labor unions, ownership of nightclubs and roadhouses, and shake-down extortion in many forms—some crude, some refined." Murder, carried out in the most atrocious ways by minor "employees" was just a by-product. It "was performed purely for business reasons . . . to discipline the gang's personnel, to eliminate competition and to dispose of 'troublemakers'—that is, law-abiding citizens who got in the way." [12]

More interesting are criminal enterprises where crime itself—its industrial performance, not only its business administration—is professionally organized. Mr. David W. Maurer, a professor of English and linguistics at the University of Louisville, Kentucky, has rendered a real service to social science by describing the organization, the techniques and the morals of "confidence men" in his book, *The Big Con*,[13] a report which is as amusing as it is alarming and which contributes more to the knowledge of our present society than many sociological treatises. It shows these trickery enterprises as true replicas of regular industrial corporations, equipped with large operating funds, staffs, agencies, fake offices (brokerage, Western Union and the like), and well-established connections with state officials (police, state senators, and so forth). It relates their professional codes of behavior, their complex functions which are in no way erratic, in no way a snatching of easy money, but involve hard work, highly specialized training and knowledge in various fields. The book conveys an impression of the fluid borderlines between respectable and illicit business, between the reality and unreality of our institutions. "The methods [of the confidence men]," Mr. Maurer writes, "differ more in degree than in kind from those employed by more legitimate forms of business." In fact, when reading this book one is seized with a kind of sociological dizziness.

Bearing in mind the general condition of our society, how can we be surprised at the frightening spread of juvenile delinquency? Adults are confused; they have lost values and the faculty of valuation; their lives are harassed and breathless, their consciousness filled with a tumult of incoherent facts. Temptations and pressures, sensations and fears, the fight for jobs, the whip of competition, the lure of money, the supreme standard of success— this is what drives them along day by day. Apartments and schools are overcrowded, families frequently broken up or on the move. The social atmosphere is loaded with tensions and hostility, with talk of war and ever more ghastly weapons, of total annihilation of cities; bombers and bombs dominate the scene.[14] What can we expect in a world of such adults from children and adolescents who need stability and a protection of their delicate growth, a long sleep of consciousness and a very gradual awakening to the handling of reality? Even under the best of conditions puberty is a dangerous age, brimming with emotions, weighted with frustrations; as one of these young gang leaders said: "Seems like when you're seventeen you're crying inside all the time." So it happens more and more often that not only notorious rowdies but apparently good-natured children burst suddenly into killing without being able to give any reasons for it. What distinguishes their acts from those of adult criminals is their utter senselessness. Albert Deutsch, in an article, *Why Do Children Kill?* [15] has assembled a long list of juvenile murderers, all of them telling their interrogators: "I don't know what made me do it. I just don't know." How should they know that it is the captive urges of their age, finding no channels but only stimulants in their environment. Small wonder also that, in defense and defiance, the children, following the prevailing social pattern and in particular the example of the gangsters, gather in collective groups terrorizing teachers and parents and whole areas of the city. Even in the most decent homes the consensus of "pals" dominates the bewildered parents.

Experts—educators, psychiatrists, jurists—seem puzzled by these phenomena. As reasons they cite lack of discipline, demoralized homes, negligent parents, inept teachers, the influence of comic books. All these, however, are secondary causes; they are themselves rather symptoms of a basic and more comprehensive determinant. It is not the perplexed parents who are mainly to blame, not the poor underpaid and overworked teachers, or the probation officers, youth consultants, judges—there are wise and dedicated people among them who sometimes against their will and better judgment are compelled to surrender mere children, just because they have no other place to put them, to penitentiaries or "reformatories," which are actually training grounds of crime and perversion. It is outrageous that boys of thirteen or fourteen should be sentenced to ten or twenty years of jail instead of being given medical and human care.[16] The primary source of all these evils is the general condition of our society, a world that has lost all coherence and consistency, and governments spending billions for armaments to defend a state of affairs in which youth, the very future of the people, is left without adequate institutions to safeguard its healthy development.

Our concept of crime has, admittedly or not, undergone a fundamental change. Psychological and sociological findings have made it actually impossible for us to identify crime with sin any longer, that is, to attribute the guilt exclusively or predominantly to free individual determination. We have learned too much about the determining factors of heredity, upbringing, social and historical environment to have a clear conscience about the enactment of penal codes. In fact, our whole criminology has come to be one big hypocrisy. The worst, just the worst criminal cases are actually medical or sociological cases—what there is of free will and individual determination begins only on a rather high human level. In the wilderness of our civilization not even a good-natured disposition is enough to assure decency. A broadly developed intelligence is needed to ponder moral problems, to have moral problems, and only he who feels ethics as a continuous problem is a person to whom ethics is a real concern—just as only blasphemers or near-unbelievers, like Job, Kierkegaard, Hopkins, Dostoievsky, Kafka, Simone Weil, are the ones to deal deeply with religion. The Prussian King Frederick II, an atheist, was the only one among his devout dynasty who took religion quite seriously.

But whatever the phenomenon of crime may be considered—a chargeable offense or a personal or social disease—our aim should be to keep it within the pale of human abnormality and to prevent it from coming too close to a status of even limited acceptedness. Whether the criminal index goes up or down is less important than the maintenance of the identity of crime as such. When the mayor of a large, old and most respectable American city resumes the duties of his high office immediately upon his return from jail, it is not so relevant from our point of view whether his conviction was an act of true jurisdiction or of political persecution, that is, whether the guilt rested with the accused person or with an abused administration of justice. What matters most is the apparent indifference toward the public status of criminality or, to put it in reverse, toward the dignity of a public office. What matters, and what is at the point of vanishing today, is the realization of human responsibility on the part of the offenders as well as on the part of the people, a responsibility that cannot be supplied or replaced by laws and penal codes, but that has to be experienced through a feeling of human community. What else is morality but responsibility in regard to the human community? In this plain postulate are comprehended all the experiences, examples and teachings of man's most advanced cultures at the stage of their full maturity.

HERE WE ARE AT THE CRUCIAL POINT. As long as people were able to communicate on human grounds, in a common language of values, the feeling of an inner human community and value-communication conferred upon every individual a definite human responsibility, responsibility to and for the human community. There existed *human responsibility* even when and where someone offended against it.

In our century, however, as a consequence of the increasing predominance of functional collectives in the individual, there have developed all sorts of *functional responsibilities,* such as the responsibility of the employee to the interests of his corporation, of the businessman to his business, of the politician to his party, of the official to his administration and his department, of the worker to his union, of the executive to the policies of his trade, of the scientist to the discipline and the methods of his science—even of incorporated gangsters to the rules and codes of the game. All these specialized, functional responsibilities have come to displace the old human responsibility, the responsibility to the human community.[17] They have come to displace it, first of all, by means of relativization, since all these various functional responsibilities seem to have an equal claim on the loyalty of the individual, equal also to that of the human community. And whenever a person feels a human responsibility colliding with a functional responsibility, there arises a conflict of loyalties, in which the pressure of the instantly effective functional collective is more powerful by far than the seemingly inconsequential demands of the human community.

An illustrative parable of this dilemma has been furnished by Charlie Chaplin in his film *Monsieur Verdoux.* Here the human feeling still prevails for a moment. Monsieur Verdoux, a little bank clerk, anxious to provide for the future of his beloved family, shifts to the career of a professional bluebeard, marrying wealthy women and then doing away with them. He wants to try out a new poison, which is supposed to leave no traces, on someone without family or friends who might inquire. He happens to find a young girl just released from jail, lonely, desperate, starving, abandoned to the street. He takes her up to his "studio," treats her to a hearty breakfast and brings in two glasses of wine, one of them containing the poison for the girl. They start a friendly conversation and she tells him her story, a story of desolation and love, of the mess and misery into which she was drawn by her love. Suddenly, he discovers a piece of cork in her glass, which she had not yet touched. He removes the glass and exchanges it for one without poison. Afterward, when he urges her to leave, much against her will but provided with money and good wishes, he pushes her out, imploring: "Go away! You have corrupted my morals!" These morals were his professional code which he had betrayed to human feelings and human loyalty, to what, in fact, constitutes true morality.

But in reality it often happens that such dilemmas do not even arise. Pending the grave decision on the development of the hydrogen bomb—which, according to a statement of competent physicists "is no longer a weapon of war but a means of extermination of whole populations," whose use "would be a betrayal of all standards of morality and of Christian civilization" [18]—Mr. Lilienthal, then Chairman of the Atomic Energy Commission, found himself prompted to protest that "Neither he nor any of his colleagues is opposing any weapon, no matter how terrible, on moral grounds or on principle." [19] Mr. Lilienthal was on the point of resigning and he could at least have refrained from taking a stand in this conflict of loyalties of which he was presently to be relieved anyway. But for him there apparently existed no conflict. The power of his functional responsibility was so strong that he explicitly denied any regard for human criteria, as if they were a disgrace.[20]

Even more frightening is the case of a prominent physicist, Professor Louis Ridenour who, carried away by his professional zeal, did not shrink from writing the following lines: "The area that can be poisoned with fission products available to us today is disappointingly small; it amounts to not more than two or three major cities per month." [21]

The functional responsibilities usually bear the mark of an objective, impersonal obligation. What imposes this obligation on the individual is an overpowering mechanism far beyond the reach of his determination and mostly even that of his group. If he does not comply with it, this is not just a personal failure; it is not confined to his personal orbit but may concern and disturb a whole complicated system. On the other hand, the individual is protected by anonymity. He is a modest little part in some huge organization, and his performance is often but a minute link in a widely extending and complex process. Much is being done today by corporations, offices and official departments which a man in his private life would still hesitate to do. Not only does the functional responsibility exert its claim on the individual, but the responsibility diffuses, it is atomized, broken up in little pieces, indeed it evaporates altogether. You cannot locate a responsibility any longer. Every individual acts under a definite order, under definite limited authorities, and the power of decision is but a combination of such restricted authorities and competences. More often than not it can hardly be established where a decision actually originated.

THE FULL EXTENT OF THE PROBLEM comes into view when we consider the extreme case of the total state. In the Nuremberg trials the perpetrators of the Nazi atrocities almost unanimously declared that they committed them on order or at least under the overwhelming influence of Nazi indoctrination. Any bit of human responsibility that was left in them was blacked out by this collective compulsion. And wherever such collective indoctrination becomes prevalent, be it Russian bourgeois-baiting or American red-baiting, a similar tendency is noticeable. The attitude of the Nazi doctors who experimented on human guinea pigs is particularly revealing because here human and functional responsibilities clashed in the most striking manner. The medical profession is unique inasmuch as its functional and human responsibilities actually coincide. A person who does not have a strong sense of human responsibility is incapable of being a good doctor. In the case of the Nazi doctors, however, the state collective availed itself of two intermediary functional collectivities: the military and science. In such a way, as has been aptly demonstrated by Doctors Alexander Mitscherlich and Fred Mielke in their book, *Wissenschaft ohne Menschlichkeit,* a discrepancy of deeper significance has been brought to the fore. There existed "a personal union of doctor, scientist and soldier. By means of military duty a usurpation of medical and human duties took place. He who had become a military chief (particularly an Elite Guard chief) had to take the war aims seriously, and that meant he had . . . to take the Nazi ideology seriously. . . . The result was a shift in guiding values. . . ." The Nazi doctors let themselves be diverted from the field of their proper activity without resistance, indeed "obedient to such a degree that they took their military duty toward a most precarious political ideology and their openly cruel and inhumane aims more seriously than their traditional duty which is one of unconditional human care." [22]

This is where another functional inducement comes in. The military collective, used and abused as an auxiliary by the supreme collective, the total state, resorted in turn to a further auxiliary collective, to science which is in itself today on the point of being alienated from, and threatening ultimately to counteract, the medical concern for the individual human being. In the trials against the Nazi doctors, an American witness, Professor Ivy, admitted a fundamental distinction between the broadly scientific and the therapeutic capacity of the physician, which implies that different commitments, different sections of the Hippocratic oath are valid, depending on the capacity that comes into play. "Professor Ivy," Doctors Mitscherlich and Mielke point out, "evidently recognizes the validity of still other lines of conduct apart from those aimed at the aid of the sick. In case of war, for instance, the medical scientist would be allowed to put his knowledge of the functional connections of the human organism at the disposal of one of the belligerent parties. This, however, basically affects medical independence, the duty to help suffering human beings impartially, regardless of circumstances. The medical scientist helps one party to damage people of the opponent party, and his practicing colleague tries again to heal the damages done. Obviously, the separation of medical research and medical practice has a bearing on the basic human obligations and is bound to destroy the ultimate meaning and effectiveness of the medical profession; the right hand no longer knows what the left hand is doing. . . . In principle then—and not only in Germany—the situation of the physician has been so thoroughly changed by technical developments and the emergence of giant collectives like the modern states, that the Hippocratic formula has lost its former unconditional validity. . . ." [23] The specialization and technicalization of medical science "has brought medicine into an indissoluble connection with technological developments in general. As a result, the physician finds himself more or less subject to all the evolutional corollaries of standardized mass societies. He not only grows more technical in his thinking and in his practice, but he even comes to decide about working ability and fitness for military service. . . . Should he take his criterions solely from the quantitatively oriented functional mechanisms that otherwise determine the present world or should he be mindful of his unchanging and timeless duties as a rescuer of human beings . . . ?" [24]

"The majority of the accused Nazi doctors," Mitscherlich and Mielke conclude, "were not sadists nor irresponsible abettors of cold-blooded schemes but men who up to the time when they yielded to the exacting demands of their political and military leaders had been scientists and physicians of perfect integrity. How else than through a deadening of ethical, human feeling could they have acted the way they did? And that this deadening of human feeling has a definite correlation with the inner development of medical research, this in fact is our thesis." [25]

In America, essentially the same conflict among military, scientific, and human loyalties has arisen in connection with the atom bomb. But here some of the leading scientists who had had a part in the development of the bomb clearly realized this conflict of loyalties, and discussions have been going on ever since as to whether a scientist is responsible, or should be made responsible for the pernicious effects of his discoveries; that is, to put it more specifically, whether a scientist should actively concern himself with the political application of his discoveries and see to it that they are used for beneficial rather than destructive purposes.

The problem is certainly a most intricate one. To be sure, no scientist should be *made* responsible for the evil effects to which society or the state puts his findings. It is the peak of absurdity when modern physics is sometimes condemned by people for having brought about a situation in which such monstrosities as the atom bomb and the hydrogen bomb have become feasible. The discovery of nuclear fission was determined by the progress of collective research, no less than the discovery of radioactivity or electricity; as soon as that stage of knowledge was reached, the invention of the atom bomb was bound to happen somewhere and sometime in the course of the big world conflagrations. Nobody could tell in 1941 whether it would not happen in Germany first. Thus, in America, too, science came to serve the military aims of the state in a conspicuous way. Although the research was conducted with all possible care for human lives, and although the result was originally intended as an ultimate resort, fatality took its course. Against the advice of conscientious scientists, the bomb was put to use in Hiroshima without warning, for political reasons. Therewith it was introduced as a regular modern weapon to be further "improved" up to the practically limitless destructive potentialities of the hydrogen bomb. In the controversies concerning the development of the hydrogen bomb the split of loyalties, to the state and to the human community, lay wide open.

While there can hardly be any doubt that scientists should not be *made* responsible for this course of events, the question remains,

and fortunately keeps stirring in personalities of keen human sensibility, whether a scientist should not *feel* responsible as a human
being for the unprecedentedly hideous results of recent discoveries,
and whether, in the face of past experiences and the enormity of
foreseeable perils, he should lend himself to such application of
his work. This is a clear case of human responsibility which we
all share wherever we stand, whatever our work. A refusal of
technical collaboration on the part of prominent scientists, especially if this refusal were openly declared by a group, an international group, would establish an example and would bring more
pressure to bear on governments and world opinion than ordinary
citizens are able to exert. Professor P. W. Bridgman, the eminent
physicist, who has written an indignant article against the imposi-
tion of social responsibility on the scientists,[26] has omitted the
crucial fact that scientists nowadays are not merely pursuing their
theoretical research, which is then put to bad use by governments;
they are themselves instrumental in the pernicious application of
their findings.

Professor Bridgman believes that a scientist should be concerned
only with his "good life" as a scientist, that is, "life of the intellect."
He should not interfere with social affairs and should decline all
social responsibility. To Professor Bridgman, the ideal society is
one of utmost tolerance: "What would be a good life for one man
would not be a good life for another. . . . No society dedicated
to a special thesis satisfies this requirement. A totalitarian society
such as that of Russia . . . is obviously not such a society." But,
Professor Bridgman goes on to say: "Neither is the conventional
Christian society, with its thesis that the good life is the one devoted
to the service of a man's fellows, and with the correlative assumption of the right of the community to impose this ideal on the
individual."

The society pictured by this distinguished scientist would be an
anarchical society even if it could still be one in which every
individual were allowed to choose his own preferred form of good

life. As things actually are, however, Professor Bridgman's "tolerant" society could only be a medley of many collective intolerances between which little choice would be left to the individual.

Professor Bridgman's views are a perfect reflection of the social condition of our day. The most frightening aspect of our present world is not the horrors in themselves, the atrocities, the technological exterminations, but the one fact at the very root of it all: the fading away of any human criterion, the disruption of the contents and substrata of human responsibility. There is a fatal correlation, a vicious circle in which we seem to be caught: Without a human community there is no human responsibility of the individual, and without such responsibility, without true morality in this purely human sense, no human community can maintain itself.

CHAPTER SEVEN

Possible Utopia

Das Notwendige ist immer möglich. Das historische Geschehen vollzieht sich, indem ein kaum Geglaubtes von Wenigen so behandelt wird als liesse es sich unmittelbar verwirklichen.

(The necessary is always possible. History proceeds in just that way, that something hardly credible is treated by a few as if it could be immediately realized.)

HOFMANNSTHAL

Let those who want to save the world if you can get to see it clear and as a whole. Then any part you make will represent the whole if it's made truly.

HEMINGWAY

Il faut une part de réalisme à toute morale: la vertu pure est meurtrière; . . . et il faut une part de morale à tout réalisme: le cynisme est meurtrier.

(An element of realism is needed in all morality: pure virtue is murderous . . . and an element of morality is needed in all realism: cynicism is murderous.)

CAMUS

OUR SURVEY has furnished us ample evidence of a powerful trend toward the disruption and invalidation of the individual. This trend, manifestly present in the most diverse currents of modern life—economic, technological, political, scientific, educational, psychic and artistic—appears so overwhelming that we are induced to see in it a true mutation, a transformation of human nature. Humanity seems to be in a state of transition from the individual form of existence to some new and larger, some supraindividual form of existence. Our present situation is strained between extremes. On the one hand new, "utopian" prospects of an unprecedented range flare up within alluring reach, on the other the peril of a loss of human control, of an engulfment of mankind in a common disaster has never been so acute as in our day. This ultimate alternative represents the climax of all the tensions between productive and destructive tendencies, which we have observed in modern developments.

We seem to be heading for, indeed, we are actually engaged in a form of life in which the group and not the person is the decisive factor; we live in a world in which the collective and no longer the individual is the standard unit. It is futile to hope for a reversal of this situation which is the result of long, consistent developments. The population of the world has been growing rapidly, by natural progression as well as through spreading hygiene. Heavily populated countries liberated from colonial patronage, such as China, India, Indonesia, have joined a closely interconnected company of nations. They hasten to become Westernized, industrialized, technicalized, following the recent Russian example, and the inevitable effect is a collective awakening of huge masses of people, stimulated even by modernized despotisms to a higher state of consciousness and standard of demands. The modern "revolt of the masses" is but a function of the industrial, technological, scientific advances. Masses have revolted time and again, unsuccessfully, throughout the ages; what helped them to their present influential status was industrialization and mechanization. In turn, the mobilization of mass production, entailing instigation to mass consumption, calls for ever wider collective organization, ever more technology and science, ever increasing complexity of groupings and preponderance of groups.

So we cannot expect a turn of this tide and we cannot even wish to stem it if we could, because this would mean abolition of so much betterment of material conditions. Indeed, it is not just the advancement but the sheer maintenance of increasing populations which will require further collective organization of the masses, scientific exploitation of natural resources, technological regulation of an indissolubly interrelated world.

We have to acknowledge this trend of events and we have to face it. Only then shall we be able to counteract its destructive effects which have recently come to outweigh the productive ones and which threaten to destroy the human quality in man, if not the physical existence of humanity. Plainly speaking, we are confronted with the crucial question: will the future belong to a *collective* or to a *community,* that is to say, to a grouping controlled by merely technical necessities, by its autonomous, in fact automatic course, or to a grouping controlled by man and for the sake of man? And what can we do to influence this development, to rescue the human quality in man?

IT IS BY NOW WIDELY RECOGNIZED that our political, social and cultural disturbances are not just so many partial disorders, but that we are passing through a critical impasse of our general human condition; on this all sincerely and profoundly attentive minds of the Western world are agreed. However, counsels for remedy concentrate mostly on a reform of the individual. They lack a sharp distinction between individual and collective circumstances and do not sufficiently take into account the inevitability of the new restrictions of individual freedom. Based as they are on the unquestioned assumption of the identity of "human" and "individual," they all aim at a restoration of the consummate individual.

It will be useful to consider some such characteristic viewpoints —psychological, sociological, biological, philosophical—as held by representative contemporary minds. They may best serve to elucidate and delimit the final conclusions of the present study.

In his book on *Personality,* Gardner Murphy winds up a thorough analysis of the present situation by venturing on the following happy-end theory: "We have talked as if we were very sure that, under the industrialism of today, the individual does not count; we have groaned in protest that individuality is being suppressed. But here is a great paradox: the vaster the organization of power, industrial or political, the greater the power of the individual who knows how to seize the helm. . . . We have every reason to deny that vast impersonal forces are going to make the future. The great individual causes extensive change; the personal factor has become of colossal magnitude. . . . Sherif suggested that when, in a crisis, the perceptual field is disorganized but is capable of being restructured around one of several different anchorage points, the individual who seizes upon one of these anchorage points can induce the group to see things as he does. During a period of successive crises, he who focusses perception in a clear, elemental way upon the means of survival may direct the whole caravan to take one route rather than another. . . . In a time of crisis the individual likely to become a leader is he who senses the prevalent needs and knows how to structure the solution. . . . The more there are of these potential leaders, the more competent they are and the more deeply they love their task, the greater the likelihood that at the points of choice . . . they will guide the pent-up energies of a confused people in the direction of genuine self-realization." [1]

It is hardly conceivable how this eminent psychologist can, in the face of recent experiences, join in the common irrational belief in the saviorship of a great personality who, irrespective of prevailing conditions, will emerge at the given moment and dispose of all the troubles. We have seen the rise and the results of dictatorial leadership; we have learned the tragic impediments and limitations of the best kind of democratic leadership. In all these cases the crux of the matter lay in the cleavage between the desires of people and the good of the people. In the modern situation, and especially in large countries, as has been indicated before, the actual demand of the public does not coincide with the real need of the nation, let alone of humanity. Hitler and Mussolini came to power not by sensing the real needs of the country, but by arousing the emotions and the resentments of the masses; they certainly sought solutions "in a clear, elemental way" by cutting through the Gordian knots of modern complexities, but in so doing they "guided the pent-up energies of a confused people" into genuine self-destruction. The outrages and errors committed by megalomaniac Stalin are now officially recognized by the Soviet government. As far as democratic leadership is concerned, we witnessed the destiny of Woodrow Wilson who certainly realized what ought to be done in order to safeguard future generations; we witnessed the desperate entanglements of worn-out Franklin D. Roosevelt who combined vision with an unusual ability to sway Congress and public opinion; and later we saw the predicament of Nehru besieged by inner and outer difficulties. All these extraordinary leaders became victims of overpowering collective pressures and circumstances and did not succeed in bringing us relief from the basic evils in our human situation. Indeed we can observe in every domain that the task of mastering the ever larger and ever more involved organizations of our time exceeds the capacity of a single man.

David Riesman, after having displayed his overwhelming material and after having stated that today "both rich and poor avoid any goals, personal or social, that seem out of step with peer-group aspirations," prevails upon himself to hope that "people may, in what is left of their private lives, be nurturing newly critical and creative standards. . . . If the other-directed people," he adds, "should discover how much needless work they do, discover that . . . they no more assuage their loneliness in a crowd of peers than one can assuage one's thirst by drinking sea water, then we might expect them to become more attentive to their own feelings and aspirations." [2] How this should come about in a society and social atmosphere like ours can hardly be gathered from Riesman's presentation.

BUT LET US TURN to more penetrating explorations of salvage possibilities. These explorations concern themselves with a *new foundation of ethics,* with the creation of an ethics workable in our modern circumstances. Serious attempts have been made in this direction by the Jungian psychologist Erich Neumann in his book, *Tiefenpsychologie und neue Ethik,*[3] and by the biologist Julian Huxley in his contributions to the book, *Touchstone for Ethics.*[4] Both of them, the former from a rather ontogenetic, the latter from his phylogenetic point of view, come to similar conclusions. The new ethics, they seem to agree, must be a *dynamic ethics* recognizing changes and differences of conditions and abandoning the rigidity of formal commandments, the reference to ever-valid absolutes and the aim at integral perfection. They stress the *wholeness of the human being* and in it the inextricable intertwining of "good" and "bad," in striking accordance with the representations by modern authors, which have been described in the previous chapter. They call for recognition of the "bad" as a legitimate part of the personality. Its remedy is treatment and integration, not expulsion and condemnation.

Neumann traces the *internal* evolutionary process of the rise of consciousness in the individual personality out of what Jung has called the collective unconscious, and he shows the inalienable dependence of the conscious ego on this persistent "collective unconscious." The "persona"—the outer, apparent personality, the "mask" personality, a product of individual conscience conforming to the demands of outer collectivities—is in conflict with the "dark side" of the personality, the "shadow," which is the actual personality, but is, on its part, populated by residues of the inner "collectives," i.e., primordial, mythical archetypes. On these premises Neumann bases his *"total ethics"*: to reach a new protective consolidation of the personality we should strive for unity of the conscious and the unconscious, a unity that would bind the lower forces as well as the higher ones. Instead of the super-ego, the "self," comprising both the conscious and the unconscious spheres, would then be the center of the personality. "Anything that leads to wholeness is good, anything that leads to split is bad." Such integration is a perpetual process of self-interrogation, self-control and psychic compensation. "The personality that, according to total ethics, has found its inner center and acquired its ethical autonomy forms with its strengthened structure and widened consciousness . . . a stronghold of stability in the flight of events (*ruhender Pol in der Erscheinungen Flucht*) which," as Neumann assumes, "will repel the onrush of collectivism and of the mass-psyche from without and from within." [5]

Julian Huxley derives his new "*evolutionary ethics*" from the directions inherent in the *external* evolution of the human being, in the development of life leading up to the *genus Homo*. The first notion that the data of evolution have impressed on its student is the fluidity of all existence, the unending change of structures and conditions, which applies to our social no less than to biological forms: "We are beginning to grasp that societies, like the individuals which compose them, and like life in general, have a time dimension. They are processes, and their direction in time is as important a part of their nature as their organization at any particular time." [6] Ethics, accordingly, cannot be stable; it has to be adjusted to changing conditions. If we raise values to abstract absolutes we achieve nothing but their actual invalidation. There are, however, certain "components of an ethics," as indicated by general evolution, which may be considered as permanent. Huxley, like Neumann, points to wholeness as a prerequisite of productivity and of the perpetuation of life. Throughout the history of life, he states, overspecialization led into dead ends, wound up with elimination of species from the evolutionary stream of life. Therefore, humanity as a whole should beware of becoming a eugenically "specialized caste society," but similarly in what concerns the individual, "We must aim at . . . the establishment of a general attitude which condemns over-specialization and the neglect of other faculties, and the working out of practical methods by which the specialist can continue to practise his specialism while yet remaining 'many-pointed.' . . ." [7] The individual should seek moral integration through "the attempt to be free from the tension caused by guilt, whether conscious or unconscious," [8] through "the resolution of all inner moral tensions in a harmonious though dynamic peace." [9] This sounds just like Neumann's inclusion of the "shadow" in the personality, and psychic balance through perpetual compensation. And just as Neumann's "self" appears to come about through a sort of agreement between the "persona" and the "shadow," so Huxley's demand "to be free from the tension caused by guilt" is supplemented by a required "adjustment of our ideas of right and wrong to our constantly enlarging horizon of knowledge and action—or in broader terms, the adjustment of the developing individual to the outer world, and notably the human community in which he lives." [10] No indication is, unfortunately, given, either by Julian Huxley or by Neumann, of how such a difficult psychic balance can be put into effect and maintained in our average daily situations, except with permanent psychoanalytic help which very few people can afford.

A third ethical inference which Julian Huxley draws from general evolution is the trend toward increasing *individuation,* which he also reckons among the moral permanences. The human individual not only is, but "will continue to be the highest product of evolution." This seems to me a bold prediction which involves Huxley in an unexplained paradox. For a further, and very important, feature of evolution, that which Huxley calls *progress,* is an increase in complexity and organization of complexity, "the capacity to attain a higher degree of organization but without closing the door to further advance." [11] Biological evolution that has come to an end with man is succeeded by "a considerable advance in the degree of social organisation. . . . What is more, the general rate of advance . . . has been growing progressively quicker. There is every reason to believe that through the attainment of this new level of conscious and social organization, the evolutionary process has taken on a new and apparently indefinite lease of life." [12] We have seen in the course of our study and we can observe every day what such a rapid increase in complexity and organization means: an inevitable curtailment of the power and status of the individual. When we consider the vast new masses of populations and problems awaiting organization, it is hard to believe that evolution will stop at the development of the individual. Huxley names among the main criteria of progress, on the biological as well as on the social level, "greater control, greater independence or self-regulation, greater but at the same time more harmonious complexity of organization, greater range of knowledge or available experience." [13] An essential question, however, remains unanswered: "greater independence or self-regulation," "greater range of knowledge or experience" *of whom?* Of the individual? This is very doubtful. Here we touch the crucial point, which needs to be further investigated.

Huxley has omitted one most important factor of progress, and that is the growing extension of units. The formation of higher organisms came about through aggregation and integration of cells into a more complex body structure. And our study has shown us that the expansion of social organization, of the range of man's reach into the universe, of man's control of natural forces, of man's introspective experience—all this goes at the expense of personality. *The gain in expansion of the genus and the loss in selfness of the individual appears to be one and the same process.* Huxley rightly regards as the principal social and ethical goal of humanity today that we must "achieve global unity of man; . . . nations must combine if man wishes truly to achieve the good." [14] Indeed, the assertion made earlier in the present book—that certain values common to the highest human cultures in their state of maturity, i.e., all values affirming the brotherhood of men, seem to be inherent in the constitution of man—this assertion is corroborated by the evolutionary tendency toward the formation of ever larger units and an ultimate fusion of mankind in a world organization. In this aim, finally, ethics and vital necessity coincide. It is, how-

ever, also the point where the extreme realization of human morality may reverse into an extreme surrender of the human quality.
Most certainly, we have to strive for a world organization, but it
will fulfill its human sense only if we manage to make it a community and not a collective.

Erich Fromm, in his book *Man for Himself,*[15] which he calls
"An Inquiry into the Psychology of Ethics," draws a picture of
the human situation, in many respects related to those of Neumann and Julian Huxley. But his observations concerning our social conditions are more radical and reach deeper. The social
process is not treated as casually and marginally as it is in Neumann's presentation, which concerns itself exclusively with the
individual, nor is it as vaguely distinguished from the individual
processes as we find it in Huxley's views. The interdependence of
social and individual life and the conflict between them stand out
more sharply. He also leads a step further toward clarification of
the ethical problem by subsuming it in the basic antagonism between life and death, productiveness and destructiveness. His aim
is, just like Neumann's and Huxley's, the integration of the personality and the elimination of the old moral struggles and he
also conceives morality as a matter of mental hygiene: "The problem of psychic health and neurosis is inseparably linked up with
that of ethics . . . every neurosis represents a moral problem.
The failure to achieve maturity and integration of the whole personality is a moral failure in the sense of humanistic ethics." [16]
"All evil strivings are directed against life," [17] and "destructiveness
is the outcome of unlived life. . . . The evil has no independent
existence of its own, it is the absence of the good, the result of the
failure to realize life." [18] "Virtue is the same as productiveness
. . . the wish to make productive use of his powers is inherent
in man and his efforts consist mainly in removing the obstacles in
himself and in his environment, which block him from following
his inclination." [19] Therefore, "if society is concerned with making
people virtuous, it must be concerned with making them productive
and hence with creating the conditions for the development of

productiveness. . . ." [20] As things stand now, "the historically conditioned social necessities clash with the . . . existential necessities of the individual," and this conflict will not be resolved "as long as humanity has not succeeded in building a society in which the interest of 'society' has become identical with that of all its members. . . ." [21]

Unfortunately, this ideal state can never be reached, not only because of the inherent nature of organization, but because of the dynamic character of all living conditions and the unmasterable differences in mentalities, stages of consciousness and tempo of grasp of individuals and generations. Yet it must be maintained as an unchanging goal. However, just like the other ethical thinkers, Fromm seems to assume that the individual and his fulfillment is the ultimate end of evolution; indeed, he expresses this conviction in even stronger terms than Huxley. "As long as anyone believes," he says, "that his ideal and purpose is outside him, that it is above the clouds, in the past or in the future, he will go outside himself and seek fulfillment where it can not be found. He will look for solutions and answers at every point except the one where they can be found—in himself." [22] But then, what does productivity mean? Does it not mean going beyond oneself, striving for something that lies ahead of oneself? Does it not in any case mean shaping a future? Man will forever, as far as he is fully alive, and that means active and productive, be on the move toward something beyond himself, for self-transcendence is his essential distinctive quality, indeed, self-transcendence is his very self-fulfillment. What makes the crucial difference is whether he transcends himself toward a humanly meaningful end, for the sake of human beings and the human community, or toward a nowhere, aimless and ungrasped, for the sake of things of his own making, for a rational mechanism, or an emotional folly, for a senseless record, for production *per se*.

WE HAVE FINALLY to consider certain concepts of *existentialist philosophy,* the only modern philosophical theory that is rooted

in the experience of our human situation and that has a bearing
on the ethical problem of this situation, indeed, claims to restore
the liberty and dignity of man and thereby to "make human life
possible." It is French existentialism which drew the ethical conclusions from Martin Heidegger's ontological theory. The present
study is not the place in which the basic assumptions of this
philosophy can be adequately analyzed. We have to confine ourselves to the arguments pertinent to our actual state of affairs and
these we find assembled in Jean-Paul Sartre's treatise, *L'existentialisme est un humanisme.*[23]

How existentialist philosophy is grounded in the shocks and
feelings of our age may be gathered from a genuine utterance by
a young woman who knew nothing about this philosophy, but
wrote to her relations in America shortly after the collapse of
Nazi Germany as follows:

"From the disaster into which we have been dragged we have
gained the painful but glorious experience that only he who is
stripped of all his possessions, only he who is so bare and alone
as he was when he entered upon this earth, so helplessly forsaken
and left to himself, only he has a notion of what actual freedom is.
Only he who has gone through the ultimate depth of human help-
lessness and desolation and through the icy cold of deadly fright
from which there is no escape, only he is able to see the sky above
him in the right proportions. . . ."

This ultimate and initial bareness of the human individual, his
primal desolation and anxiety, this is precisely the point of departure of existentialist philosophy. From it Sartre derives his theory
of freedom. His basic axiom is: existence precedes essence; which
means that existence is the fundamental reality, the only reality
which is a certainty, and that therefore we have to start from a
point of sheer subjectivity. He takes it for granted that there is no
God, there is no creator of the universe and maker of man. Hence,
there is nothing before and above man's, or to be more exact,
the human individual's existence. There is actually no generality
of man, no *genus humanum,* which, according to Sartre, could

only have arisen from a general design of the divine creator. Since there is no God, there is no common "human nature." What we call "human nature" is just a human concept devoid of any reality. Really existent is only the individual I. Thus, Sartre concludes, "there is a being which exists before it could have been defined by any concept and . . . this being is man, or, in the words of Heidegger, the human reality." [24] Man, therefore, is at first nothing at all, he is nothing but what he makes of himself, he is nothing but what he wills himself to be. Man is first just "what launches itself toward a future and what is conscious of projecting itself into the future. Man is at first a project which lives itself subjectively, instead of being a moss . . . or a cauliflower. . . ." [25] Man, accordingly, is capable of choosing what he is going to be, of creating, "inventing" himself by way of this choice.[26] Man is *free*; there is no determinism besides his own determination. He is, as it were, "condemned to be free." Therein consists his peculiar dignity. But in making his choice he has implicitly entered into a commitment, a responsibility not only for his own life, not only for what he has chosen himself to be, but a responsibility for all of humanity which, by his choice, he wants to be alike to himself. "Choosing is at the same time affirming the value and validity of what we choose." [27] By choosing to be a Catholic, or a communist, by choosing to get married, one automatically wants everybody else to be Catholic, communist, or married: "And if I decide . . . to get married, to have children, even if this marriage depends entirely on my personal situation, or on my passion, or on my desire, I thereby commit not merely myself, but the whole of humanity to monogamy. . . . By choosing myself, I choose man." [28]

What concerns us mainly in this argument is the special emphasis on choice and responsibility. The theory, however, enticing as it may be, is an artificial construction abounding in inconsistencies and fallacies. There is first a basic confusion about the meaning of "willing," on which the whole conception of man's choosing and freedom to choose hinges. On the one hand, choosing is considered by Sartre not identical with an act of conscious will:

"What we usually understand by willing is a conscious decision which, for most of us, is posterior to what [one] has made of himself. I may wish to join a party, to write a book, to get married— all this is but the manifestation of a choice which is more original, more spontaneous than what is called will." [29] What is it then in man that performs the act of choosing, and how can this act be free, how can it be real choosing, if it is not an act of conscious will, indeed, of thinking and deliberation? There is no liberty, no liberation without deliberation. In fact, Sartre manipulates his concept of choosing by juggling with the double meaning of, on the one hand, "*choix original et spontané*" ("original and spontaneous choice") and, on the other, as it is spoken of at another point in the treatise, "*choisir son engagement et son projet en toute sincérité et en toute lucidité*" [30] ("choosing one's commitment and one's project in complete sincerity and complete lucidity"). Moreover, reference is made in the course of the argument to the Cartesian *cogito:* "There cannot be any other truth at the point of departure than this: I think, therefore I am; it is the absolute verity of consciousness attaining to itself." [31] Here, existence is identified with thinking. But only one or the other is possible: either the *cogito ergo sum* is the fundamental verity; then choosing must be an act of consciousness. Or, if choosing is "an act more original, more spontaneous than conscious will," then it is not undetermined, but conditioned, and that means that the human individual is dependent on something beyond him.

Here is where a second ambiguity comes in: while the individual is supposed to be entirely of his own making, "Man who attains to himself through the *cogito* implicitly discovers also all the others, and he discovers them as being the condition of his own existence. . . . In order to obtain any truth about myself, I must pass through the other person. . . . The other person is indispensable for my existence. . . . In this manner we presently discover a world which we shall call the inter-subjectivity and it is this world in which man decides what he is and what the others are. . . ." [32]

Again, there is said to be no human nature, no peculiar quality common to all men, human nature being a concept which could have reality only as a design of God; but since God does not exist, human nature is an intellectual substitute for the divine concept, devised a posteriori by philosophers, and no reality corresponds to it. The only reality, in the existentialist view, is the human individual and his subjective existence. However, existentialism cannot do without a specific reality common to all men, a "human reality," a "human condition"; and Sartre as well as Heidegger speak constantly of "man," a general term. What they actually refer to is by no means the concrete human individual, but an abstraction, an *individuum generale,* as it were. An *individuum generale* who is of his own making, who is nothing but his own invention and therefore free, but conditioned by the existence of others and the "pressure of circumstances" which condemns him to choosing and does not allow him to choose not-choosing; conditioned by "the totality of limits *a priori* which delineate his fundamental situation within the universe, the necessity to be in this world, to be at work in it, to be in the midst of others, to be mortal." [33] An *individuum generale* whose choice is "spontaneous" and pre-conscious, but comes about by man's attaining to himself through thought; whose subjectivity is an "inter-subjectivity," whatever that may be.

The resulting ethics of existentialism is by necessity relativistic and formalistic, in spite of Sartre's attempt to escape this consequence by a final juggling. There cannot be a commitment binding for all men, there cannot be a valid common aim unless there is a human nature, a true reality and quality common to all men. If the ultimate ethical criterion is to be the subjective choice of the individual, the self-choice by which he chooses his potential world, then all these subjective choices are of equal validity, that of the humanist and that of the fascist, that of the communist and that of the anarchist. To evade this conclusion, Sartre resorts to a logical trick: by the very act of choosing freely, he says, I am committed to promote freedom throughout. If I do not do it I am insincere and inconsistent. "When I declare that freedom in every concrete circumstance can have no other aim than to will itself, if man has once realized that in his desolation he establishes values, he can no longer will anything else than freedom, freedom as the basis of all values. . . . And by willing freedom we discover that it depends entirely on the freedom of others. . . . I cannot aim at my own freedom without aiming at the freedom of others as well." [34] This is simply not true to fact. Unlimited freedom of the individual, as it existed among the ruling circles in the first centuries of the modern era, is not only quite compatible with the subjection of others, it is indeed dependent on and inversely proportionate to the subjection of others. If an antihumanist, a Fascist, declares that he chooses unfettered freedom for himself and his particular group, he is perfectly consistent in wishing to subjugate others. The radical anarchist, on the other hand, who espouses unbridled freedom for all would, by his very consistency, end up in the actual inconsistency of creating an impossible, self-destructive world.

So this existentialist theory which claims to have recovered human freedom, dignity and responsibility remains wholly in the abstract. Its human individual starting from scratch is not the concrete individual who walks our streets; he is a pseudo-concrete individual, an artifact with the attributes of concreteness. The actually concrete individual does not start from scratch, but is largely conditioned by inner and outer circumstances, those of his heredity, those of his historico-social situation—we have seen in what degree his freedom is collectively restricted in our day—those of a very real human nature which is the ineluctable premise for what the existentialists call "human reality" or "human condition." If every human being is supposed to be capable of "attaining to himself through thinking" and of "living himself subjectively instead of being a moss . . . or a cauliflower," there must be a particular disposition common to all men, distinguishing them from other beings, a common quality that capacitates them for their peculiar position in the universe; there must be a genus, a distinct and very real entity to be called man. This supra-individual entity is the only one from which the individual can derive the amount of personal freedom and choice which is granted him. It is the only one whose inherent criterion confers on him dignity and commitment. There is one profound verity which the existentialist theory has brought to the fore: that every single human being is responsible not only for what he *does* but for what he *is,* including what happens to him; he is responsible for his whole being, his mode of existence. Responsible, that means in regard to man, to the human community; for responsibility, if it has any meaning at all, implies a reference to a criterion higher than self. Such human responsibility for one's whole being is of course a transcendent responsibility, that is to say, it is beyond any law and specific convention.

THE CONCEPT THAT REACHES FURTHEST into the core of our modern situation is that of Albert Camus. He too starts out from the existentialist experience of the decomposition of our life's foundations, and he shares certain premises with Sartre and Heidegger; but he dares to ask the ultimate pragmatic questions and arrives at conclusions of his own. His argument is set forth in two essays: *Le mythe de Sisyphe*[35] and *L'Homme révolté.*[36] The genesis of his thought from personal experiences can be felt throughout and is explicitly stated in the preface to *Sisyphe.* He begins with the description of a *"mal d'esprit,"* an evil of the mind, as prevalent in our age, the phenomenon of alienation, which he calls "the absurd" and which he follows up in its various forms of appearance. From the contemplation of our modern situation, which originally put him on his way, he is led to an inquiry into man's existential situation as such. The connection between the most personal and the most general problems is more evident in his thinking than anywhere else in the literature of existentialism—with the exception of its founding father, Kierkegaard.

Camus sets out by asking the fundamental question which he rightly regards as the crucial problem of philosophy, but which only in our age has become every man's concern: whether this life of ours has a meaning, that is, whether or not it is worth living. "The meaning of life," he declares, "is the most urgent of all questions," and this question implies the problem of suicide.

The doubt concerning the meaning of life extends today, as I have stated before, far beyond philosophical speculation; it has spread to the people at large. Life, on its physical, unconscious level, finds its meaning in itself, in the pleasures and satisfactions of the body, in the simple joy to be. And the closer life is to nature, the more spontaneous and variegated its contentment, the less is it likely to awaken from its slumber of self-sufficiency. The plain fellow of former ages, moving and working within natural surroundings, was able to enjoy at least the gratuitous gifts and chances of nature and the full use of his physical energies. He was benumbed by physical life, and for the unbearable burdens of his servitudes religion opened its resplendent compensations. The average man of today, the average man of all classes and stations, carrying on his daily drudgery in a world of artifacts which have crowded out nature and pushed off the divine, he, "in a universe deprived of illusions and of intelligibility," has come to be increasingly estranged.

At a previous point in our investigation we observed the ghostly, characteristically modern experience of monotony and repetition. We found it depicted by various modern authors—Strindberg, Alberto Moravia, Elisabeth Langgässer and J. D. Salinger among others—we saw its impact effective in the mood and mentality of people in all walks of life. Camus describes the various ways in which such weariness begins to stir an at least semiconscious, "instinctive" cognizance of the "laughable character of that habit . . . to perform the gestures that existence commands, the nonsensical character of that daily agitation and the uselessness of suffering." [37] He records "that strange psychic condition where the void becomes eloquent, where the chain of daily gestures breaks and the heart looks in vain for the mesh to reconnect it. . . ." The daily routine is easily pursued most of the time. "But one day the 'why' arises and there everything begins, in that lassitude tinged with amazement. . . . The lassitude concludes the acts of a mechanized life, but at the same time it initiates movement and consciousness . . . everything begins by means of consciousness and nothing is valid but through consciousness. . . . The simple 'worry' (*Sorge*), as Heidegger puts it, is at the beginning of things." [38]

There are other avenues leading to the same worry. Camus notes the sudden awareness of time that befalls us, the panicky feeling that we are tied to time. We constantly live toward the future which we should dread because it is death in disguise. Man in his youth "was craving for the morrow when his whole self should have rejected it." We can live only by ignoring that we are destined to die: "Under the mortal flare of this destiny futility looms." [39]

We further come to realize that the world is impervious, we feel the strangeness, the irreducibility of objects, and "how intensely nature, a piece of country, can disown us. . . . The primeval hostility of the world . . . reverts upon us. . . . The world escapes us by becoming itself again. These sceneries masked by our habit retreat into what they are, they withdraw from us. . . ." In like manner, human beings may "secrete something non-human. In certain hours of lucidity the mechanical aspect of their gestures, their senseless pantomime dulls all that surrounds them." [40] All these sensations, so many varieties of the existentialist "*nausée*," express what Camus calls "the absurd": The manifold alienation of man, "this divorce between man and his life, between the actor and his scenery, this is precisely the feeling of absurdity." [41] And it arises from a special susceptibility in modern man, sharpened by the conditions of our age.

However, what Camus is concerned with is not so much the description of this multiform estrangement, it is the conclusions to which it leads. Two alternatives seem to present themselves after the shattering experience: suicide or redintegration. Does the absurdity of existence call for escape, through suicide or through hope, in spite of it all? Does the absurd require us to die voluntarily, or should we go on living by some surrogate reason or unreason? Most people, ordinary people, are inclined to return to "normal," since the body's resistance to annihilation is stronger than all arguments: "We acquire the habit of living before we attain to that of thinking," and "the body preserves this irretrievable precedence," [42] this prevalence of the "sweet, friendly habit of existence" (*"süsse, freundliche Gewohnheit des Daseins"*), the loss of which Goethe's Egmont bewails before his execution.

There remain other kinds of evasion: hope "for another life which one has to 'merit,' or the delusion of those who do not live for life itself, but for some great idea which surpasses it, sublimates it, gives it a meaning and betrays it." [43] And for those who cannot get rid of their full consciousness, who must go on thinking, there remains what Camus calls *"le suicide philosophique,"* the "philosophical suicide."

In order to evaluate such acts of thought as those supposedly committed by Jaspers, Chestov, Kierkegaard, Husserl, he examines our intellectual situation and begins with stating the nowadays well-established limits of reason. Our scientific knowledge he sees, at the astronomical as well as at the subatomic frontiers, fading away into metaphors and hypotheses; he sees it forever in flux, as a permanently transitory approximation. Being what it is, it appears settled down in hopeless conflict with that deep desire for comprehensive comprehension, that "exigency of familiarity" with the universe, that "nostalgia for unity," that "hunger for the absolute" that is inherent in human thought, indeed, in the unconscious sentiment of man. Again we are confronted with the absurd. Yet in dealing with this situation Camus reveals himself to share the positivistic premises of existentialism: "That heart in me, I can feel it and I can conclude that it exists. This world, I can touch it, and again I conclude that it exists. At this point all my knowledge comes to an end and the rest is construction. . . ." That means reliable reality is just what you can touch with your senses, and the ultimate feeling of existence of self, with its "worry"; nothing beyond that: "Forever I shall remain a stranger to myself. In psychology as well as in logic there are verities but there is no truth. . . ." [44]

From this point of departure he proceeds to his critique of the different ways of "philosophical suicide," which he characterizes as so many ways of speculative evasion. All existential thinkers quoted by Camus have realized the futility of reason, all of them are seen to have recourse to some transcendent entity as *raison d'être:* Husserl to his "extratemporal essences" of innumerable phenomena, Chestov and Kierkegaard to a deity whose loftiness consists precisely in His incomprehensibility, indeed in His inconsistency, arbitrariness, inhumanity. Chestov is quoted as saying: "We address ourselves to God only to obtain the impossible; as to the possible, humans suffice." Such deity, to Camus, shows all the features of the absurd; He demands, in the old way, the *sacrificium intellectus.* In point of fact, it could be said that Tertullian's *credo quia absurdum* has arrived, in the modern situation, at a *vivo quia absurdum.*

This is particularly true of Camus' own position. Camus rejects the "philosophical suicide"; he refuses to accept any transcendent as *raison d'être,* but seeks to remain within the pale of this world and to maintain himself on his scarce certitudes. He likewise discards the alternative of physical suicide, because this also, in its ultimate consequence, resolves, dissolves the absurd, implying acceptance. "The point is, to die irreconciled and not of one's own accord." Camus' solution is to live on in the face of the absurd and at the same time reject it; to live on without hope but also without resignation, to live in constant awareness and persistent revolt. Absurd man has "unlearned to hope. This hell of our present has come to be his kingdom." [45] The consequences are threefold, and again, as with Sartre, human dignity and liberty are the issues. First: defiance stretching over a lifetime restores man to his distinct excellence and pride. The magnitude of absurdity exalts the man who resists it. Second: There is, generally speaking, no human freedom, because death is an insuperable barrier and living toward the future drags one toward death. But to live the life of a man sentenced to death, to live it in full consciousness; to live without a morrow, against the morrow, to live a sheer present, a sequence of presents, this is what liberates me, what affords me individual freedom of mind and action. "Deprivation of hope and future means an increase in human availability." [46] Third: this freedom enables us to live more intensely. "It is an error to think that the amount of experiences depends on the circumstances of our life. . . ." It depends solely on us, on the degree of our lucidity. "To feel one's life, one's revolt, one's freedom, to feel it as strongly as possible, is to live and to live as fully as possible. Where lucidity reigns, the scale of values becomes unnecessary." [47] Observation, registering, remains the essential task. These are the tenets of Camus' *homme absurde*.

Camus, however, does not stop at the personal concern; he proceeds to contemplate the broader implications of his argument, turning from inner to outer life, from personal to public life. After having resolved the question of suicide, he goes on to investigate the problem of its outward equivalent, murder; more specifically, the modern variety of logically calculated, organized, legitimized murder. "The realization of the absurd, inasmuch as we derive a line of action from it, renders murder at least indifferent and, consequently, possible. If one believes in nothing, if nothing has any meaning, if we cannot assert any values, then everything is possible and nothing is important. . . . Nothing being true or false, good or bad, the rule of conduct will be to prove oneself the most efficient, that is, the most powerful." [48] Killing, therefore, appears to be at first a logically admissible consequence of the position of absurd man. Camus attempts to demonstrate that this argument does not hold: absurd man has rejected suicide on the grounds that it is flight from or surrender to the absurd. Life, to him, is the only indispensable value, permitting as it does the "desperate confrontation of human interrogation with the muteness of the world. . . . To say that life is absurd, consciousness must stay alive." [49] But now Camus goes on to ask: "How can one, without making a considerable concession to the desire for convenience, reserve for oneself the exclusive benefit of such an argument? As soon as this boon [of life for consciousness] is recognized as such, it belongs to all men. One cannot grant a logical coherence to murder if one refuses it to suicide." [50] This, however, is the weakest link in Camus' chain of thought: either recourse is made here to Sartre's precarious theory of automatic *engagement*, the "choosing of man by choosing oneself"; or a new value slips in, unnoticed, without which the whole argument crumbles, the value of human decency, of moral, not intellectual honesty which derives from conscience and not from consciousness.

In reality, man cannot maintain an attitude of purely meditative revolt, a life just for the sake of consciousness. A whole epoch, starting from Descartes' total methodical doubt (Camus also refers to Descartes), has gradually come to realize the instability of all values, of the divinity as well as the rationality of our world. It has not, however, watched the spectacle of absurdity in quiet, detached lucidity; it enacted its doubts, it proceeded to act, individually and collectively, to stop the scandal, to transform the world, one way or the other, and to set up some order, rational or irrational. Experience and emotion developing into concerted action, hardening into rigid doctrine, ended up in terror, in legitimized murder.

Camus studies, in his second treatise, the various forms of *l'homme révolté* and the different ways of revolt, metaphysical, artistic, socio-political. And he finds that all of them went out of bounds by establishing and seeking an absolute, by running amuck and getting stuck in some murderous institutional doctrine. "The ideologies guiding our world today are born in the period of scientific absolutes. Our factual knowledge, on the contrary, justifies only a thinking in relative terms. . . . Approximative thinking is the only one that produces reality." [51] The fact that all idea, all action pursued beyond a certain point denies and reverses itself, teaches us that there is *"une mesure des choses et de l'homme,"* a limiting measure of things and of man. Against the *démesure,* the excessiveness, unrestraint of all modern movements and ideologies, their reckless exceeding the capacities, and disregarding the well-being, of concrete, present man, Camus puts *mesure,* the measure of man, the sense of proportion, the poise and self-assertion of human life within its limits. He demands that we should constantly be on our guard, constantly in the state of revolt against *démesure.* The revolt against the absurd in its various manifestations is no contradiction to *mesure;* on the contrary, all revolutionary movement must, in order to stay alive, turn again and again to its primary revolt, to its first, spontaneous emotion from which it has drifted astray and out of real life; it must gather new inspiration from this original feeling that keeps it within the bounds of life. Such perpetual revolt against the revolutionary degeneration of revolt, indeed, against all forms of *démesure,* is the attitude we should seek to maintain.

In an address which Camus gave in New York in the spring of 1946, he made plain the connection of his concept with his personal experience, the birth of his revolt from the *résistance.* "We all sanctify and justify [murder and terror]," he said, "when we permit ourselves to think that everything is meaningless. . . . This is why we have sought our reasons in our revolt itself, which had let us without apparent reasons to choose the struggle against wrong. And thus we learned that we had not revolted for ourselves alone, but for something common to all men . . . there was in this absurdity the lesson, that we were caught in a collective tragedy, the stake of which was a common dignity, a communion of men, which it was important to defend and sustain . . . if this communication of men with one another, in the mutual recognition of their dignity, was the truth, then it was this communication itself, which was the value to be supported. . . ." [52]

Camus' theory concerning the nature of our human predicament and the conclusions to be drawn from it seems to me the straightest and most consistent argument among all those assembled here in our summary of the various points of view representing the trends of our day. It is also the most comprehensive, inasmuch as it reaches from an immediate, indeed, metaphysically immediate personal experience to its implications for our world situation at large. In his theoretical search Camus does not recoil from envisaging the extreme practical consequences; he faces them with courage and honesty. Starting out from clearly existentialist premises, he has finally arrived at a truly humanistic position. The survey of his line of reasoning carried us to a point from which an attempt can be made to delineate what aims should be followed, what course of action taken, lest humanity be left to decay and self-destruction. Our survey of the different contemporary theories furnished us much of the necessary equipment of discourse and a certain consensus of prominent opinions, all of which facilitates the following argument.

Not more than rather general directions can be presented in the conclusion of this study, and they are bound to be what is called utopian. In point of fact, however, any proposition that has not become a reality as yet, that has not found a rooting place on earth, is "utopian." What makes the crucial difference is the distance to realization, the greater or lesser potentiality of a design. Even the historical utopias of the sixteenth and seventeenth centuries, which were parables, had some bearing on the reality of their age and were intended to point a way to the redress of evils. Today, "utopia" is closer to reality than ever, in fact, it begins right at our doors. Not to speak of our technological and scientific wonders which were inconceivable to our own generation a few decades ago, but the very utopia of former ages, united and co-ordinated humanity, has assumed such an imminent urgency under the threat of mutual and common annihilation that it appears equivalent to sheer survival. Not only the facts assembled in this book, but the conclusions reached by all truly responsible minds of our time call for more utopian thinking, that is, for efforts to contrive possible approaches, approximations to that ultimate imperative utopia.

Camus, in his fight against *démesure,* against the degeneration of revolt into the rigidity of a systematized doctrine, demands that we should watchfully maintain the delicate and resilient balance, the ever provisional, ever approximative condition of life in process.

Such counsel shows Camus in marked agreement with the tendencies of psychological and biological ethics. But this anti-utopian
demand is in itself, alas, utopian; it is an aim, valid as such, but
hardly ever attainable. Who can, even for himself, achieve such
a constant balance, and particularly when, in the course of collective action, he tries to make himself heard and heeded! Any
change in public life comes about only through gross overemphasis.
Any concept regarding social order in our immensely complex and
extensive circumstances can be devised and acted upon only in a
stably instituted form. It is, to be sure, of vital importance to bear
in mind the relative character of all rigid principles, to accept their
relativity as a guiding principle above all principles. We cannot,
however, dispense with those goals of established perfection, those
provisional models of the absolute. Without them there can be no
approximation.

EXISTENTIALIST THINKING is the result of total doubt and total
disillusionment. And it is to its credit that it tried to revert to a
tabula rasa, an in fact impossible *tabula rasa,* of all premises and
assumptions of our age-old life; that it attempted to start from
scratch, from a most elementary certitude which is said to be the
individual's feeling of existence.

It is, however, this very start, this basic fact that seems to me
contestable or, to be more exact, incomplete. Very much depends
on this starting point: its difference changes the whole picture.

When I try to delve into my innermost feeling, my initial feeling
of self, I find that at bottom there is not just a feeling of sheer
existence, or of sheer thinking, the Cartesian *cogito.* There is, immediately and simultaneously, something more. There is implicit
in my feeling of existence a feeling of *organic* existence, of organ-
icity, of *wholeness.* Distorted, stunted as it may be by the wear and
tear of modern life, the original form is still traceable as it was
present in the bud of youth: a ball of radiating strength and capacity; all-sidedness, all-potentiality; coherence, correspondence, cooperation of all my organs and faculties. A young healthy human

being feels the unity of body and mind, the one present in the other, and the mind governing the body in a still naïve, unconscious, spontaneous manner; neither intellect nor brute force are autonomously prevalent as they appear later through the division of organic powers. He feels the unanimity of all his energies which he can set in motion wherever and however he wishes.

Such elemental feeling of organic existence shines forth in the beautiful, masterly, fully animated bodies of "primitive" people in whom the face is not predominant as yet, or better, in whom the whole body is face and has the playful, controlled expressivity of a face. It is apparent in the innocent gracefulness of their movements and gestures, and it projects itself into their world: primeval people, until the Greeks, saw the world animated throughout by corresponding organic beings; they saw the whole of nature alive. They addressed themselves to living beings; they could hardly conceive of any other form of existence, and only gradually they learned the first alienation, the distinction between living beings and inanimate things.

The many forms of alienation which developed subsequently in the course of human history and which have been discussed in previous chapters were so many ways of breaking up that original feeling of organic wholeness in the human being. The crucial alienation, according to Marx, occurred in the division of labor. Camus, following Marx, calls it the original *démesure*. Specialization and collectivization pervading all our social life, the cleavage between spirit and body as established by Christianism and widened by Protestantism, and the ever more elaborate, more penetrating rational and perceptional analysis of the data of human life and its environment—these were the main agencies that brought about the modern situation and the awareness of the "absurd," from which existentialist thought takes refuge to its primal certitude of sheer existence. Yet this basic certitude, this inexpressible, inexplicable, however analyzable, feeling of sheer existence and the various shades and manners of being into which it is split by Heidegger, all this is in itself abstraction, intellectual

projection of the modern bareness of self into an imaginary main-
spring of all things human. In order to arrive at this prime certitude, the ontological concept of sheer existence had to be isolated
from the actually basic experience which is that of a naïve wholeness.

If this applies to the human being in his personal and generic
youth, it is all the more true of mature man who lives in a state of
fully unfolded consciousness. The ground on which he lives is not
just a spot of sheer being, of being in, or "being thrown" into,
existence, nor is it the function of thinking; it is an inner space, a
latent arena, an area of self, which may be designated as a feeling
of identity. Such identity of self consists in the silent presence of a
person's whole background and surroundings in every moment of
his life and his move into a future; it comprises the total potentiality of his experiences ever ready to be called into function,
in short, the immeasurable avenues of his memory and of his
interiorized world. Identity is the feeling of personal wholeness on
the conscious level. Therefore, starting from a basic feeling of
existence is no such start from scratch as it is pictured by the
existentialists. The most genuine feeling of existence is in itself
infinitely complex and comprehends the whole microcosmic universe which is given us in latency even when we enter the world.

This entails the invalidation of a second existentialist premise
shared by Camus, and that is the identity of meaning with total
rationality, an assumption which is itself a heritage of rationalism.
Since we have discovered the limits of reason, so it is argued, since
we have to give up hope that we may ever be able to achieve a
completely rational comprehension of our world, the only possible
conclusion is the total incoherence, the total absurdity of our
world. Now while it is true that our present world and human condition has reached such a degree of incoherence that it seems
further than ever beyond our rational control, indeed beyond any
kind of coherent comprehension; while it is true that the individual
is lost in this maze and despairs of a meaning of his life; while all
this is incontestably true, it does not follow that we have to cast the

huge shadow of our present situation on life as such and on the
world as a whole and for all time. In the course of human evolution
and the manifold differentiation which it implied, the human being
has by necessity become estranged from his basic wholeness. His
world, previously animated by living spirits, has become a world
of objects and products. The spirits of nature have merged into one
all-embracing God lifted from the earth and banned from present
life. This involved the separation of spirit and body, the first move
toward the replacement of divinity by pure rationality. And again,
in its attempt at world domination, in the course of its pursuit
of power, intellectual and actual, reason has come to reveal its
limitations, its incapacity to penetrate the whole of life and of the
universe which has proven to be in perpetual flux and continually
escaping the state of established rational comprehension. Reason,
just like God before it, had to abandon its claim to omnipotence.

Sheer rationalism, the assumption that it should be possible to
grasp the world by purely rational means and so rationally to pre-
dict its course in all details, this belief, as expressed by Laplace's
concept of an imaginary God-like all-computor, was itself an
alienation and accordingly absurd. The original feeling of wholeness prevailing in generic and individual youth, the presence of
mind in the sensitive body and the mind's innocent control over
the body, teaches us the unity of mind and body and the true role
and function of reason. Reason is an organ of control and guidance, a spearhead of a body, of a living being. It elaborates and
develops the natural impulse to assertion and expansion of self,
the urge of the human being to control and integrate his environment, an ever broader environment. A life without the control of
reason is no less a defection from wholeness, no less an alienation
than a wholly rational life. But reason, in order to be valid and
effective, must ever again recur and refer to that basic experience
of wholeness, must probe its course in view of that basic experience. What Camus demands of the revolt—that it should, on guard
against *démesure,* ever rejuvenate itself at the source of its initial
emotion—the same is true of reason, this vanguard of human en-

deavor. As soon as reason tries to be self-sufficient, it deviates and increases alienation and confusion, it fosters incoherence and finally sheer irrationality.

We cannot grasp life and the world by purely rational means. It would be a horror if we could; it would be the end of life. For life consists in and persists through tension, perpetual tension between luxuriance and control, change and establishment, reason and the irrational which surges incessantly from unfathomable grounds. Life is a constant challenge to control. It escapes us while we live it, it moves with us, in our very investigation and rational control, which is part of it, in infinitum. It is inherently a *coincidentia oppositorum,* and thus paradoxical, otherwise it could not subsist for one moment. Life without tension, without hundredfold tension, is no life at all, and all after-life promised to the faithful is, in fact, nothing else than a sublimation of death. The existentialist experience was certainly a great contribution to the realization of the paradoxicality of the human condition, but the outright repudiation of this paradoxicality on the part of the existentialists, including Camus, is a residue of their rationalism. What we have to revolt against is not the paradoxicality of our human condition as such, it is the particular state of alienation, of all-pervading alienation, which is the distinctive feature of our age; it is the total loss of control over our life, our loss of wholeness and thereby our loss of meaning.

Human life in its naïve beginnings carried its meaning in itself. The question of meaning arose together with the concept of sheer humanity as implied in the concept of one universal God or of one underlying world substance; it arose from the realization of the futility, changeability, imperfection of human life in the face of the eternal absolute. This meant the genesis of the moral problem, i.e., the problem of human conformance to the perfection of the absolute. In the perfect, self-existent absolute, wholeness was embodied and sought. Judaism and original Christianity established it as a goal to be reached on earth in the advent of the Kingdom of

God and thus gave a concrete meaning to the futility and imperfection of human life. Man was seen to have lost his naïve harmony
through his fall, in fact rebellious rise, into consciousness and free
will, that is, through his becoming man. Human will, once risen
into existence, was now committed to restore consciously the for-
feited state of perfection and harmony by achieving the brotherly
unity and community of men. Subsequently, Augustine lifted this
goal from the earth into heaven and thus beyond human life which
he pictured as an exile for the faithful and a sphere of unredeem-
able corruption for the rest. In such a manner he actually deprived
human life of its meaning. For the ascetic mortification of the
saint does not establish a meaning *of* life, but a meaning *beyond*
life, the profession of a supra-human absolute. If we set aside
Jesus' teaching of the brotherhood of men, i.e., of the human
community here below, what remains in Christian eschatology is
just a substitute for meaning, a solace and relief from the meaninglessness of life.

Later, Christian eschatology was supplanted by the secular
eschatology of reason. Rationalism in its exuberant beginnings
produced the belief in an ultimate state of human perfection and
happiness through reason. The idea of progress toward this mun-
dane absolute, and the ideologies engendered by it, provided generations with a meaning of life. This again passed away in the
failing of reason. It is time for us to recognize that reason alone
will not furnish us with a meaning of our life, but that, on the
contrary, the unmastered growth of rationality has led us straight
into its present meaninglessness. This meaninglessness has been
greatly enhanced by the very fact that an ever-increasing number
of people, quite apart from those who are involuntary slaves of collective toil, have given their lives to the fascination of rational
techniques *per se* without asking for a meaning of their work any
longer, without raising the question of meaning at all.

If we want to regain control over our world, if we want our
life to have a meaning, we have to be true to our basic feeling of

wholeness. The human being must again address his life to an organic entity, and in the present situation this can be nothing else than the human community.

THE BASIC EXPERIENCE OF OUR AGE is the dynamic nature of our world. The absolutes have vanished; we have learned that we are living, man has always been living, unawares, on a floating ground. The ancient problem of man's relation to the absolute, man's falling off from, falling short of the absolute appears to be abolished by the fact that even in the deepest foundations of the universe there is no absolute to fall off from. This experience, once it has arisen, cannot be eradicated. We are bound to settle on the floating ground; we shall have to learn how to live in the relative. We must look for a stability within the unstable.

The only absolute reality that seems to be left is, paradoxically speaking, a fragmentary, incomplete, dynamic absolute, an absolute not resting on firm foundations but moving with the universal process. It appears to be a happening, an ever-recurring occurrence, however not only happening as such, not only Whitehead's "event" which signifies just a "spatio-temporal unity," but a peculiar mode of happening, a tune, a melody of structure or arrangement, a formal tendency of happening, that assumes full reality only as embodied in temporally and spatially limited existences. Such a tendency, a tendency to form closed systems, stations of wholeness, however fragile, changing and transient, we find manifest in the atom as well as in any living form. It is an all-pervading tendency, settling down, "crystallizing" again and again; and we may conceive the whole universe as such a floating system of wholeness, somehow coherent, interconnected even underneath its apparent cleavages. How could it persist otherwise, how could it exist—for existence as such is some sort of coherence. Such universal coherence, with its microcosmic homologues, is the only form in which we could, in a non-anthropomorphic manner, visualize the divine in our age.

Now such a station of wholeness, crystallization of wholeness, is *man,* the *human form*; and this statement implies that man is to be regarded as something real and as an entity of its own. Not only to the existentialists, but to all the ethical thinkers whose theories we have discussed, the identity of man with the human individual is a matter of course and, accordingly, their concern centers exclusively or primarily on the human individual. Contrariwise, it appears to me necessary that we draw a sharp distinction between the human individual and man as a peculiar organic form. Man, I contend, is a reality, an entity in itself, not a mere idea, abstraction, "construction." In his capacity as a reality, man is neither identical with "mankind," i.e., the sum total of all human beings, nor is he plainly identical with the merely biological species or *genus homo* which is defined by specific "generation," by intercopulation and certain anatomical, behavioral and communicative characteristics such as brain size, upright gait, difference of foot and hand, language, specific pathology, "extra-uterine infant-development" (Portmann), and so forth. Although such physically evident delimitations confirm the existence of man as a distinct organic form, the biological species as such is nothing more than a bunch of external characteristics common to the individuals who belong to it. The reality which I have in mind means something beyond that: an entity in itself, apart from the individuals.

Such a concept must of course be unacceptable to the prevailing, strictly positivistic point of view according to which reality has but one level, the level of facts, which may either be directly perceivable by our senses, or ultimately derived or inferred from sensorily observed phenomena and facts. Therefore the world is seen to consist of so many single individual beings, phenomena and facts, while all entities which are sensorily imperceptible or unverifiable have no genuine reality, at best only a derivative one. They are mere abstractions made by men in order to bring some order into the multitude and multiplicity of single phenomena and to make them manageable for the uses of our life. Sartre and Camus, each in his own way, have driven this view to its extreme. To be sure, their prime certitude is a feeling of existence, or the

Cartesian *Cogito,* which are not perceptions of our outer senses, but rather data of our inner life. However, irreducible, elemental experiences as they are, they have a character similar to outer perceptions; they can be attributed to an inner sensorium. "That heart in me," Camus says, "I can feel it and I can conclude that it exists. . . . This world, I can touch it and again I conclude that it exists . . . the rest is construction." And Sartre asserts, as we have seen, that in reality there is no such thing as human nature; a human nature is a fiction devised by men.

Actually, the discoveries of nuclear physics have taught us the unreliability of our sensory experiences. It is a truism today that what I touch is not what I touch. The crucial point, however, cannot be seen in the fact that nuclear research has come to move in domains far beneath sensory perceptibility—the results of the most intricate instrumental experiments can still be brought back into the realm of immediate perception. The decisive turn appears to be that this research has arrived at a borderline where observables are affected by observation and where facts have become a matter of interpretation. Certainly science has possibilities, not available to the disciplines dealing with human matters, to verify concepts through practical application. But it turned out that even practical applicability is no guarantee for the correctness of the picture of reality, from which it was derived.

In point of fact, reality has many levels. As has been pointed out before, we have the most stringent evidence that a group is something essentially different from the sum total of its members, that it shows a behavior entirely of its own. A nation is something else and something more than all its component individuals, living and dead; it has developed an invisible focus of its own, involving special customs, attitudes, values. On the one hand, the personality of any French individual contains elements which cannot be regarded as characteristics of the French nation as a whole. On the other hand, the existence of this nation extends not only far beyond any single one of its individuals, but beyond the corporate body of all its individuals; it resides in a living spirit manifesting itself in traditions and institutions, in a focal vitality and productivity just as much as in a specific disposition pervading all individual Frenchmen. *"La France est une personne"* ("France is a person"), as Michelet felt. The same is true in a limited degree of modern collectives, of occupational and functional groups, which also produce certain reactions of their own, different from their individuals —or better, from the individual parts that are left to the members of such groups.[53] There exist therefore sub-individual and supra-individual levels of reality which we have to take into account. *Reality is a multilevel affair; we live simultaneously on different levels, and developments on the different levels are constantly interacting.*

The present book is not the place to go into the details and broader implications of this notion, which would take us far into epistemological regions. This has to be treated in a different context. I have to confine myself to the one conclusion pertinent to our problem and indeed crucial for its possible solution: There exists man, an organic form, an organic being which manifests itself in a specific human quality, or human nature, a being which had a definite and definitely known beginning and accordingly may have a definite end and may be replaced by some other and more complex organic form. Man must be viewed not as a theoretical abstraction, but as a huge individuality in the realm of organic forms, an individuality which has developed distinct characteristics setting it apart from other forms.

This concept carries important inferences. First of all, if there is man as an organic entity, if there is a human nature, there is also a distinct development, a coherent and consistent career of this specific entity. In other words, there is history, history as a coherent unity, a notion which in our century has been completely lost in the overcrowding and complexity of factual material and through the scientistic tendency among theorists of history to search for historical laws of nature. What is left are rubbles of happening, happening without a substratum, without a being to whom it should happen, or a variety of insulated peoples and "cultures" rising and falling like animal species, lacking inner relationship and uniting quality. But if there is history in the sense of a coherent evolution of man as a definite and real organic entity, then the ideas and concepts which developed in the course of the human career assume the character of real attributes and attitudes of man, of vital processes going on in this vast organic being. Consequently, certain fundamental values also, as they evolved in different parts of the world at the peak of human maturity, appear to be more than just products of the inner experience and theoretical speculation of single personalities; they emerge as an expression of the fundamental coherence of man as a whole. All the ups and downs, all the schisms and struggles and antagonisms notwithstanding, a homologous basic design can be found in the Chinese and Hindu teachings, in the Stoa, in Judaism and in original Christianity and in their secular transformations, the theories of the "age of reason" and of socialism.

Julian Huxley notes among the main factors of evolution: "increase in control over the environment"; "increase in capacity to experience reality—both outer and inner reality," and this, he adds, "is not merely a quantitative process but in some sense a qualitative one, since it leads to the emergence of consciousness both in individual life and in evolution." [54] All this points to a further factor of evolution, not mentioned by Julian Huxley, and that is a progressive expansion of scope of the organic being. The individual infant growing into consciousness wakens to a realization not only of his outer relations to an ever more extended environment, but also of his inner relations, of the coherence of his inner being. Once he speaks of himself as an I, this conscious realization of himself as a coherent being is completed. In the same manner, the "we" as applied to all humans at the points of highest cultural maturity, the concept of the brotherhood of men, expresses a conscious self-realization of man as a whole.

This self-realization, however, has remained up to now a mere inner experience fully alive only at the peaks of consciousness, in the most advanced and sublime minds of humanity. It has never as yet ripened to an actual realization, a "materialization" of the human community. On the one hand, when we look at our present world, we seem farther than ever from this materialization. On the other, the very real alternative of total annihilation has made this materialization an imminent necessity. The picture gained from our inquiry has made it pretty evident that evolution, the expansion of scope, does not stop at the individual, as the wishful thinking of our sociologists, psychologists, biologists and existentialists like to assume. The distinctive trait of human nature is an inalienable tendency toward transcendence of self. This impulse has been the principal instrument of human evolution and has eventually driven the human being into his manifold collectivization. All the symptoms which we have observed indicate that we are in a state of transition from the individual form to a broader, supraindividual form of existence. The experience of inner, human community fades away under the pressure of collectives which, as has been pointed out before, are purely external, mechanical groupings for partial and functional purposes, partial not only in the sense of specialization, but also inasmuch as they tend to stifle the inner, human part of the human being. A collective will never be able to restore meaning to human life; it will never afford a true control of man over his world grown out of bounds.

Our task, therefore, appears to be to establish the human community, to bring it from the state of potentiality into the state of actuality and accomplished wholeness, to make it as real as the collectives are today; to transform the anonymous, unmastered collective consciousness as it now exists, dispersed among so many institutions and disciplines, into a controlled consciousness and conscious self-control of the whole human community.

SUCH AN ATTEMPT will have to start from the top, that is, from our mental condition. The present anarchy derives ultimately from the *state of our learning.* Let us recall the chain of effects.

The basic principle on which modern science rests and which has been adopted by all sciences, including the humanistic disciplines, is strict factuality, which implies neutrality in regard to values, refraining from valuation. The establishment of this principle has been one of the great achievements of modern science and nobody in his senses would want to discard it. However, like all principles pursued to the end without any check and counterbalance, it has, from a certain point, brought the human mind into a perilous condition. What happened is this: Since interrelations of facts, indeed facts themselves are by no means self-evident and unambiguous, interpretation, i.e., theory, cannot be avoided. But, unless overwhelming verification produces a certain consensus, a democracy of theories has come to prevail to the effect that the very aim at a broadly unifying theory is resented as an infringement of the civil liberties of other theories. In addition, ever-sprouting specialization has narrowed down the range of research and vision. The result of this combination: democracy of views and shrinking of the scope of research, is a loss of distinction between essential and non-essential, a loss of the criterion of essence, a bewilderingly increasing accumulation of unconnected facts and theories and methods, and, finally, pluralism, an outspoken disbelief in coherence, in a unified structure of our world.

In this manner we have lost all control over the state of our learning, all orientation in the vast wilderness of factuality and, since there exists no whole any longer in which to determine anybody's or anything's position and role in this world, our hugely expanded knowledge ends up in suggesting that, apart from practical purposes, everything is meaningless.

The disorganization and at the same time immense proliferation of our learning, and the steady progression of analysis have exerted an unsettling influence on the state of mind of people at large. The impossibility of drawing any meaning from the mass of material and reasoning assembled in our age has given rise to desperate movements, like futurism, Dadaism and surrealism, which, as we have seen, in order to go back to the roots of life and start afresh, attempted first of all to destroy all meaning wherever it could still be found in the conventional uses of language and action. The existentialist experience and ensuing theory is another consequence of analysis and despair. Thus, loss of meaning produced disillusionment with illusory meanings, weariness of meaning, intentional destruction of meaning and ultimate crumbling of meaning and coherence in the very texture of daily life. All these movements herald a panicky mood which looms underground in people's minds and may one day break down the last barriers of civilization if developments are left to drift the way they are.

To remedy this situation seems a rather precarious task for two reasons: first, because the mass of our knowledge is not stable but is constantly on the move, constantly gaining and losing ground and, second, because we cannot stop specialization which is the very frontier of our advancing search. Something, however, can be done, and that is to counteract the inordinate course of developments. We cannot, and should not, stem the progression of life. But we can and should prevent it from self-defeat. We can and should do everything possible to keep our balance, the human balance; and that is, to keep developments under human control.

This would mean, in practical terms, that we try to correct the evil effects of boundless analysis which predominates in the modern sciences by a methodical effort toward *synthesis*.[55] Analysis is humanly productive, that is, meaningful for human life only as long as it is held in check by synthesis. Specialization, the inevitable concomitant of analytical research, is of the greatest value if its results are constantly integrated in a unified picture of our world, which alone can furnish us the orientation needed for the conduct of human affairs. If, however, analysis is carried on exclusively and unrestrictedly, if it lacks the control of organized synthesis, then it is bound to lead into disintegration of our knowledge, our mind, and our very life.

We have indeed arrived today at a most dangerous state of confusion, and with the daily emergence of new special disciplines, interdisciplines, sub-disciplines and theories widening and hardening into "isms," most of them fighting or disregarding each other, the anarchy is growing ever further.[56] The need for remedy begins to be widely recognized; until now, however, the facilities for serious synthesis studies have been lacking. To be sure, scholars and scientists get together occasionally to discuss the mutual relations of their compartments; conferences are being held as, for instance, the Conference on Science, Philosophy and Religion, the Interdisciplinary Conference of the Viking Fund, the meetings of the Institute for the Unity of Science at Harvard University. For a long time isolated studies have been undertaken by individual scientists and scholars concerning the correlations between different fields. Niels Bohr examined the applicability of his complementarity principle to the data of non-physical disciplines, Wolfgang Pauli compared certain cosmological and psychological concepts, Schroedinger, Delbrück, Linus Pauling, Pascual Jordan, F. C. von Weizsäcker, Lancelot L. Whyte among others explored the connections between physical and biological phenomena. European sociologists have not surrendered entirely to the rational fancy that it is possible to grasp human conditions by purely quantitative methods. Nor do they shy away from broad interpretations of factual material. As a shining example of this I want to point to the eminent German sociologist, Alfred Weber, too little known in the Anglo-American orbit (only recently the work of his famous brother, Max Weber, has been introduced into America); in his elaborate studies on "cultural sociology" (*Kultursoziologie*), Alfred Weber established connections between multifold data from all social and cultural spheres; and, what is even more important, all his extensive research is aimed at the understanding and redress of our critical human situation.

But conferences and isolated endeavors are not enough. No decisive advance in synthesis can be expected from professors who are absorbed by their teaching or by their specialized research. Synthesis study requires the full time and energy and a concerted effort of scholars and scientists who should expressly specialize, as it were, in general outlook and would have to be trained in diverse disciplines. Scholarships should be made available to facilitate such training, and institutes should be created in which synthesis studies may be carried on by methodical teamwork of regular working communities.

An Institute for the Integration of Studies would have three main tasks:

1—*Clarification and co-ordination of fundamentals.* Basic concepts such as time, space, causality, matter, fact, reality, existence, perception, instinct, person, and so forth, concepts which in the various disciplines and theories have evolved into widely divergent, esoteric or indeterminate senses, should be re-examined and clarified by comparing and co-ordinating the different uses. The present Tower of Babel of our sciences calls for translators and interpreters, for the establishment of a common, coherent language of concepts, which is the prerequisite for mutual understanding and co-operation. Synthesis students would have the function of catalysts, of human enzymes in the body of our learning. Such co-ordination of concepts is by no means a purely formal, terminological operation. By comparing the various applications of a term we may discover substantial interrelations and we are drawn into the depths of basic problems.

2—*Study of the convergences and correspondences in the findings of different disciplines, and evaluation of the findings of any one discipline with regard to their implications for other disciplines.* Such studies may reveal the fact that there are more interdisciplinary correspondences than could become apparent in the present state of confusion and lack of communication; they may come to demonstrate that fundamentally the universe is not pluralistic, but a true *uni-versum*: although it is certainly pervaded by an immense multiplicity of forms and systems, some indications seem to corroborate an underlying conformity and coherence in this multiplicity. Intrinsic homologies have appeared between the organic and the inorganic world and the borderlines between them have become more and more fluid. A host of problems present themselves to synthesis studies: What do the results of nuclear physics signify for the sciences of man (the social and historical sciences, psychology, the humanities), what do they imply for the concept of science as such, for the nature of fact, phenomenon, reality, observation? What can history learn from biology, psychology from linguistics, and vice versa? What clues may the study of the development of human consciousness and, on the other hand, evolution theory furnish each other? What are the subtle analogies or homologies that may be recognized—as against the differences —in physical and biological phenomena? To what extent are the methods of one discipline applicable to and fruitful for the data of other disciplines?

3—The result of all such studies should be the establishment of what H. A. Murray has called a "*strategic hypothesis*," in order to keep a permanent check on the usefulness of specific "tactical" research and to prevent specific research from degenerating into aimless automatism; in other words, to restore to the sciences the criterion of essentiality. "If we are devoted to humanity," Professor Murray writes, ". . . it is imperative that we apply, as physicians do, whatever wisdom, knowledge and skills we have or can acquire to the task of . . . checking, if not curing, the present ominous epidemic of antagonisms. Consequently for our time, a 'strategic hypothesis' might well be defined as one which is strategic not only in respect to the advancement of knowledge and theory, but in respect to the advancement of fellowship, social integration, and ideological synthesis." [57]

This does not mean, of course, that any general theory, dogma, or ideology, should be imposed on studies. Research must develop in complete liberty and must currently correct the general hypothesis which in turn may serve as a guiding and co-ordinating viewpoint. Analysis and synthesis should help each other along and work in close touch. Since ours is a dynamic world, moving more rapidly than ever before, since the results of our research are perpetually changing and progressing, the task of integration is a permanent one. Institutes for the Integration of Studies should therefore become permanent establishments.

Scholars and scientists will continue to follow whatever line of research they choose. But the sheer existence of a rallying place, of an organized effort to achieve coherence, would emphasize and strengthen the spirit of synthesis and recover in people the sense of essence and meaning. It would act as a constant reminder of the common aim: a unified picture of our world, which is the indispensable prerequisite to the formation of a human community.

SUCH REDRESS of the state of our learning lies within the range of immediate feasibility. It is a matter of funds and of understanding on the part of those who would be able to provide them.

We are not so fortunate in regard to the necessary remedies in the *social and political domain*. The realization of these cures appears to be very remote indeed. The road to the world order that would save us and after which we have to strive is encumbered by so many emotional and dogmatic hindrances—by massive states of mind of peoples and individuals, by resentments, prejudices, political passions, ideologies, entrenched habits and interests, traditions and worn institutions—that the goals to be reached seem utopian in the highest degree. And yet, when we examine with detached and unbiased care the course of actual events and the direction in which it points, the order is reversed: what is commonly called "realistic" appears in fact utopian, because it is bound to lead us into a state which will be impossible to endure. What is usually called utopian, but what an increasing number of farsighted and responsible minds support—among those quoted here, Julian Huxley, Erich Fromm, Albert Camus, Alfred Weber— is actually realistic in so far as it seems the only alternative to ultimate ruin.

No previous human generation has been confronted with such extreme alternatives—alternatives presented by man's own creations. On the broadest level, that of international relations, the unceasing advancement of atomic weapons in combination with the progress of aeronautical technology leaves us hardly any choice but that between the nought and the millennium; that is to say, between an almost certain annihilation of human civilization and the creation of a firmly established supra-national order, *world gov-ernment* and the *realization of the human community*. In the na-tional sphere we see the same inexorable dilemma approaching in the rapid spread and perfection of automation. Here we shall have to choose between a degenerate capitalism, which will have to resort to fascism, and a *democratic socialism,* the *realization of the national community.*

On the *international* scene the present armaments race in nu-clear and missile weapons has by far exceeded the range of reason, indeed, of human practicability. The contest in the production of weapons, the use of which, as everybody knows, must result in irretrievable common disaster, takes place on a wholly unreal, imaginary ground. The effectiveness of these weapons has, in fact, reached the saturation point. From the moment when it has be-come possible to exterminate at one stroke any of the vital cultural and economic centers of the world, it has also become rather irrelevant how much the area of destruction and fission poisoning can be extended and the means of delivery of such destruction can be improved. Both partners of this sinister game know perfectly well the prohibitive risks they would be taking in unleashing the deluge. Both regimes know that they could not survive it. They must know that a full-fledged atomic war would be self-defeating from the outset because of the peril of sustained radioactive fall-out which would affect the whole globe and the belligerents themselves. And yet the mad contest goes on for every inch of "superiority," regardless of what it would mean in practice; atomic tests go on with a revolting indifference to the justified anxiety of the people of the world. In point of fact, the atomic contest has come to be a nonsensical competition for world records, an exchange of bluffs which neither of the contestants believes and yet dares to call. This does not preclude the possibil-ity, indeed it may even enhance it, that events get out of hand and automatically, as it were, start off the cataclysm.

From the point of view of detached reason it is not understand-able what in such a situation a further advance in destructive power could add to the deterring effect of the bomb, indeed, it appears highly questionable whether these weapons still have a deterring effect. Surely it is not such superiority any longer that could bring the West closer to that "position of strength" from which negotiations are expected to be successful. For a long time the crucial actions of the Russian power game have been moving on an entirely different plane, in the sphere of political propaganda and influence. On this much more important front the West has been losing rather than gaining ground and here neither armaments nor old-fashioned diplomacy are likely to save it and get the world nearer to lasting peace. The reason for the West's failure lies in its fundamental attitude, and what would be needed is a radical change of approach.[58]

It has to be granted that the West is in a much more difficult position than the Soviet Union. Great Britain and France are encumbered by their colonial and commonwealth involvements, America and France by the nature of their democratic procedures. Ever so often the destiny of the world hinges on the domestic competition of the American parties and every second year Western policies are somewhat paralyzed or at any rate unfavorably affected by forthcoming American elections. Granted also that Russia takes reckless advantage of her more favorable position. But a clumsier use of similar methods, intrigues and support of unpopular governments, attempts to press neutral countries into partisan alliances, all this will not help us to stem the Communist expansion and to ward off the frightful danger of the world becoming a huge Soviet collective.

The thing to do is to raise an idea and hold it against the manipulated Soviet ideology: *the idea of the human community as against the universal collective*; to raise it not with words, with high-sounding declarations of which people everywhere are sick and tired. There has been too much of such oratory with no, or contradictory, action behind it. To make this idea convincing, it would need the infusion of a new spirit into our political methods, a spirit of psychological imagination and pedagogical intent. Its premise is the notion that in the present world situation it is ultimately the peoples that count and not the governments, and that therefore it is the confidence of the people of the world which we must win over to our cause rather than the interests of governments. Every move of our policy would have to be considered under this aspect and in view of its psychological and exemplifying effect at large.

What that means in concrete terms is this: we have built a whole system of alliances in different parts of the earth and a circle of air bases directed against the Communist bloc. All these defenses, however, have a somewhat quixotic character. The alliances are built on figures and rhetoric and treaties which, in the parliaments of the respective countries, were pushed through with the greatest difficulty; this alone would suffice to evidence their unpopularity. The peoples of the European continent, apart from their economic limitations, are weary; they live in the midst of outer and inner ruins, vivid demonstrations of what war means. They know by experience that a modern war does not solve anything, but leaves things worse than before; they know in particular that another world war would spell the end of Europe. They are thus, understandably enough, quite unfit for crusades. In the very improbable case of a Russian attack on Western Europe, the European NATO divisions, as far as they exist, are most likely to behave like the French did in 1940 and to prefer another occupation to total devastation of their countries; if they would fight at all, it would be in a civil war which can be expected to break out everywhere as a first result of the conflagration. Therefore, the system of military alliances has been a psychological miscalculation. In the special case of Germany it was worse than that; it was a bad lesson, morally. To ask a people a few years after it had been condemned for its militarism and its ruthless pursuit of power politics to rearm for another power contest, against its will, or at least against its best intention, plainly as a measure of expediency, this is education for cynicism; no mutual trust and reliance can come of it.

As to the Western air bases in foreign countries, they are most evidently unsafe; the resentment of populations against them is pretty general, if only for fear of becoming the target of atomic attacks.

But apart from the inner precariousness of defense blocs and air bases, the whole emphasis on military action is wrong. All these NATOS and SEATOS and Bagdad Pacts are not only militarily weak, they are being outflanked politically like so many Maginot lines. Obviously Russia does not want or need direct military involvement. The main contest takes place in a different sphere, and there the military obsession has maneuvered the West into an awkward position. People all over the world are longing for peace and security. Precisely this constitutes the Russian lure while the West clamors for crusading alliances. The Russians are in the rear of our military defense lines, in the minds of people. What the slowly awakening peoples of the East demand is national independence and better living conditions; their belated nationalism is a reaction to colonialism. The introduction of Western formal democracy on which we insist is to them at best a secondary concern; by now, most of these countries have parliaments anyway, if only as a matter of prestige. The only promising, indeed, possible line of policy is therefore to help the rising populations to both national independence and well-being, to anticipate and surpass the Russians in economic aid and spreading prosperity, but above all in sincerity, which means not to force or lure nations into formal alliances, but to welcome them, oblige them, and draw them closer in their capacity *as independent nations*. Disinterestedness is our best interest. The sharply manifested grudge against neutral India has been one of America's gravest mistakes.

Alliances only provoke counter-alliances and the fateful tension never ends. Since we have to have peace—the other alternative being total destruction—let us act accordingly. Peace cannot be achieved through breeding hostility, through a poker game on the grandest scale, the stake of which is the future of man. Our first concern must be to ease the tension that weighs heavily upon the

world, that poisons and corrupts international conduct and paralyzes all constructive designs. The more independent prospering
nations there are in our world the better. They are badly needed
as intermediaries and media of reconciliation; their sheer existence
in great number and variety could gradually soften up the cohesion
of the Soviet bloc, indeed, the rigidity of the Soviet system and
mentality, which encircling hostility turns stiffer and tighter. Only
when the present tension is eased, when independent nations have
again become a factor in world affairs, a gradual formation of
a world authority, a true supra-national authority, could be en-
visaged.

If the West continues in its present political tracks, it has hardly
a chance of success. All odds are against this course of action.
Only by candidly embracing the cause of the human community,
by veering carefully, without jeopardizing its own security, toward
the realization of the human community, will it be able to prevail
over Soviet dogmatism and lead the world out of its perilous chaos.
Such a new policy would also and mainly involve a new attitude of
the West toward the United Nations. It would require that we
take the idea of the United Nations quite seriously; that we do not
use it just as a convenient instrument for the promotion, through
intrigues and pressures, of one power bloc against the other, and
as a forum for oratory and the exchange of invectives, but that we
try to invigorate it by all possible means, to make it strong and alert
enough to step in immediately with an effective world police force
whenever a country is attacked. It would mean that we treat the
United Nations as a first step in the direction of a supra-national authority, that we submit to its decisions even when they are against us;
that we shape our own policy within the organization according to
the real situation, and do what needs be done, regardless of who
is for or against it. An incident like the representation of present
China by Formosa suffices to let the whole institution appear
farcical and invalid.

The impediments to a reasonable and beneficial policy are
certainly enormous. Our only hope is for statesmen who would be

willing to take the right kind of risk, the risk of losing positions and votes; who not only would know what ought to be done but would act according to the best of their knowledge, without regard for party interests; who would dare to make an unpopular decision if they deem it necessary and then go to the people and tell them their reasons.

In a review of Lewis Mumford's courageous book, *In the Name of Sanity,* Reinhold Niebuhr wrote: "If we compare mankind in its present situation to a man walking on the narrow edge of a precipice where any misstep may spell disaster, Mr. Mumford's prescription for sanity would seem to be analogous to advising the man about as follows: 'You haven't a chance to escape disaster by walking on the edge of the precipice. Your only chance is to fly. I know you haven't any wings, but you must sprout them. The impossible must become possible in an extreme situation.' " Now, in point of fact, man has no wings, but he has indeed learned to fly. To counsel a world government is commonly regarded as equivalent to "reaching for the moon." But is not this very metaphor obsolete, is it not on the point of losing its metaphoric character; and does this not clearly demonstrate the stupendous change in our situation? Are we not about, in technological reality, to build cosmic satellites, to envisage interstellar communication? Are we not actually, practically, "reaching for the moon"?

Technology, which has an inherent tendency toward unification of our globe, has paved the way for the realization of the human community. Technically, this community is feasible today,[59] not only feasible but in fact indispensable for our survival—this distinguishes the utopia of our age from all previous utopias. What prevents the achievement of the human community is no longer its technical impracticability, it is only man himself, irrationally backward, emotionally blinded, dogmatically narrow-minded man.

NATIONALLY NO LESS THAN INTERNATIONALLY technology has invalidated the old order which was based on unbridled competition. This order has proved incapable of mastering our modern social situations; its "natural selection" has ceased to further the progression of life, to produce a generally beneficial balance of advantages. Through the military use of atomic fission and thermonuclear fusion, technology has rendered the power contest of states and ideologies perilous to the extreme. Similarly, through the development of automation, technology has made the power contest of economic interests, i.e., capitalism, imminently dangerous.

Capitalism had its great moment when it carried broadly human aspirations, that is to say, as long as it helped, with all its abuses, to liberate the human being from inveterate feudal bonds, as long as it promoted equality and human rights and betterment of material conditions, which at that time were believed to bring about not only the happiness but the perfection of man. In America, particularly, capitalism was the invaluable vehicle for conquering and mobilizing her continent and exploiting its immense resources. Capitalism, by harnessing the individual interest to this task, has indeed "made this country great." The American dream of personal success meant more than just personal success, more than sheer money and economic power; it meant implicitly the prodigious advance of human possibilities, the seemingly boundless chances of "self-made man."

In favor of this traditional "American way of life," people can often be heard saying: We have to stick to it because this is what made our country great. These people are not aware of the fact that their very argument compromises their cause. They forget, and like to forget, that a nation is no more static than an individual, it grows and changes and conditions change with it. What may be good for a young person is by no means advisable for a person at the height of maturity. Similarly, the same principle which in an early period led a nation to the peak of its capacity will at a certain moment change its effect and become most harmful. So, while it is undoubtedly true that capitalism made America great, it is more than doubtful whether it can keep it great in the present age of the nation and of the world.

Capitalism has reversed itself; it has become self-defeating. The symptoms are numerous and too obvious to be overlooked even by staunch supporters of the system. First of all, free enterprise is no longer individual enterprise. "The capital is there," so we read in Adolf A. Berle's revealing book, *The Twentieth Century Capitalist Revolution,* "and so is capitalism. The waning factor is the capitalist." [60] Individual ownership of enterprises is vanishing and giving way to corporations and "concentrates," i.e., collectives.

Along with this, other important changes have developed: 1—*Splitting of ownership and producership* whereby—this is a truism today—not the owners but the managers have become the decisive factor. "When an individual invests capital in the large corporation, he grants to the corporate management all power to use that capital to create, produce, and develop, and he abandons all control over the product. . . . He is an almost completely inactive recipient. . . . Were the American system entirely one of ownership and production by large corporations, every individual would have a job under the direction of corporate managers. . . ." [61] Berle himself draws the conclusion: "There is a striking analogy between this and socialist theory. Under socialism, all productive property is held or 'owned' by the agencies of the socialist state; all individuals receive pay or benefits. Planning, development, creation, production, and so forth is done by the political agency. . . ." [62] In order to fully evaluate this "analogy" we have to bear in mind that the big corporations dominate the scene. "The ability of the large corporation to make decisions and direct operations overflows the area of its ownership. Its power travels farther than its title—in fact, a great deal farther. . . ." And "the mid-twentieth-century American capitalist system depends on and revolves around the operations of a relatively few very large corporations. It pivots upon industries most of which are concentrated in the hands of extremely few corporate units." [63]

2—This power of the corporations is increased by their *emancipation from previous controls.* They have freed themselves from the necessity to appeal for credit in order to provide capital. "Major corporations in most instances do not seek capital. They form it themselves." [64] Consequently they have become independent of the "judgment of the market place."

3—They have further been able to rid themselves of the checking power of free competition. This again is a fundamental change: *the restriction of free competition.* To be sure, there still exists competition, competition between giant corporations, as between General Electric and Westinghouse, or General Motors and Ford, and competition between materials, as between steel and aluminum. However, as Berle rightly states, "competition means one thing when thousands of tradesmen, craftsmen or farmers are offering their wares to thousands of customers. It means quite another when four or five large units are grinding against each other. The result of the competitive system when many units were involved was to push out the least efficient units, or perhaps the worst-placed strategically. The result of great corporations fighting each other is either consolidation, or elimination of one of the units, or acceptance of a situation in which the place of each is approximately respected. . . ." [65]—which means "oligopoly." Each of these alternatives is fraught with danger. (The picture is in some respect analogous to that on the international scene which is dominated by the conflict of two colossi.) "A struggle between giants may wreck hundreds of thousands of lives and whole communities. In a system of individual entrepreneurs the men squeezed out of one market may readily turn to another; in the highly organized concentrate, changeover is always difficult and expensive, and often impossible." [66]

4—This leads inevitably to *planning,* another socialist feature. The state has to step in to secure the balance of national economy. Many industries had to submit grudgingly, in critical moments even beggingly, to government control. Indeed the big corporations themselves have to resort to planning on a large scale; expansion in breadth of organized production involves extension in temporal length of projecting. In addition, the government has had to assume maintenance of the balance between the two dominating economic factors, industrial oligopoly and the great industrial labor unions.[67]

Once more, Berle himself proceeds to the ominous conclusion: "Clearly, if business organizations like the modern corporation are not automatically limited by economics, a political problem of first importance is in the making." [68] He pins his hope on the restraining force of public opinion. Public opinion, however, is itself to a large extent shaped by the turn of mind and the interests of the great corporations, particularly when the government is composed of big-business men. The present Secretary of Defense, Mr. Wilson, has naïvely confirmed this state of affairs when he identified "what is good for General Motors" with "what is good for America."

Thus, the twentieth-century capitalist revolution turns out to be the American version of collectivism. Under certain conditions it may, in its external features, come dangerously near the Russian form of collectivism which, on its part, is not real communism in the Marxian sense any longer—or, as they insist, as yet—but political state capitalism. This is not to deny the great differences: The Russian kind of conformism is overtly authoritarian and dogmatically rigid; the American kind of conformism is covertly compelling—as by a natural process—and technically flexible. But conformism it is, here and there. Under both systems, only in different ways, a person is forced to sell himself. The Russian way leads to mental enslavement and ideological stultification, the American way leads to all-pervading functionalization and commercialization whose pernicious psychic, moral and political effects have been indicated before. Erich Fromm has, in his books, assembled an overwhelming mass of evidence on the harmful influence of twentieth-century capitalism. This thoroughly collectivized capitalism is not likely to rescue our world from the peril of becoming a total collective; it is, on the contrary, training the people for it. Capitalism has ceased to help us to human ends. No longer does the adventure of personal success carry a general, pioneer meaning. It has become a purely singular, private striving for material advantages: money, objects, status and influence. The degeneration of the American dream is pathetically pictured in

Scott Fitzgerald's *Great Gatsby* and in Arthur Miller's *Death of a Salesman.*

WITH ALL THESE CONSIDERATIONS, however, we did not even touch as yet upon that greater revolution which will bring matters to the peak and will confront us with an inescapable alternative. Compared with this technical revolution, that is, *fully accomplished automation,* all political and social revolutions, all men-borne revolutions, appear as minor incidents. In our over-civilized areas decisive revolutions are not made by men any longer, they are made by objects. And while our politicians have their eyes fixed on the danger of Communists aiming at the "overthrow of the government," they are little aware of that creeping revolution of things which will shake our social order to the ground and call for basic decisions.

To characterize the effects of this "second industrial revolution," suffice it to quote one of the creators of automation, Professor Norbert Wiener of the Massachusetts Institute of Technology, who wrote in his book *Cybernetics*:[69] "Taking the Second Revolution as accomplished, the average human being of mediocre attainments or less has nothing to sell that it is worth anyone's money to buy." In his new book *The Human Use of Human Beings* we read: "The intermediate period of the introduction of the new means . . . will lead to an immediate transitional period of disastrous confusion. We have a good deal of experience as to how the industrialists regard a new industrial potential. Their whole propaganda is to the effect that it must not be considered as the business of the government but must be left open to whatever entrepreneurs wish to invest money in it. We also know that they have very few inhibitions when it comes to taking all the profit out of an industry that there is to be taken, and then letting the public pick up the pieces. This is the history of the lumber and mining industries and is part of . . . the traditional American philosophy of progress. Under these circumstances, industry will be flooded with the new tools to the extent that they appear to yield immediate profits, irrespective of what long-time damage they can do. We shall see a process parallel to the way in which the use of atomic energy for bombs has been allowed to compromise the very necessary potentialities of the long-term use of atomic power to replace our oil and coal supplies, which are within centuries, if not decades, of utter exhaustion. Note well that atomic bombs do not compete with power companies. Let us remember that the automatic machine . . . is the precise economic equivalent of slave labor. Any labor which competes with slave labor must accept the economic conditions of slave labor. It is perfectly clear that this will produce an unemployment situation, in comparison with which . . . even the depression of the 'thirties will seem a pleasant joke. This depression will ruin many industries—possibly even the industries which have taken advantage of the new potentialities. However, there is nothing in the industrial tradition which forbids an industrialist to make a sure and quick profit, and to get out before the crash touches him personally. Thus the new industrial revolution is a two-edged sword. It may be used for the benefit of humanity, but only if humanity survives long enough to enter a period in which such a benefit is possible. It may be used to destroy humanity, and if it is not used intelligently it can go very far in that direction. . . ." [70]

Professor Wiener expects this development to take about ten years to be completed, unless war interferes, which would, in his opinion, accelerate the process. To my mind it seems impossible to conceive of anything that would happen after another full-fledged war. Anyway, whenever automation will have reached its final stage, another moment of ultimate peril will have arrived. Then the latent panic of the people, all the passions and furies now fairly held in check or channeled toward expedient goals, may break out into the open, and no committees investigating un-American activities will be able to stem this tide. The communist regimes will be greatly favored by automation. Although they too will encounter socio-psychological difficulties, they will be in a position to gradually adjust their strictly controlled population and economy to the new technical situation and indeed to profit from it by easing the living conditions of their peoples. In the West, however, a crucial choice will present itself between a dictatorially collective order—fascism or communism—on the one side and, on the other, the true human community which can only be achieved through democratic socialism.

For this kind of order, the only one that could save us, we are not in the least prepared. To be sure Professor Wiener tempers his gloomy picture with a dash of optimism and notes that in meetings with representatives of business management he has been "delighted to see . . . awareness on the part of a great many of those present of the social dangers of our technology and the social obligations of those responsible for management to see that the new modalities are used for the benefit of man, for increasing his leisure and enriching his spiritual life, rather than merely for profits and the worship of the machine as a new brazen calf." [71] However, all the good will on the part of management will not suffice to meet the requirements of a situation which is bound to uproot our social order. Once more, what is needed is a fundamental change of mind, a new aim to be introduced into our whole civilization. Take the problem of leisure, which will be crucial. People may suddenly find themselves expelled into leisure as into an exile, abandoned to leisure without having the proper use for it, without knowing any longer that leisure is not idleness, a hole in time, a hollow time to be filled with meaningless doings, radio, TV, movies, cards, magazines, sports and gadgets. Having lost the sense of meaning altogether, how should they be prepared to focus their attention on "spiritual values," which is an empty word unless it means shaping one's whole life according to a supra-personal end, something beyond individual success and pleasure. There is no enjoyment of spiritual values without a feeling that what is experienced is of serious consequence to one's life and conduct. There is no leisure that may give an average person real satisfaction and fill the inner void left by his present kind of work unless the breach is abolished between leisure and work, so that leisure may support and supplement meaningful work. This is possible only in a truly socialist order in which work is more than a profitable individual job but is serving a common human end. Where in present education or entertainment can we find a preparation of the minds for this necessary change of aim? Education follows the current trend toward "vocational training," that is, making young people fit for advantageous careers; entertainment, the means of communication, appeal to the lowest standard of demand. How could it be otherwise in a social system that in all its parts is guided by the commercial point of view? Nothing less will do than a radical change in our whole outlook and social attitude.

SOCIALISM has been in the air for a long time and since the emergence of the most influential of all socialist theories, Marxism, many versions of social reform have been advanced and attempted, the social situation having developed into a much more intricate complex than the earlier socialist theories, including the Marxian, had assumed it to be. Paternalism is obsolete; it does not remove the basic, psychic and human, disturbance. Class struggle is obsolete; the events of our century have shown that there are more than two classes, and the most important, most dangerous class turned out to be a third one, not foreseen by Marx in its great significance, the lower middle class with its fluid borderlines and fluctuating mentality. We have seen how capitalism has changed its character fundamentally and, although persisting as a system and state of mind, has lost its human substratum, the capitalist; it has turned into a huge collectivistic machinery of employees. On the other hand, we have seen how the dictatorship of the proletariat has resulted in the establishment of a vast totalitarian collective, which, partly owing to its struggle for existence, partly however to its basic doctrine, concentrated mainly on material power, competing with capitalism in all features of the common collectivistic trend, fostering hostility in the world and disregarding the mental needs and inner development of the human being. The materialistic concept is but a residue of the preceding rationalistic view that improvement of material conditions will by itself produce the happiness and perfection of man.

None of the current social prescriptions will be a really effective cure for our basic evil. The New Deal with its PWA and Welfare State—which in fact was a last-ditch fight for the preservation of capitalism—English Fabianism, the various forms of Christian Socialism, all of them have certainly done a lot of good, but none of them has been able to influence the calamitous course of events. Sharing of profits will not suffice, nationalization of the means of production will not suffice, participation of the workers in management will not suffice. All this will be of no avail without a fundamentally new attitude.

Such new attitude, the new spirit that is required, can be found already in existence in various parts of Western Europe. We may see it at work in the flowering communities of the *"communitarian movement"*; communitarian, not communist—this difference in terms and features signifies precisely the difference between community and collective. When we turn from the prevailing reality of our world situation to the live "utopia" of these communities, which have spread all over France and to Western Switzerland, Belgium and Holland, it is as if we would step out of a nightmare into a scene of bright sunshine. Only a rough outline of this movement can be given in the context of my argument; it may serve to exemplify by a concrete case what a genuine community means and can achieve in our day. For more details I want to refer to the beautiful report on the movement by Miss Claire Huchet Bishop in her book, *All Things Common.*[72]

Like French existentialism, this movement arose from the desperate, chaotic condition of France after her defeat in 1940. It is closely linked with the experiences of Nazi terror, concentration camps and the Maquis. It was born from *suffering,* as "companions" of the movement repeatedly affirm: "The Community of Work was born out of the revolt of proletarian people meditating on their own suffering." [73] Indeed in their suffering, the experiences of generations and ages, of our whole recent world, seem to have accumulated to produce finally the fruit of this movement. It is as if, unknowingly, all the reasons for failure of the social experiments of previous centuries had been taken into account.

Unlike existentialism, this movement is based not on theory but on sheer practice; it is action from beginning to end, action prompted by utter necessity. A man who had known destitution and desolation since his early childhood, who, as a young worker, had acquired "a firsthand knowledge of what bosses are worth and also workers," decided, together with his wife, to try and build a business of their own. "We sold all our furniture to buy machines. . . . We slept only three or four hours at night. . . . We had no money, no backing, the banks refused to accept the drafts. . . ." [74] Finally they "stuck it out."

So far this is no more than the familiar American success story, a story of personal courage and perseverance. But the man, Marcel Barbu, is an unusual man. From the outset he sensed vaguely what is wrong in our society. He was aiming at something more than personal success, he was striving for a new "style of living." In his own shop he introduced a factory council and a wage rating approved by all. He wanted to go much further, but his workers were not interested; they were satisfied with what they had.

The real start on his venture became possible only in the revolutionary situation after the catastrophe of 1940 when the ordinary frame of life had broken and everything was in a state of flux. "Barbu tried to find some mechanics in Valence. He could not find any. So he went out into the streets and coralled a barber, a sausagemaker, a waiter, anyone except specialized industrial workers. . . . He offered to teach them watch-case making [his own trade] *provided* they would agree to *search* with him for a setup in which the 'distinction between employer and employee would be abolished.' " [75]

It was the point of departure and a crucial point indeed. How difficult it is to overcome the age-old, deeply entrenched distrust of workers of "the boss," be he ever so selfless and well-intentioned, may be gathered from the dramatic story of another Community of Work, the vineyard community in La Londe-les Mauves. The original owners of the old and famous enterprise, two brothers named Ott, who undertook to transform it into a community but, being at first the only experts capable of handling the business, were retained in charge of it, suddenly faced an irrational outbreak of misgivings on the part of the workers; only their calm and patient understanding prevented the ruin of the venture and the business.[76]

Barbu's group started their common search for means to abolish the distinction between employer and employees by stipulating that everybody "should be free to tell the other off." The disputes that arose led them to further highly important steps. They found out that in order to keep people together an agreement about an "ethical minimum" was required: "Unless there was a common ethical basis, there was no point to start from together and therefore no possibility of building anything. To find a common ethical basis was not easy because the two dozen workers now engaged were all different; Catholics, Protestants, materialists, humanists, atheists, communists. They all examined their own individual ethics, that is, not what they had been taught by rote, or what was conventional, but what they, out of their own experiences and thoughts, found necessary. 'All our moral principles,' they declared, 'have been tried in real life, everyday life, everybody's life . . . we distrust philosophers and doctors.' " [77]

In this way they actually found a common "ethical minimum," and it turned out to be a new, somewhat enlarged version of the Decalogue. This in itself is a very significant and revealing happening. The Decalogue has become in our modern world a legal, religious, traditional convention pushed back by the turmoil of daily life into remote corners of people's minds. Except in very rare persons, it has ceased to be a living motive. It had to be discovered afresh, out of present, practical circumstances and in answer to practical necessities, in order to be brought to real life again. And having thus become an indispensable element of a practical undertaking and its daily maintenance, it was bound to be taken very seriously; it "meant business." The two last paragraphs of this new "Decalogue" are particularly worth mentioning:

"Thou shalt fight first against thyself, all vices which debase man, all the passions which hold man in slavery and are detrimental to social life. . . ." "Thou shalt hold that there are goods higher than life itself: liberty, human dignity, truth, justice." [78]

The second point that has to be stressed is the fact that here people of the greatest variety of creeds, opinions, party affiliations are bound together by a common engagement in work and life, which has become possible only because the common aim has revived and mobilized the human part of the self as against the collective part. They are free not only to think and express themselves, but to belong to parties and vote as they please. It does not affect the human community which directs their daily lives. While collectives leave behind a human rudiment in people, these communities conversely release a collective overplus.

In the further course of their practical experiment there evolved a whole elaborate constitution, a "Rule," of the community, establishing a "General Assembly," a "Chief of Community" elected by the Assembly for a term of three years, a "General Council" and "Council of Direction," a "Court of Justice," an "Assembly of Contact," and, most important of all, the "Neighbor Groups": in their regular meetings and discussions common opinions and decisions take shape. A new system of checks and balances was worked out as well as quite novel principles of economic order.

There is common property of the means of production, or, to express it more correctly, their owner is the community. A strong feeling prevails that "The community is a real person," "not an organization but an organism." Its meaning and ultimate aim consists in its very life and prosperity, and implicitly the life and prosperity, inner as well as outer prosperity, of all who form part of it; that is to say, neither financial profits are the goal nor assertion and expansion of power, nothing beyond the human good, and just this. There is, accordingly, no division of ownership and producership. The "companions" are not stockholders; they are remunerated, and part of the sales value is distributed among them, according to their "human value," their "value as men," which consists of their professional value plus their social value. A system of remuneration with coefficients has been worked out: ". . . the professional value comes out of the multiplication of the professional coefficient by the professional rating. The rating is evaluated by the professional teams, each man grading himself and the team grading him. The social value comes out of the multiplication of the social coefficient by the social rating. The social rating is evaluated by the General Council . . . it is revised every three months. The social value includes the [educational] courses followed (physical, intellectual, artistic, philosophical, religious), the sense of fellowship, mutual aid, the ability to perceive the common good and work for it, the sense of responsibility, etc." [79]

This can be fully understood only in combination with the new, peculiar concept of work, which has been evolved by these communities. "Work," to them, is "not only professional work," it is "any human activity which has value for the group." Consequently, the educational courses taken after professional working hours are valued and paid as Work. "The Community of Work"— so they call themselves, applying the word in that broader sense— "is a community of families. The work the wives do at home *is* Work; housekeeping has professional value to the community. In addition, wives can also contribute to the Community socially. So, like the industrial producers, they are rated professionally and socially and receive an allotment on their total human value. As for the children, they grow, and that is work too. So they too have to be 'paid.' A sick person who follows the doctor's instructions is paid. The work of a sick person is to get well." [80]

There are other directions worth mentioning, which have formed from their experiences: all essential decisions have to be reached by unanimity. "Unanimity," as one of the communities declared, "is not a voting system. It is a method of work." [81] The majority rule, to them, is another form of tyranny, it means domination of the minority by the majority. They go very far in applying their principle as their judicial practices show, which are remarkable in several respects. "The Court does not judge the fault, but the man. Therefore, the same fault may bring different verdicts according to the culprit. What is to be kept in mind by the judges is the common good on one side, and, on the other, giving the culprit a maximum chance to make good. The verdict is rendered on unanimous agreement: judges and culprit alike. What is the good of a sanction simply submitted to and not really understood and accepted?" [82] Such is the feeling of the communitarian people.

This brief summary of their main features shows the spirit of the communities. What guides them is, according to their words, "a spirit, not a set of beliefs." There are, to be sure, certain distinct principles accepted by all the various Communities of Work that have developed following the example of Marcel Barbu's original community, Boimondau. These principles, however, have evolved not from *a priori* thinking, but out of, and in the course of, practical experiences; they are constantly improved upon and modified according to changing circumstances. They have been worked out not by intellectuals, but by plain, average people; group pictures included in Miss Bishop's book are hardly distinguishable from those of any agricultural or union meeting, or middle-class family reunion, or football team. The only initial disposition of these thoroughly ordinary people was good will, sincerity, and the desire to live a human life, a life of free human beings, which today as they came to know could only be achieved by being together and working together in a human community. Again and again in the different communities we hear them say: "The biggest satisfaction is to work together. One is not alone any more. All of us are like one man." "The Community . . . it's not to be alone any more . . . to feel each other's elbows." "All the pleasure consists in being together." In all these utterances we sense the relief from the desolation of the "lonely crowd." Of course, not to be alone any more means more than just the permanent company of a team.

It implies the special mode of this working and being together. It means that by being together in this special way they are themselves again; by living and working in such a community in which they are integrated and which is their tangible common cause, they are not just performing a collective function; they are leading a meaningful life. In order to improve the community they are called upon to improve themselves. "A Community of Work does not mean plant community, enterprise community. The members might decide to do something else. The work, the plant, the field [in the rural communities] is but the *economic expression* of a group of people who wish to search for a way of life better suited to present living conditions and to a fuller expression of the whole man. It is true that there is no Community of Work without work, but the work comes second in the title: 'We do not start from the plant, from the technical activity of man, but from man himself.' " [83]

What distinguishes these communities from co-operatives is that their aim is not financial gain. What distinguishes them from the social experiments of the nineteenth century, from Robert Owen's colonies and Fourier's phalansteries, is that, as stated by Barbu's community, Boimondau, they "have not retired from the world in a sort of select and self-sufficient ghetto. We are not retracing our steps to a former state of civilization. We want machines—more and better machines—we like machines . . . on the other hand we are thoroughly integrated in the civic life of the nation . . . we participate in all citizen activity at Valence. . . ." And, "We do not stem from the thoughts and ideas either of intellectual or of religious apostles. Only experience born out of suffering has been and is our teacher." [84]

This is probably the reason why these communities have outlasted and overcome all the tremendous difficulties, economic, political and human, which confronted them. Barbu's initial community, for instance, was destroyed by the Nazis; he himself was put in a concentration camp while other members joined the Resistance; afterward they rebuilt the community. And, of course, the story of each of these communities includes critical situations, financial and legal troubles, personal failures and frictions. However, they not only survived them all but keep multiplying and prospering, economically no less than humanly. It has by now become a large movement. There are industrial as well as rural Communities of Work and there are combined industrial and rural communities. Religiously inspired working communities which had existed before have joined the movement and assimilated themselves to the communitarian ways; they have adopted the communitarian rules and methods and have arrived at a point where they are ready to accept persons of different creeds, even atheists, if only they aim at the same form of life. By living communitarian one can just as well live the gospel, as one can live socialism, or humanism. "Community," one of the religious communitarians said, "is the modern form of the church!" There are successful businessmen and industrialists who have begun to transform their enterprises into Communities of Work because they feel, as Monsieur Pierre, a prosperous building contractor in the North of France did, that "piling up profits for oneself is dull." "If you are a born pioneer like me," he says, "what do you do? You go communitarian. Mind you, I don't think it is the solution of the whole world problem. But it is the first step in the right direction." [85] Attempts have been made to turn even "limited companies" (*sociétés anonymes*) into communitarian units—a technically intricate experiment. The ambitious project of Adriano Olivetti, the head of the well-known typewriter factory and founder of the Italian *Movimento Communità,* who wanted to shape his whole country along communitarian lines, at the time of his death had not advanced beyond the pale of theory.

It would, of course, be preposterously rash to assume that the methods of the communitarian movement would, in their present form, be applicable to structures of larger proportions, to national and supra-national conditions. The communities themselves are more modest. They are not campaigning against capitalism or for a world revolution; they believe that capitalism will die of itself. They strictly confine themselves to their own limited aim, that is, forming oases of human community in the midst of a collectivized world, islands of unanimity in a sea of raging hostility, and they do not go further than such occasional sighs: "If everyone did the same in France and in the world [as we do] there would be no problems left." And yet, without any propaganda, the movement grows, which seems to indicate that indeed, as Miss Bishop says, "a trend of thought is in the air."

The reason why I have dwelt so elaborately on this movement is because it furnishes us a living example of the new spirit that alone could save us. Whatever part this movement may be destined to play in future world developments, it has given us, even by its present achievements, a few most valuable lessons regarding our socio-economic, our political, our moral problems.

Socially, economically, it demonstrates the fallacy of the age-old capitalist contention that profit and power are the only incentives to work. Appeals to self-dedication, indeed self-sacrifice, have always been successful if directed toward meaningful common ends, sometimes even humanly objectionable ends, such as national and racial glory, or ideological ascendancy. Particularly under modern, generally collectivistic conditions, people evidently work better and more happily in a real community of work; they appear to be, consciously or unconsciously, frustrated and bored to work just for a living, as employees of anonymous business enterprises, which is the destiny of most people under the system of modern, collectivistic and bureaucratic capitalism. There are cases of members of a Community of Work who left their community in order to work for higher salaries in capitalist factories and after a short while returned to their community because "they were bored."

Besides, it is obvious that Communities of Work will be much less vulnerable to the effects of automation. In such communities, "When more machines are used and more perfected ones acquired it does not mean turning men out while increasing production. It means increase of production, same number of workers, same amount of money or more, and shorter professional hours. This is so because profit is not the goal." [86] And, because "fullness of the development of man" has been the goal from the beginning, the use of leisure will be no problem.

POLITICALLY, the communitarian movement throws into strong relief the flaws of our *democratic process*. Our present democratic system has become a system of splits. There is a split, corresponding to the economic division of ownership and management, between the people (the owner of the state) and its government (the management of the state). The people has grown increasingly remote from the actual conduct of its affairs, which is in the hands of collective groupings, the parties or, more specifically, the party machines. There is a second split between the common, human good, the good of the national community as a whole, and the interests of collective, professional groups; the former is supposed to be represented by the official, political parliament, i.e., Congress, the latter are represented by the unofficial pressure groups, the lobbies. We leave aside the frequent antagonism between executive and legislative.

Certainly, the people have more effective means to exert their influence on the government than the owners of a corporation have with respect to its management. The people as a whole can actually assert their will through the elections. They have this opportunity, however, only every second year; they decide on persons and not on issues, and on candidates whom they have hardly a chance to choose, but who are presented to them by the party machines or by self-salesmen making handshake rounds. In the elections, as well as in current affairs between the elections, the manifold collective, professional interests are in conflict with the interest of the country as a whole and more often than not prevail over it; the effects of the general commercialization of public life make themselves felt. And the electoral power contest of the parties invites demagogy no less than totalitarianism does.

The present state of affairs is the result of the perpetuation of provisions which were meant for a population of much smaller proportions and of an entirely different social and economic struc-

ture. The nation today has in all respects outgrown its original conditions. An adequate study of the problem goes far beyond the
scope of this book. I can only venture a few indications in what
direction a remedy might be sought.[87]

The communitarian movement has shown that a group of people
are very well capable of thinking reasonably and fruitfully deciding
on issues of common concern, provided they act as an organic
community and not as collective masses. The guiding principle of
all reform must be to prevent people as much as possible from
becoming irrational collective masses and to put them in a position
to resolve matters in rather small circles, as real communities of
work and life. In this capacity they should be enabled to currently
decide, or influence decisions on issues and not only on persons
to whom authority is delegated. Indeed, a deeper understanding
of issues is even needed for properly judging the personalities of
delegates. Delegation cannot be avoided, but the aim should be
to build up delegation from the bottom, that is, from small communities upward through a hierarchy of ever higher communities
and to strengthen and control such delegation through directions
on issues. Small communities may send their speakers, or representatives, into the next higher council, and so forth up to the top,
so that a perpetual contact prevails, a come and go, between the
lowest and the highest, the smallest and the broadest community.
This dynamization and actualization of democracy would abolish
the present split between ownership and management in the political domain. It would require thorough, methodical information to
the people on the issues concerned. Such current information may
become possible through increase of leisure as a result of automation, and it would, in turn, teach people the meaning and productive use of leisure. The fateful cleavage between work and leisure
would be healed.

There would be a correspondingly good effect on the negative
side: this rotating process of democracy, this exchange of guidance
from above and below, instruction reaching down from administrators, scholars, scientists, and influence reaching up from the small

est circles—this permanent and regulated process of democracy would invalidate, or at least reduce, the hysterical hubbub of election time, that hotbed of demagogy, which casts its evil effects over the whole preceding year and over the whole national and global scene. It would, instead, introduce a certain amount of steadiness and calm reasoning into the conduct of public affairs. Hardly any other way is conceivable of how the desires of people could again be made to coincide with the good of the people.

I am perfectly aware of the fact that all this must appear quite unrealizable as seen from our present state of affairs. It should be taken as an aim, presupposing a conjunction of economic, political and moral reform, which again points to that fundamental change, the change of spirit and attitude.

WHATEVER SPECIFIC REFORM we may be pondering, we are ultimately referred to the *moral problem* which, however, must be seen in a much broader sense than usual. Morality should be cleared of all the conventional cliché attaching to the word; it has to be re-conceived as factually as possible. Just as the communitarians were led by their practical experiences to the rediscovery of the Decalogue, a new, effective concept of morality must be derived from the experiences of our age. Certainly, such regeneration on a national and supranational scale is very different from the application of personal experiences to a community of two dozen people. And yet, it follows just as clearly from the realization of the evils that plague our world: collectivization, functionalization, commercialization, disruption of all human and organic coherence. The awareness of these overpowering tendencies instructs us to strive, wherever we stand, for the prevalence of the human point of view over all other particular and functional points of view; to work as much as we can for human integration, in politics, in economy, in education and learning—not, to be sure, by relinquishing the least of our scientific, scholarly, artistic, technological standards, but, on the contrary, by raising them to the level of a new wholeness. Such an effort implies the revival of human sensibility, of a susceptibility to all things human, which is on the point of vanishing today. As has been pointed out before in this study, values are only special rationalizations of something much deeper and much more comprehensive, much more dynamic and much more living, of a general feeling for what is human, a response to what is human. Response fosters responsibility; there is a close connection between the two. All morality valid for our epoch can be comprehended in these two terms: *human response* and *human responsibility.*

Values are worth nothing if taken separately and literally, cut off from the attitude and sensibility which is their generative ground. Formal moralities are preaching stuff and as such rightly abhorred. Not only must old venerable values constantly be re-interpreted, re-adjusted to changing conditions, but from new situations new evils have grown which are not covered by the Ten Commandments or by the conventional ordinances of the churches; new evils which in those less advanced ages of man no lawgiver could have foreseen and which are far more pernicious than the good old sins.

There are certainly in the world today many decent, progressive, kindly clergymen of all creeds, who work for the good in public and private life and take what they teach very seriously. But if they fail to teach people how to apply Sunday rules to Monday jobs (and who could possibly live up to this desperate task!); if they sometimes have recourse to morality in the age-old guise of respectability: churchgoing and a presentable family life, be it underneath what it may; there is danger that they achieve nothing else than to provide a good conscience where there should be no easy conscience.

The effectiveness of ecclesiastical guidance can be measured by the effect of Pope Pius XII's admonition concerning the abolition of hydrogen tests: none of the governments glorying in their Christian faith paid any attention to it.

The real evils at the bottom of present anarchy, outer and inner anarchy, cannot be wiped out by codified rules or spiritual prescriptions. They call for a *moral hygiene* much more comprehensive and at the same time more subtle, corresponding to physical and mental hygiene, indeed, supplementing psychic hygiene. As we have seen, modern psychology and biology have arrived at a dynamic ethics combining both moral and mental therapy, and treating moral defects like psychic and physiological disorders. Good and Bad can no longer be regarded in a black-and-white fashion as neat opposites, sins and virtues; scientists as well as artists have discovered their complex intertwining and their social and constitutional conditionality. Moral hygiene is a matter of balance and integration in the whole human being and in the whole human community. It implies the creation of social circumstances in which a human being can lead a meaningful life and may be moved by the general atmosphere to regain his capacity for human response and responsibility. It therefore comprises, if only as aims and efforts, all the reforms, intellectual, socio-economic and political, which I ventured to trace on the foregoing pages.

No watchword more telling could be found for the goal to be reached than the maxim of a Dutch communitarian school: "Cooperation between those who naturally oppose each other."

WE FINALLY HAVE TO FACE THE QUESTION: what will be the *future of the individual?* As far as I can see, the destiny of the individual will depend on whether collective or community will prevail in the world to come. If developments continue in their present trend toward ever more inclusive collectivization, capitalistic or totalitarian, the individual is in the gravest peril; he will be increasingly hollowed out, deprived of his vital strength. The only way to safeguard the individual, even in a somewhat restricted position, is the realization of the human community. No other choice remains in a world which under any circumstances will be a place of ever growing, ever more awakening and preponderant masses of population, requiring ever more complex organization.

Naturally, even in an accomplished community the role of the individual will not be the same as it was in the individualistic age, between the Renaissance and the nineteenth century. The individual will no longer be as autonomous and self-sufficing as he was in that period; he will no longer determine and represent the essential action of his world; not the individual but the community will be the decisive unit. He will not rule any longer, he will have to serve, but in a community he may serve a human aim which is implicitly his own, not an alien purpose imposed on him from without. He will be able to develop freely, to contribute his development to the common development and bring his influence to bear on this development. Indeed, the eminent individual with his special ingenuity will continue to be the vehicle, the spearhead of common advances. No essential evolutionary gain is completely lost; transformed, it continues to be operative in all future progression. Thus, the fully matured individual will, within the framework of the community, preserve an indispensable function. The community, "recoiling for a better leap," will have to resort to the sources and resources of the individual. Of course this will never be smooth going; frictions are bound to occur, and the maintenance and readjustment of balance will remain a perpetual concern.

Anyway, no other alternative will be left to us: unless we want to be collectivized, we shall have to live as communities, free and human communities. Man's career started from communities, original, pre-individual communities. Out of these primeval communities slowly, gradually, the individual evolved, disengaged himself from the common bonds and came to concentrate in his accomplished self the human quality, the human form. This distinct human quality, however, is synonymous with the faculty of perpetual self-transcendence, which is plainly expressed in the human being's gift of self-reflection, of conceiving himself as an I. Thus, the individual in his manifold Promethean, or Faustian, ventures became re-entangled in trans-individual interconnections. The period of adolescent self-concentration was followed by a period of self-expansion and dispersion, of exploration and analysis, eventually of specialistic and functionalistic combinations. And now, after a long era of boundless centrifugalism, it seems imperative to shift the emphasis to centripetalism again, that is, to the recovery of the lost wholeness. The original community was a whole, the accomplished individual was a whole, the goal is to reach wholeness again in the *consciously* achieved community, a community on a higher level and with a broader scope.

This evolutionary passage, actually traversed by man, is prefigured in the Biblical story of man transgressing the bounds of nature into forbidden consciousness, expelled from innocent harmony and set on his path toward the conscious attainment of harmony again, i.e., of the accomplished brotherhood of men. As it is said in Heinrich von Kleist's beautiful parable *Über das Mario-nettentheater* (On the Puppet Show): "Thus we have to eat a second time from the tree of knowledge in order to recover our state of innocence. . . ."

We must learn to live with the tragic awareness that living forms are mortal, as mortal as individual beings. Yet something persists in the dignity of the human form crystallizing in its sublime moment. In the fullness of form time is abolished: its moment of life is eternity.

POSTSCRIPT

This new edition of *The Tower and the Abyss* would have called for a thorough revision of the text, had this not, for technical reasons, been unfeasible. I have, therefore, added a few notes in which some of the points most needful of amplification or clarification are briefly developed.

—E. K.

Society (Chapter One)

The distinction drawn in this chapter between the two basic types of groups, with their different effects on the individual, may help to clarify a general term that is used widely in a very vague and confusing manner: the term *society*. It fluctuates between the two opposing types, the organic form *community* and the functional form *collective*.

Commonly *society* denotes an assemblage of either genealogically or "sociably" connected people—whether a traditionally developed elite, such as the European nobilities, internationally related through intermarriage; or the financial elite of the American "Social Register"; or the even more loosely connected, undetermined and shifting, convivial company of cocktail parties and "café society."

The French *société,* as depicted by generations of great authors, from Saint-Simon, Madame de La Fayette, and Choderlos de Laclos to Balzac and Marcel Proust, issued from the *curia regis,* the counseling court of the French kings, and kept expanding until, in the eighteenth and nineteenth centuries, it came to comprise also the money aristocracy of the bourgeoisie. So the concept of "society" first evolved as a term applied to limited groupings that had come about naturally through the gathering around the monarch of subjugated feudal grandees and appointed legal advisers, who distinguished themselves through a tradition of manners and standards of conduct. (The word *société,* implying what subsequently came to be called *haute société, bonne société, le grand monde,* or simply *le monde,* seems to have made its initial appearance in the seventeenth century, when it was used in this sense by La Bruyère in his *Caractères.*) To be sure, since Roman times the term *societas* has also been used, in Roman, Canon, and English Common Law, to designate certain purposive, legal, or economic associations.

It was only much later, however, as a result of the social upheavals in the wake of the French and the Industrial Revolutions, that our modern theoretical, "sociological" concept of society evolved, as developed by Comte, Spencer, and the socialist thinkers. The *sociological* interpretations of "society" are legion. They range from "social organism," "social order," "social environment" to—I quote some definitions mentioned by Professors John W. Bennett and Melvin Tumin in their book *Social Life, Structure and Function* (1948), pp. 164, 170, 173—"the largest number of people who interact for the solution of problems vital to human survival and continuity . . . who share a common culture pattern and institutional framework"; or "a pattern of interconnected institutions, viewed as a unit"; or "a master network of social relationships and behavior." Bennett and Tumin themselves refer to society as "man's instrument as well as man's condition" (p. 185), which makes it appear as something in between natural growth and intentional association.

Generally, however, modern sociologists tend to stress the purposive aspect, and seem to follow the concept of the German sociologist Ferdinand Tönnies, who, in his book *Gemeinschaft und Gesellschaft* (Community and Society) termed "society, *Gesellschaft*" a "mechanical aggregate and artifact," an essentially purposive association of individuals who are in no way intrinsically related to each other, in contradistinction to "community, *Gemeinschaft,*" which he sees as a "living organism," "a natural association of human individuals based on consanguinity and lasting sexual relation, or on neighborhood, or on intellectual sympathy and cooperation."

These selected quotations show that the term society lends itself to the most diverse interpretations, according to the context in which it is used. In our context I would deem it appropriate to retain the fluid characteristic of society, its being an intermediary, a medium between organism and organization, in fact a very *medium*. Society may be called the complex of human environments of the individual, national or universal within his own epoch, in which interrelations and interactions of individuals, groups, and institutions take place.

This vast complex is the domain in which the "social sciences" operate, and so it is also the sphere with which David Riesman and his collaborators confront the individual in their book *The Lonely Crowd*. I wish to refer to this brilliant study as a supplement to and support of what I have outlined in the first chapter of the present book. But, significantly, the problem of social relationships is approached by Riesman and his co-authors solely from the point of view of the individual, thus implying that the individual is the only basically valid social unit. The authors are particularly interested in what they call the "modes of conformity" of Western man, the varying ways in which Western man is led to conform to his social environment. This is a very American and thoroughly modern kind of concern, and it is in itself a symptom of the social condition, or "social character," of the man of our age, as Riesman describes it.

He distinguishes three "modes of conformity" as historical stages, connecting them—rather problematically—with demographic phases of population growth and decline. "The society of high growth potential," so he writes, "develops in its typical members a social character whose conformity is insured by their tendency to follow tradition: these I [D.R.] shall term *'tradition-directed'* people, and the society in which they live: a 'society dependent on tradition-direction.'—The society of transitional population growth develops in its typical members a social character whose conformity is insured by their tendency to acquire early in life an internal set of goals. These I shall term *inner-directed* people and the society in which they live: a society dependent on inner-direction. Finally, the society of incipient population decline [the present society?] develops in its typical members a social character, whose conformity is insured by their tendency to be sensitized to the expectations and preferences of others. These I shall term *other-directed* people and the society in which they live one dependent on other-direction."

I am a little doubtful about whether this aspect of social conformity is as relevant to earlier periods of history as it is to our own epoch. In the period of "tradition-direction" the problem of the incipient individual was rather how not to conform to the omnipotent clan or tribe or polis, how to achieve his individuality and transform, advance, improve his community. The "inner-directed" man, that is, the socially and intellectually pre-eminent person, who alone was able to develop "an internal set of goals," was even less concerned with conformity. His foremost, indeed even his sole aspiration was the inner and outward assertion of his personality. It is only in our age, in which masses and collectives predominate, that conformity, social adjustment has become a focal issue.

David Riesman deals mainly with the American scene and with American man; and in the course of his investigations he seems to have reached the conclusion that a fundamental change has occurred in the character of American man. This conclusion appears to me of particular importance. It is not often that someone envisages such a fundamental change. My concern in the present book was with man in general, the condition of modern man. And I have ventured to show that a fundamental change is going on, not only in the character of American man, but in the character and condition of the man of our age, of whom American man is but a conspicuous exponent.

Schizophrenia (Chapter Three)

The Eichmann and Auschwitz trials furnished many more examples of the personality split described in this chapter. One of them seems to me so gruesomely striking that I feel it should be mentioned in this context.

Inge Deutschkron, a reporter at the Auschwitz trials, relates in her book *Denn ihrer war die Hölle, Kinder in Gettos und Lagern* (Köln 1965) the story of the arrival of 150 Jewish children in Auschwitz. "The group looked like a kindergarten class on an outing," reported the witness, Marina Wolff. "They halted in a meadow in front of the crematorium. A female Nazi guard told the children to undress, to fold their clothes neatly so that they could each find their own after the shower they were going to take. Suddenly a little five-year-old girl threw a big red ball into the air, and a game started in the warm September sun. After a while, the guard, just like a kindergarten teacher, clapped her hands and told the children to stop playing now because it was time to have their bath. The children obeyed and rushed down the steps to the crematorium. A little boy, less than two years old, was unable to get down the steps. So the guard took the child in her arms. . . . The little boy played with the blond hair of the good-looking guard, and feeling at ease in her arms he laughed with joy. A moment later both were out of sight. Shortly afterwards the guard came out of the crematorium and walked calmly back to the camp. The ventilators shrieked and the operation was completed. . . ."

Alienation (Chapters Four and Five)

While the general phenomenon of alienation is given increasing attention in recent literature, the widespread acceptance of "avant-garde" works has fostered the impression that the special alienation of the artist from his audience is a thing of the past. Indeed the products of such collective movements as "pop" art and "op" art, "beat" literature and *musique concrète* are eagerly received, not only by the volatile crowd of intellectual snobs who, craving the new and afraid of missing the next fad, actually produce it, but also by lively young people in need of outlets for their exuberance and weary of faded conventions.

All this, however, does not get at the core of the matter. What has happened is not so much a greater readiness, or capacity for understanding on the part of the public, but a radical transformation of art as such, an approximation of "avant-garde" work to the level of daily experience: our fragmented existence and its patent discordances, the prevalence of life machinery over life itself, and hence its increasing mechanization.

Again, this new mode of creation is plainly neither the result of compliance with the human situation, nor a contrivance of sensationalist fakery—although it greatly favors it; it is, as indicated in the text of this book, a result of convergent developments within and outside the arts. The "avant-garde" exposes the reality in which we live—this has always been the function of art. At the same time, however, it is itself both a product and a victim of the processes that have led up to the present reality. The complexity and uncertainty of man's secularized existence, fostered by popular, scientific, and technological developments and the concomitant hypertrophy of psychological and conceptual analysis, found shape in the uncertainty of the means of communication, of language, and so of the artistic languages. These languages have in themselves become problematic, and more and more—since form is "the shape of content," as Ben Shahn has rightly put it—have become identical with the problematic substance of reality itself. Thus, lettrism, the programming of "beauty," linguistic mechanization, "pop" and "op" art, concrete and electronic music, seem to spell the end of art, as we have known it for millennia, and to herald new, unforeseeable structures. In these circumstances, the alienation of the artist merges with the general alienation of man from man, the "loneliness of the crowd."

Camus (Chapter Six)

In his preface to a new edition of *The Stranger* (1955) Camus has given us his own interpretation of the novel; he did not intend, he says, to picture Meursault as a mere "drifter." Meursault, in his view, is a man who "refuses to lie. . . . He tells the truth, he refuses to exaggerate his feelings." "The truth at stake is as yet only negative, the truth of being and feeling. But without this truth, no conquest over oneself and over the world will ever be possible. It would not, then, be much of an error to read *The Stranger* as the story of a man who, without any heroic posturing, is willing to die for the truth. Once, paradoxically . . . , I said that I had tried to symbolize in my character the only Christ of which we are worthy."

Admirable and appropriate as this intention is, it seems to me to have remained in the abstract. It does not come forth as the dominant theme of the story. In the novel, Meursault is certainly unwilling to lie, he is "true to his feelings," but what pervasively and strikingly appears, and what seems to me of deeper significance with regard of our present human condition, is that he has hardly any human feelings to be true to. Actually, he is true to his lack of feelings. It is as if, in order to expose the conventional offensiveness of truth, Camus had had to choose a case of complete apathy; this however, was bound to blur the intended meaning.

No matter what situation or relationship Meursault is involved in, he shows no real concern, no inner response or even preference. When the manager of his firm offers him a better position in Paris, he says "yes," but adds: "actually, I did not care." Giving up his studies was "of no real importance." When his girl friend asks him whether he loves her, he says "I do not think so," but if she wants him to marry her, he says he would not mind because, again, it is of no importance. His arguments for putting his mother into an asylum are certainly quite reasonable, and even the fact that at her funeral he is only bored and hungry, could be quite compatible with true sentiment; but at no point does he show the slightest sign of affection or sympathy for a mother against whom he had no grievance. Nor does he show more than a fleeting interest in any human being. Significantly, his encounter with the Arab whom he kills is as accidental as the killing itself is unnecessary: his revolver goes off automatically, as it were, in a reflex of uncontrolled irresolution.

So it seems not primarily his lack of conventional hypocrisy that makes him a monster to other people, but rather what lies behind his truth, his complete lack of human response. (He himself concedes that he "never had any real imagination.") He does not die *for* the truth, he dies *of* it. And the only "passion," if indeed one can call it that, which in the end, rather abruptly, breaks out of him, is a passion for indifference, the "brotherly indifference of the universe."

Population Explosion (Chapter Seven)

Among the forces that have contributed to our present human condition there is one that has been treated too cursorily in this book: the rapid growth of world population. It has become a problem of utmost urgency. To deal adequately with it in relation to the various developments discussed in the text would by far exceed the proportions of a supplementary note. I must confine myself to some brief indications.

In Europe, the "population explosion" started, as is well known, in the wake of the Industrial Revolution, for diverse, still controversial reasons that cannot be gone into here. But the general determinants of an ever accelerating population growth are, to my mind, unmistakable. They can be found, ultimately and in summary, in the development of democracy, nationalism, science, technology, and industry. All of these processes were interdependent and interacting, all can be traced back to a common source: to the development of enlightenment, that is, the tendency to subject all matters of life to rational treatment.

By democracy must be meant not only the political system itself, but the presence in government of the masses of the people, the pressure of whose amorphous moods makes itself felt even on authoritarian regimes. Since the revolutions at the end of the eighteenth century, the status of the masses has been raised once and for all, their influence, their national and more and more nationalistic self-assertion has increased. Attention to the material well-being of the people and urging them to beget children in order to boost the international importance of the nation and to add to the number of potential soldiers, has been the order of the day.

The rise in the *national* status of the masses has been accompanied by their *international* ascent, which was the effect of the class struggle. Enlightenment, the rational approach, not only fostered political democracy, it developed modern industry, which from its inception was closely, and ever increasingly, linked to technology and science. The very same revolution that produced modern industry laid the foundations of the organization of the working class and its striving for social and economic democracy. Thus in general, through the increasing prevalence of science and technology, the rational disposition has contributed to the awakening of the masses, to their mounting awareness of human rights, and that implies, of racial equality; finally to the dissolution of colonialism and the liberation of colored peoples.

In the initial stages of modern industry the use of child-labor furnished an incentive for begetting children who would become providers. Now, the needs and aspirations of newly liberated peoples tend to favor population growth, apart from the fact that seemingly improved circumstances allow their natural inclinations free rein, while actually the worst economic deficiencies persist. By promoting hygiene, improving living conditions, and raising the social status of the people, science and technology stimulate the increase of population in areas where the population growth has been inhibited or where the mortality rate has been high. We also have to take into account that the climate of democracy has given rise to the sort of mentality, never quite extinguishable, that no longer looks with indifference and a quiet conscience on the mass starvation of colonial and subject populations. At least some hypocritical aid has been offered in emergency cases, which must be regarded as a kind of progress. The result of all this, however, is the accelerating overpopulation of our globe.

So the very endeavors that have been intended and expected to produce better human conditions—that is, science, technology, and

democracy—are now, due to their not being controlled by an awareness of our human condition as a whole, on the point of becoming
a grave menace to the survival of humanity. Our disciplines, in their
pursuit of overspecialized, autonomous aims, have come to disregard the broader implications of their work and to lose sight of the
ultimate purpose of all knowledge: the guidance of human conduct.
The drive toward total rationalization of our life and mechanization
of all techniques, mental as well as instrumental, upsets the balance
of human nature. It has exceeded the scope of the individual and
his capacity for understanding. The rapid growth of the population
and the concomitant collectivization of all our practices and
institutions have complicated the task of government, and have
diminished the contacts between government and people, thereby
jeopardizing true democracy.

This is the point at which overpopulation poses the greatest threat
to humanity. The democratic process ceases to be an exercise of
reason. It becomes a more and more irrational pressure exerted by
parochial groups of an uninformed population on a bureaucratized
government, a government just as professionalized and overspecialized as any other segment of the population, and no less affected
by the general incapacity of individuals to grasp our entire world
situation. The government itself is increasingly indoctrinated by
pressure from a citizenry that it has itself, under the pressure of circumstances, set out to indoctrinate. More and more it is pushed into
ideological and nationalistic arms races, into short-range manufacturing of emergencies and expediencies, the cutting of Gordian knots,
and that means, toward the rule of violence and irrationality. In the
measure to which the masses grow and prevail, true democracy fades.

We have in our midst influential people who in all seriousness
contemplate an atomic war as a means of solving the population
problem. Reasonable human remedies would be: cultivation of the
vast stretches of untilled, but arable, or even still presumed unara-
ble, land all over our globe, to take care of the food shortage; perseverance in birth control and the teaching of contraception, and
reminding civilized people who keep thoughtlessly multiplying of

their responsibility for the future of human generations, including their own; an international anti-poverty program, and an international division of labor, to prevent the unrestrained industrialization of our entire globe and the consequent neglect of land cultivation, as a result of the new countries' aspiration for future independence; last but not least, a world organization capable of regulating and administering such measures. But all this that would promote human welfare and preserve human dignity seems too long and too complex a procedure, requiring too much moral and mental stress, for the technocratic minds of our social strategists. We have arrived at a stage of a-humanity where people have become inured to exterminating human beings like vermin, whenever and wherever they are in the way of a preferred ideological or economic system.

Notes

Introduction

[1] "Every one of your relationships to man and to nature must be a definite, distinct expression of your real individual life, corresponding to the objective of your will." Karl Marx, "Nationalökonomie und Philosophie" in *Der historische Materialismus,* Die Frühschriften ed. by S. Landshut and J. P. Mayer, Leipzig, Kröner, 1952, v. I. p. 360.

Chapter One

[1] "*Ille* [Democritus] *atomos, quas appellat, id est, corpora individua propter soliditatem censet in infinito inani. . . ."* De Finibus Bonorum et Malorum* I, VI,17, and other passages.

[2] The etymological conjectures of the word *persona* show its complexity. They range from πsóσωπον (*prósōpon*), which means "face," "mien," "external look," or περì σῶμα (*peri sōma*), "the body's periphery," or *personare,* "to sound through," to *per se una,* "one in itself," which is identical with "individual," "indivisible."

[3] Various abstractions of the word "person" evolved in professional, legal and dogmatic usage. In ancient Rome *persona* came to designate also the official position, the "capacity" of a man, his rank, his "distinction." In 13th and 14th century France it denoted the professional office of the minister (*parsoune*), an interpretation which seems to have survived in the English usage of "parson."

Likewise, the abstract use of *persona* in jurisprudence had its origin in ancient Rome, where *persona* came to denote "legal man," "legal person," or even (still informally, not as *terminus technicus*) a "body corporate," i.e., a "juristic person," "artificial or conventional person," representing a body of persons or an impersonal aggregate of property, like a firm, which is legally considered on the same level with real, "natural" persons. Even in such group interpretations a "juristic person" figures as a single entity in opposition or relation to other single entities. A person appears here to be equivalent to an abstract individual.

In Christian dogma the term assumed a spiritual character when it was used to interpret the trinity in the one deity. God the Father, God the Son and God the Holy Spirit were characterized as persons—they could never

309

have been represented as individuals. Tertullian (2nd to 3rd century A.D.) introduced this usage while attempting to express the three grades, forms, or modes of the one deity. Undoubtedly the legal term, which meanwhile had been formally established, was on his mind. This dogmatic interpretation influenced Boethius (480?-524? A.D.) when he defined "person" as "the individual substance of a rational nature" (*naturae rationabilis individua substantia*)—nature being used in the sense of the "specific difference that gives form to anything." The elaborate exposition of Boethius' very elucidating concept of "person" may be found in his tractate *Contra Eutychen et Nestorium*, chapters I-III (*The Theological Tractates*, with an English translation by H. F. Steward and E. K. Rand, The Loeb Classical Library, London, Heinemann and Cambridge University Press 1946). About the whole history of "person" cf. the exhaustive study by Hans Rheinfelder, "Das Wort 'Persona,'" *Beihefte zur Zeitschrift für Romanische Philologie*, 77, Halle (Saale), 1928.

⁴ For a detailed account of the various interpretations see Gordon W. Allport, *Personality, A Psychological Interpretation* (New York, Holt, 1937), p. 28 *ff*. Bergson's interpretation is not quite unequivocal. To him "person" is unquestionably the *moi*, the ego, but the ego is doublefold: in its essence, its depth, it is one and a whole, but its contacts with the outer world divide it into distinct moments and situations. Cf. *Essai sur les données immédiates de la conscience* (19th ed., Paris, Felix Alcan, 1920, pp. 97-106: "Les deux aspects du moi").

⁵ C. G. Jung, *Die Beziehungen zwischen dem Ich und dem Unbewussten* (Darmstadt, Reichl, 1928, 63 *ff*.).

⁶ Gordon W. Allport, *op. cit.*, p. 48. Gardner Murphy in his outstanding book, *Personality, A Biosocial Approach to Origins and Structure* (New York, Harper, 1947) also emphasizes uniqueness, selfhood and wholeness as basic features of personality.

⁷ "Hence," William McDougall writes in his book, *The Group Mind* (New York, Putnam, 1920), Chap. 2, p. 31, "though we may know each member of a group so intimately that we can, with some confidence, foretell his actions under given circumstances, we cannot foretell the behavior of the group from our knowledge of the individuals alone."

⁸ The expression "tribal self" which conveys the phenomenon very well I borrow from W. K. Clifford, without accepting his certainly outdated interpretations.

⁹ William Halse Rivers, *Instinct and the Unconscious* (England, Cambridge University Press, 1924), p. 95 *ff*.

Chapter Two

¹ The term "rationalization" is most commonly used in the economic sense, indicating, according to Webster, "the organization of a business or industry upon an orderly system, to avoid waste, to simplify procedure, to coordinate parts, etc." In the present context the term is also applied in a

broader sense following the general meaning of the word "rationalize": "to make something conformable to principles satisfactory to reason" (Webster). The general codification of the operation of reason, of the "normative formal principles of reason," is logic which in all its forms (epistemological, pragmatic, symbolic, or mathematical) involves abstraction. Science is logical treatment of empirical material.

[2] The aim appears to be an "exact social science," a "social physics," based on the assumption that "the behavior of people in large numbers may be predicted by mathematical rules." John Q. Stewart, "Concerning 'Social Physics,'" *Scientific American*, May, 1948.

[3] F. Stuart Chapin, "Sociometric Stars as Isolates," *American Journal of Sociology*, LVI, No. 3, November, 1950.

[4] *New York Times*, October 21, 1950.

[5] (London, Falcon Press, 1950), p. 11.

[6] Cf. F. J. Roethlisberger and William J. Dickson, *Management and the Worker, An Account of a Research Program Conducted by the Western Electric Company, Hawthorne Works, Chicago* (Cambridge, Mass., Harvard University Press, 1947).

[7] G. R. Taylor, *op. cit.*, p. 36 ff.

[8] Cambridge, Mass., Harvard University Press, 1945, p. 76.

[9] C. Wright Mills, *White Collar* (New York, Oxford University Press, 1953), p. 204 ff. Under these circumstances morons seem to have a golden opportunity. Dr. Ruby Jo Reeves Kennedy, sociologist at the Connecticut College for Women, gave the following report before the American Association on Mental Deficiency in Boston: "The typical male moron is a semi-skilled worker earning between $35 and $55 a week, compared with the U.S. average industrial wage of $51.50. He gets to work on time, gets along very well with people smarter than he is. Movies are his favorite entertainment, though he also listens to the radio regularly. He marries at an average age of 21.9 years, a wife who went farther in school than he, and has an average of one child. . . . The female moron makes more money than the normal woman industrial worker, but does not save her money." (Quoted in *Time*, May 31, 1948.)

[10] John P. Marquand, *Point of No Return* (Boston, Little Brown 1949), p. 478 ff. Cf. also the following passages: "Charles could hear his father's voice . . . 'The system, Charley. You have to beat the system.' . . . It was true—the harder you pursued happiness, the less liberty you had, and perhaps if you pursued it hard enough, it might ruin you. . . . No one had told the school children that freedom of choice was limited. He could see himself hurrying, always hurrying, and he would be hurrying again tomorrow. . . . It was not what he dreamed of, there in Clyde, but if he had to start all over he would not have acted differently. . . ." p. 526 ff. "He was thinking about security, a popular word still, even when nothing was secure. The foundation of everything was shaky and yet there were always plans on top of those shaky foundations, pathetic plans, important only to an individual." p. 534 ff.

For an informative over-all picture of the situation of the executive, see the article by Perrin Stryker, "How Executives Get Jobs," *Fortune,* August, 1953. More material on the tendencies discussed above, also on scientism and the doubtful value of tests, may be found in William H. Whyte, Jr.'s *The Organization Man* (New York, Simon and Schuster, 1956).

[11] David Riesman, *Faces in the Crowd* (New Haven, Yale University Press, 1952), p. 382 ff.

[12] Gertrude Stein, *Brewsie and Willie* (New York, Random House, 1946), pp. 108 f.

[13] There is only one instance which could be compared with these collective performances and that is their prototype: the rigorously exact rank-and-file marching of military units, which was introduced by the drilling methods of the Prussian army in the eighteenth century. It is a fairly recent phenomenon that people are attracted by such complete merging of individual human beings into a collective body in action and by the mechanical precision of this spectacle.

All other working combinations, the orchestra or the traditional ballet, for example, are based on an entirely different principle, on the organization of subtle diversity, which is the principle of every work of art. Peculiar border line cases were the great Russian theatres of the 1920's, under the leadership of Meierhold, Vachtangov, Tairov, Granowsky. These groups achieved performances of the utmost artistic perfection. Every move, every detail of the scene were fixed in relation to all others and to the whole; the scene was composed like a painting in motion: what happened downstage left corresponded to something upstage right, and so on. This was accomplished by a routine of sometimes over a hundred rehearsals, but the utter discipline of action did not in the least impair the vitality and apparent spontaneity of the performance. Although these representations were the result of the strictest and most meticulous training, the work of the group was animated by enthusiastic cooperation and thorough common dedication. Lugné Poe, the director of a famous Paris theater, introduced the Vachtangov group to the French audience by saying that these were not just actors as we know them, "they are monks, devoting their life to their art." These groups could be considered as a blend of community and collective. They were collectives inasmuch as they underwent a most rigorous training and acted as a whole, intricately connected group. On the other hand they were a true community in that they were inspired by a genuinely common concern and each one of them identified himself completely with and felt individually responsible for this common cause.

None of these truly artistic combinations transformed the individual into a streamlined automaton.

[14] Sidonie M. Gruenberg, "Homogenized Children of New Suburbia," *New York Times Magazine,* September 14, 1954.

[15] *PM,* July 13, 1946.

[16] J. D. Salinger, *Franny,* in *Franny and Zooey* (Boston, Little, Brown, 1961).

[17] Erich Fromm, *Man for Himself, An Inquiry into the Psychology of Ethics* (New York and Toronto, Rinehart, 1947), p. 74.

[18] *Op. cit.*, pp. 68-78. Regrettably, Fromm's most recent book, *The Sane Society*, came to my knowledge too late to be discussed in the context of this study. It contains important material and conclusions corresponding to and supporting certain points raised in Chapters Two and Seven of the present book.

[19] Karl Marx, "Deutsche Ideologie: Feuerbach," *Der Historische Materialismus*, ed. by S. Landshut and J. P. Mayer (Leipzig: Kröner, 1932), II, p. 23 ff.

[20] Karl Marx, "Nationaloekonomie und Philosophie," *op. cit.*, vol. I, p. 292.

[21] *Op. cit.*, I, p. 357 ff.

[22] The Italian *commedia dell'arte*, historically the first professional theater group, formed in the middle of the sixteenth century, also developed "types," but we need only compare these types with those of the German expressionist plays to see immediately the fundamental difference: the types of the *commedia dell'arte* were *human*, not functional types, basic forms and attitudes of the human being; they were derived from different regions in Italy where each of these character-forms were predominant. In Bologna, the university town, the prevailing figure was the doctor, the scholar, the ridiculous pedant; in Venice, the center of Mediterranean trade, it was the old merchant Pantalone; in Naples, which at that time was ruled by the militant Spaniards, it was the captain Spavento, the "miles gloriosus" and killer of Moors; in Bergamo, the city of pack-carriers, it was the two stupid and roguish servants Arlecchino and Brighella, and so forth. A profession in that age was not a functional capacity; it was identical with a genuinely human disposition that had grown out of the traditional climate of an ethnic community. It was the specific local and historical situation that made the Spaniards into hidalgos and the Venetians into merchants; and individuals were still very strongly rooted in these communal traditions which shaped their personality to a considerable degree. So, in the view of the people for whom these comedies were produced, a man from Venice was necessarily concerned with trade just as a man from Bologna must be connected with learning. In the comedies of Molière (and Goldoni), which derived from the old Italian comedy, the protagonists are exponents of purely human attitudes divested of any regionally professional features: the "misanthrope," the "hypochondriac," the "miser," the "bourgeois gentilhomme," and so forth. The difference from collective types such as the "bank teller," the "officer," the "engineer," the "revolutionary" is self-evident.

[23] Quoted by Gerard Piel in his article, "Scientists and Other Citizens," *Scientific Monthly*, 1954.

Chapter Three

[1] The convictions of his home and his time inculcated in Luther a repre-

sentation of God the Father and Jesus as stern and even cruel judges whose just wrath must be appeased through the intercession of the saints, and dread of the omnipresent influence of the devil and his retinue of evil spirits. Indeed, God and devil appeared to move in a blurring twilight, their contours merging and their actions often difficult to distinguish. Luther's father suspected that the thunderstorm vision, which induced young Luther to become a monk, was a work of the devil. And Luther himself once complained: "When I looked for Christ it seemed to me as if I saw the devil."

[2] *Wochenpredigten über Matth. 5-7, 1530-1532.*

[3] But Luther could have found another passage in Paul: I Cor. 7, expressing the very opposite: "Art thou called being a servant? Care not for it: but if thou mayest be made free, use it rather. . . . Ye are bought with a price; be not ye the servants of men."

[4] *Ermahnung zum Frieden auf die zwölf Artikel der Bauerschaft in Schwaben,* 1525.

[5] *BA* IV, 1, p. 479, quoted by Ernst Troeltsch, *Die Soziallehren der christlichen Kirchen und Gruppen* (Tübingen, Mohr, 1919), p. 582; Engl. transl.: *The Social Teaching of the Christian Churches* (Glencoe and New York, 1949), Vol. II, p. 872.

[6] *Immermanns Werke* (Leipzig und Wien Bibliographisches Institut), *Münchhausen,* Part I, Book II, chap. xi, pp. 254, 255.

[7] Jean Stafford, "The Maiden," *Children Are Bored on Sunday* (New York, Harcourt, Brace, 1953).

[8] Friedrich Wilhelm I, *Erlasse und Briefe* (Leipzig, 1931), p. 24.

[9] Heinrich von Treitschke, *Politik* (4th ed.; Leipzig, Hirzel, 1918), Vol. I, Book I, chap. ii, p. 69.

[10] Cf. Sir John Maynard, *Russia in Flux* (New York, Macmillan, 1948), chap. xv, p. 278 ff.

[11] Bruno Bettelheim, "Individual and Mass Behavior in Extreme Situations," *The Journal of Abnormal and Social Psych.,* Vol. 38, 1943.

[12] H. Rauschning, *The Voice of Destruction* (New York, Putnam, 1940), pp. 16 ff., 252, 83 f.

[13] The term "schizophrenia," since its creation by Bleuler, has come to designate the most diverse pathological and semi-pathological psychic conditions; often enough it has been applied rather loosely and arbitrarily. Therefore, it seems to me necessary to state that in the context of this book the term will be used in accordance with the original meaning of the Greek composite: splitting (*schizein*) of the mind (*phren*), to characterize a psychic state which could not be termed more simply and clearly any other way.

[14] *Commentary,* I, No. 3, January 1946.

[15] Bettelheim, *op. cit.* Cf. also Eugene Kogon, *The Theory and Practice of Hell* (New York, Farrar, 1950), p. 127.

[16] Bettelheim, *Op. cit.*

[17] Christopher Rand, "Letter from Korea," *The New Yorker,* March 5, 1951.

[18] Ernst v. Schenck, *Europa vor der deutschen Frage* (Bern, Francke, 1946), p. 140 ff.

[19] Einsatzgruppen-Trial, U.S. Military Tribunal II-A, Case No. 9, *Trials of War Criminals before the Nuernberg Military Tribunals, Oct. 1946–April 1949,* Drexel A. Sprecher and John H. E. Fried, Editors, Washington, D.C., U.S. Government Printing Office, Vol. IV (1950), pp. 500, 501.

[20] *Loc. cit.,* p. 468.

[21] *Loc. cit.,* pp. 503, 504.

[22] *Krupp Trial,* U.S. Military Tribunal III, Case No. 10, Judgment July 31, 1948, *loc. cit.* vol. IX, 1950, pp. 1409, 1410.

[23] Germaine Tillion, "À la recherche de la vérité," *Ravensbrück,* (Neuchâtel, Les Cahiers du Rhône, 1946), p. 25 ff., p. 45 ff.; cf. also Kogon, *op. cit.,* p. 269.

[24] Report, *New York Herald Tribune,* November 15, 1947.

[25] (New York, Schuman, 1949).

[26] On gassing, the same Hoess stated: "Our improvements over Treblinka consisted in the fact that we had built our gas chamber to accommodate 2000 people at a time. Children of tender age were invariably exterminated because we could not use them as labor." (Report in *PM,* March 16, 1947.)

[27] Germaine Tillion, *op. cit.,* p. 54; cf. also Count Folke Bernadotte, *The Curtain Falls, Last Days of the Third Reich* (New York, Knopf, 1945).

[28] Sadism was not particularly prevalent; it developed, wherever it did, as a by-product. SS men were systematically drilled in the complex techniques and varieties of torture. Cf. Benedikt Kautsky, *Teufel und Verdammte, Erfahrungen und Erkenntnisse aus sieben Jahren in deutschen Konzentrationslagern* (Zürich, Büchergilde Gutenberg, 1946), pp. 79, 83 ff., 87 ff.; Germaine Tillion, *op. cit.,* p. 25; Eugene Kogon, *op. cit.,* p. 31; on the "psychological Death Head training," see German edition *Der SS-Staat* (Stockholm, Bermann Fischer, 1947), p. 26.

[29] The only historical case inviting comparison with the Nazi situation is the Catholic Inquisition. Indeed, there exist certain similarities: mass-extermination of opponents, economic exploitation of the victims and enormous profits made on such occasions by popes and secular rulers (the French King Philip IV's expropriation of the Knight Templars), spread of fear among the populations, and unflinching obedience on the part of the clergy to the orders of the Church—all this in blatant conflict with the spirit not only of original Christianity but even of the early Church which prescribed that religion be defended *non occidendo, sed moriendo,* "not through killing, but through dying" (Lactantius, Div. Inst. V. 20). Such similarities, however, prove quite superficial, merely phenotypical, when considered against the fundamentally different background of the Inquisition. The genesis of this institution is intrinsically connected with the gradual stabilization of the Christian dogma, most especially the theory

of salvation. It was Augustine who inaugurated the Inquisition with the establishment of the principle that "there is no salvation outside the Church" (*extra ecclesiam nulla salus*) and that therefore people's orthodox faith should be watched and searched. But the decisive turn was his fateful interpretation of Luke 14:16-24: "Then the master . . . said to his servant: 'Go out quickly into the streets and lanes of the city, and bring in hither the poor, and the maimed, and the halt, and the blind.' And the servant said, 'Lord, it is done as thou hast commanded, and yet there is room.' And the Lord said unto the servant: 'Go out into the highways and hedges and *compel them to come in,* that my house may be filled. . . .' " On this little passage, the *Coge Intrare,* Augustine based the right, indeed the duty of the Church to use force against heretics (Augustine, epist. 93,5); it was because of this interpretation that for centuries many thousands had to die on the stake and in crusades. This derivation, however, shows the original meaning of the Inquisition: purgation, salvation, expulsion of evil spirits. We must take into account the spiritual climate of the centuries of the Inquisition, when to almost everybody—Catholics, Luther and the early Protestants, even to scholars and scientists—the world seemed to be populated by so many incarnations and emanations of the devil, demons, incubi of all sorts. Heaven and Hell as well as witchcraft were established reality and even most ruthless and secular-minded popes were not free from haunting fears of supranatural forces. Dreadful and loaded with abuses as the Inquisition was, it could not produce a schizophrenia such as we observed in the Nazi state. Apart from the difference between the long-grown traditional power of a dogma which dominated people's minds for centuries, and a makeshift collective indoctrination devised for specific political purposes, there is this decisive divergence: In the epoch of the Inquisition everyone lived within the same universal pale. There did not exist side by side two disparate worlds between which an individual could be torn asunder, such as the gruesomely utopian world of the Third Reich and the world of modern technological civilization and conventional middle-class values. Therefore, no comparable psychic rift could develop between a collectively functional and a private personal life.

This schizophrenic phenomenon, however, is by no means an exclusively German characteristic. Chapter Four will show that the socio-psychological texture and atmosphere of our world is such as to foster it also in other places under certain conditions. As David Rousset, himself a former inmate of Nazi concentration camps, says in his book, *L'univers concentrationnaire* (Paris, Éditions du Pavois, 1946), p. 186 ff.: "German society, owing to the power of its economic structure as well as to the severity of the crisis that undid it, has undergone a decomposition as yet exceptional in the present conjuncture of the world. But it would be easy to demonstrate that the most characteristic traits of SS mentality and its social foundations may be found in quite a number of other sectors of universal society. To be sure, less accentuated and not on the scale of the developments in the great Reich. But it is only a question of circumstances. . . ."

[30] "I am over and over again surprised at the amount of humaneness in every respect, naturalness, individuality, humanity which this people has retained under such pressure, the women even more than the men, the old people of course more than the young ones, the peasants more than the workers, but in no layer is it altogether absent. A wonderful people—one must love them." Helmut Gollwitzer, . . . *und führen wohin du nicht willst, Bericht einer Gefangenschaft* (München, Chr. Kaiser Verlag, 1953), p. 165 ff.

[31] "An examination of the foregoing regulations establishes clearly enough that the inaugurators and first sponsors of the system, if they were guided first and foremost by the exigencies of the dogma, were guided also by certain principles of humanitarianism and did indeed believe themselves to be inaugurating a work which must conduct to the betterment of mankind. Man, they believed, could and must be educated up to a desired type; this desired type being of course the type which would make possible the full realization of the dogma of the Russian Bolshevik Communist Party and the existence of a society conforming to the tenets therein laid down. This education, they believed further, could and must be achieved by the ennobling process of man's own labor. The obligation laid upon man to maintain himself by his own labor could not and must not be thought of as constituting a punishment. Far from being this, it is to be thought of as a mystical opportunity; and the act of labor as containing in itself purifying and regenerative qualities. In the nature of things, then (in the opinion of these men), the lagier system, which makes labor compulsory, is not only well suited to the reformation of common criminals; it is, above all, superlatively suited to the regeneration of 'political' ones; of all persons, groups of persons and layers of society, that is, who remain imperfectly receptive of Marxist doctrine. . . . This belief, this unswerving conviction, that by restraining intellects from admitting any alternative points of view and by restricting and preventing the use of an inquiring and active mind, they are doing something creditable and of abiding value, runs through the whole of official action within the Soviet Union, and is the key to much that would otherwise be incomprehensible or starkly incredible. . . . As so often happens, it is just those very features which out of all this theory were meant to be the most humanitarian and to have the greatest influence for good which lead to the greatest abuses and the greatest misery." *The Dark Side of the Moon,* with a Preface by T. S. Eliot (New York, Scribner, 1947), p. 119 ff.

Compare also Elinor Lipper, *Eleven Years in Soviet Prison Camps* (Chicago, Regnery, 1951) and Jerzy Gliksman, *Tell the West* (New York, Gresham Press, 1948).

[32] Charles Plisnier, *Faux Passeports* (Paris, Corréa, 1937), p. 257 ff.

Chapter Four

[1] Bruno Bettelheim, "Individual and Mass Behavior in Extreme Situations," *The Journal of Abnormal and Social Psychology,* Vol. 38, 1943.

[2] Germaine Tillion, "A la recherche de la vérité," *Ravensbrück* (Neuchâtel, Les Cahiers du Rhône, 1946), 20 (65).

[3] Ernst Jünger, "Uber den Schmerz," *Blätter und Steine* (2nd ed.; Hamburg, Hanseatische Verlagsanstalt, 1942).

[4] Friedrich Nietzsche, *Der Wille zur Macht.*

[5] A parallel to Jünger's strange formalization of a psychic attitude is to be found in a person whose roots and aims are entirely different from Jünger's: Simone Weil, whose ardent desire for metaphysical support, for some ultimate belief, could not prevent her from questioning the true existence of God. She clung to a faith without a real object, to faith, to martyrdom as an attitude *per se,* giving support and comfort by its very function even if addressed to an absent or imaginary deity. *"Il faut que l'âme continue à aimer à vide, ou du moins à vouloir aimer, fut-ce avec une partie infinitésimale d'elle-même. . . . Mais si l'âme cesse d'aimer, elle tombe dès ici-bas dans quelque chose de presque équivalent à l'enfer."* ("The soul must continue to love in the emptiness, or at least it must continue wanting to love, be it with an infinitesimal part of itself. . . . But if the soul ceases to love, it falls even on this earth into something almost equivalent to hell.") Simone Weil, *Attente de Dieu* (Paris, La Colombe, Editions du Vieux Colombier, 1950), p. 48. To Simone Weil faith was *"une fidélité à vide,"* "a fidelity in the void." *La Pesanteur et la Grâce* (Paris, Plon, 1948), p. 28.

[6] An attitude has been observed in German soldiers of the Nazi armies where depersonalization went so far as to seize upon the whole of the man's consciousness, in fact upon the whole man; where extreme and coldest factuality existed without a second consciousness:

"A Swiss physician who participated in one of the sanitary expeditions performing hospital service on the German side of the Eastern Front has told me with all indications of the deepest, one would almost say metaphysical, dismay, how detached these young people were. Even in the face of death some of them had to be positively urged to send greetings to their relatives. One had the impression that they were altogether incapable any longer of realizing the difference between life and death. Stoically they appeared to endure the most gruesome pain and suffering. There was a contradiction, difficult to describe, between this ability and a complete psychic apathy from which one would have rather expected that these young people would no longer be capable of offering any inner resistance to physical suffering. But just as indifferent were they toward the suffering of others. The 'elimination' (*Umlegen*) of prisoners, for instance, was no longer a humanly valued act but simply a question of expediency and of transportation.

"I remember at this occasion the description of a Swiss who witnessed the battles in Northern Italy. During his account all signs of horror of a totally incomprehensible phenomenon were manifest in his face—and the phenomenon here were the German soldiers. Not that they defended themselves, not that they took harsh action and 'finished' the opponents who sometimes in superior numbers attacked from all sides and performed every possible ambush—it was not that which had so horrified this man. But he had seen their faces, these faces which had petrified into death masks where not a stir of feeling, not even a stir of hate, no primitive bloodthirst, no fear, no enthusiasm could be discerned any longer. It was this which had instilled fear in the man—a fear that may never leave him whenever and as long as there might be German soldiers." Ernst von Schenck, *Europa vor der deutschen Frage, Briefe eines Schweizers nach Deutschland* (Bern, Francke, 1946), p. 141 ff. p. 135.

[7] Albert Camus, *Le mythe de Sisyphe* (Paris, Gallimard, 1942), pp. 74, 89, 131.

[8] Ernst Jünger, *op. cit.,* p. 209.

[9] *Ibid.,* pp. 204, 206.

[10] Erich Fromm, *Escape from Freedom* (New York and Toronto, Rinehart, 1941), p. 250 f.

[11] Stephen Crane, *Stories and Tales* (New York, Vintage Books, Knopf, 1955), pp. 186-190.

[12] Ernest Hemingway, from *In Our Time* (New York, Scribner's, 1930).

[13] Ernest Hemingway, *The Sun Also Rises* (New York, Scribner's, 1926).

[14] Ernest Hemingway, *Death in the Afternoon* (New York, Scribner's, 1932).

[15] The actual explorer of this experience, the author who stirred it in Baudelaire, was the German romanticist E. T. A. Hoffmann with his *Kreisleriana*. Baudelaire quotes a passage from this piece in *Salon de 1846* (Curiosités Esthétiques, Oeuvres complètes, éd. de la Pléiade), p. 607: "Not so much in dream but in the state of light delirium preceding sleep, particularly after having listened to music for some time, I sense a unison between the colors, the sounds and the perfumes. It appears to me as if all these were engendered by a ray of light and must then unite in a marvellous concert. The scent of deep red carnations affects me with a strange magical power; unaware I sink into a dream-like state, in which I hear as if from a great distance the swelling and fading of the deep tones of the basset horn." (Translated directly from *Kreisleriana*.) The influence of Baudelaire's "Correspondances," in turn, is noticeable in Rimbaud's poem "Les Voyelles" ("The Vowels").

[16] André Gide, *Anthologie de la poésie française* (New York, Pantheon Books, 1949), Préface, p. x.

[17] Arthur Rimbaud, *Oeuvres Complètes* (éd. de la Pléiade; Paris, Gallimard, 1951), p. 257.

[18] *Poems of Gerard Manley Hopkins,* ed. Robert Bridges (2nd ed.; London, New York, Toronto, Oxford University Press, 1941), p. 61 ff.

[19] *Ibid.,* p. 62.

[20] Walt Whitman, *Leaves of Grass,* Book II: "Starting from Paumanok," (2).

[21] *Ibid.,* Book I: "Inscription;" "One's-Self I Sing."

[22] From "A Pact," *Selected Poems of Ezra Pound* (New York, The New Classics Series, New Directions, 1949), p. 27.

[23] *Ibid., Canto III,* p. 103 f.

[24] *Ibid., Canto XLIX,* p. 147 f.

[25] *Ibid., Canto XIV,* p. 117.

[26] T. S. Eliot, *The Complete Poems and Plays,* "Preludes IV" (New York, Harcourt, Brace and Company, 1952), p. 13.

[27] *Op. cit.,* "Landscapes II: Virginia," p. 94.

[28] *Op. cit.,* "Landscapes IV: Rannoch, by Glencoe," p. 94 f.

[29] *Op. cit.,* "The Waste-land III: The Fire Sermon," p. 43 f.

[30] *Op. cit.,* "The Waste-land IV: What the Thunder Said," p. 48.

[31] *The Collected Poetry of W. H. Auden* (New York, Random House, Inc., 1945), p. 110 f.

[32] *The Collected Poems of Dylan Thomas* (New York, New Directions, 1953), p. xvi f.

[33] Marianne Moore, *Collected Poems* (New York, The Macmillan Company, 1952), p. 57 f.

[34] E. E. Cummings, *Poems, 1923-1954,* "XAIPE, No. 35" (New York, Harcourt, Brace, 1954), p. 448 f.

[35] *Op. cit.,* "W (ViVa), No. XXXVI," p. 248.

[36] *Op. cit.,* "XAIPE, No. 71," p. 468.

[37] Georg Heym, *Dichtungen* (München, Kurt Wolff Verlag, 1922), p. 125.

[38] *Die Dichtungen von Georg Trakl* (1st complete ed.; Leipzig, Kurt Wolff Verlag), p. 136.

[39] *Ibid.,* p. 146.

[40] Gottfried Benn, *Statische Gedichte* (Zürich, Verlag der Arche, 1948), p. 32 ff.

[41] Paul Éluard, *Selected Writings,* "Poésie Ininterrompue," trans. Lloyd Alexander (New York, New Directions), pp. 165, 173, 203.

[42] Pierre Reverdy, *Poètes d'Aujourd'hui 25* (Paris, Éditions Pierre Seghers), pp. 85 f.

[43] *Ibid.,* p. 198.

[44] René Char, *Hypnos Waking,* Selected and Translated by Jackson Mathews (New York, Random House, 1956), pp. 264-267.

[45] *Op. cit., Four Quartets,* "Burnt Norton II," p. 119.

[46] *Op. cit., Four Quartets,* "Burnt Norton V," p. 121.

[47] *Op. cit., Four Quartets,* "East Coker V," p. 129.

[48] Jorge Guillén, *Cántico* (Madrid, Ediciones del Arbol, 1936), pp. 86 f.

Chapter Five

[1] *Correspondance de la Marquise du Deffand,* ed. M. de Lescure (2 vols., Paris, 1865), I, p. 381 f., letter 212.

[2] *Op. cit.,* Vol. I, p. 426, letter 228.

[3] *Op. cit.,* I, p. 322, letter 182.

[4] *Gorki par lui-même: Images et Textes,* ed. Nina Gourfinkel, (Paris, Éditions du Seuil, 1954), p. 14. We find a similar image in Pascal: "The greatest philosopher of the world on a plank larger than necessary, but suspended over a precipice, will be overwhelmed by his imagination, much as his reason will reassure him of his safety. Few people would be able to stand the idea without blushing and sweating. . . ." (Lafuma 104).

[5] *Oberman,* Lettres publiées par M . . . Sénancour, nouvelle édition (Grenoble and Paris, Arthand, 1947), I, p. 8.

[6] *Op. cit.,* I, p. 25.

[7] *Op. cit.,* I, p. 5.

[8] Compare the following passage from André Gide's novel *Les Faux-Monnayeurs: "Si je me retourne vers moi, je cesse de comprendre ce que ce mot veut dire. Je ne suis jamais que ce que je crois que je suis—et cela varie sans cesse, de sorte que souvent, si je n'étais pas là pour les accointer, mon être du matin ne reconnaîtrait pas celui du soir. Rien ne saurait être plus différent de moi, que moi-même. Ce n'est que dans la solitude que parfois le substrat m'apparaît et que j'atteins à une certaine continuité foncière; mais alors il me semble que ma vie s'alentit, s'arrête et que je vais proprement cesser d'être."* ("When I turn to myself, I do no longer understand what this word means. Never am I anything else than what I mean to be—and this changes incessantly, so that, if I were not there to familiarize them, my morning-self would not recognize my evening-self. Nothing could be more different from myself than myself. It only happens in solitude that occasionally the substratum appears and I attain to a certain basic continuity. But then it seems to me as if my life would slow down and stop, and I am actually going to cease to be.")

[9] *Oberman,* I, p. 5.

[10] *Op. cit.,* I, p. 9.

[11] Yale French Studies No. 13, Spring-Summer, 1954 (New Haven, 1954), p. 42 ff.

[12] *I Manifesti del Futurismo, Prima Serie* (Milano, 1919), p. 4 ff.

[13] *Op. cit.,* p. 92. The futurists already wanted to let loose the irrational, the unconscious, "free association," not only in artistic expression, but in life itself. The surrealists, in their initial stage, made a special point of concerning themselves with life rather than art which they pooh-poohed: they aspired to overturn life as a whole. Their heroes were figures like Jacques Vaché who never wrote a single line or painted a single stroke, but who lived surrealism in a sequence of incoherent, senseless acts. He shoveled coal in the shipyards of Nantes and immediately afterward appeared in impeccable evening dress in the lowest joints in the city. At a performance of a play by Apollinaire in 1917 he showed up in the attire of a British officer and threatened to shoot into the audience. Impressed by this act, André Breton declared in his *Second Surrealist Manifesto* that "The neatest surrealist act would consist in going down into the street, revolver in hand, and shooting at random into the crowd." However, as was to be expected, this whole "anti-literary, anti-poetic, anti-artistic movement pro-

duced," as Maurice Nadeau states in his *Histoire du Surréalism* (Paris, 1945), "nothing else than a new literature, a new poetry, a new painting—something very different from what we had been promised . . . and that," adds Nadeau, "is what drives you to banging your head against the wall." All this was somewhat anticipated by Rimbaud and his adventurous life.

[14] *Op. cit.,* p. 96.

[15] Cf. my article, "The Transformation of Modern Fiction," *Comparative Literature,* VII, No. 2, Spring, 1955.

[16] For example, Jules Laforgue in his poem, "La Guitare."

[17] Baudelaire still believed in an Absolute whose reflection may be grasped here on earth in the beauty of an artistic creation. For Mallarmé this Absolute dissolves—together with beauty—into infinitely, if indistinctly perceptible reflexes, frictions, interplays between the words, whereby man relinquishes his control to the autonomous "initiative" of the words. Thus, finally, the sensations themselves become Absolutes. I quote two passages revealing the essential attitudes of Baudelaire and Mallarmé.

Baudelaire: *"C'est cet admirable, cet immortel instinct du Beau qui nous fait considérer la Terre et ses spectacles comme un aperçu, comme une correspondance du Ciel. La soif insatiable de tout ce qui est au delà et que révèle la vie, est la preuve la plus vivante de notre immortalité. C'est à la fois par la poésie et à travers la poésie, par et à travers la musique, que l'âme entrevoit les splendeurs situées derrière le tombeau; et quand un poème exquis amène les larmes au bord des yeux, ces larmes ne sont pas la preuve d'un excès de jouissance, elles sont bien plutôt le témoignage d'une mélancolie irritée, d'une postulation des nerfs, d'une nature exilée dans l'imparfait et qui voudrait s'emparer immédiatement, sur cette terre même, d'un paradis révélé."*

("It is that admirable, that immortal instinct for Beauty which makes us consider the earth and its spectacles like an epitome, like an *echo* of heaven. The unquenchable thirst for a beyond which life reveals is the most vital proof of our immortality. It is both through poetry and *across* poetry, through and *across* music that the Soul catches a glimpse of the splendors which lie beyond the grave; and whenever an exquisite poem drives the tears to the rim of the eyes, those tears are not a sign of extreme pleasure, they rather testify to restless melancholy, to a craving of the nerves in a being, exiled into imperfection, which wants to seize immediately, here on earth, a paradise revealed.")

"Notes Nouvelles sur Edgar Poe," chap. iv, quoted in *L'Art romantique,* XX, Théophile Gautier, *Oeuvres Complètes de Baudelaire* (Paris, Bibliothèque de la Pléiade, 1951), p. 1023.

Mallarmé: *"L'œuvre pure implique la disparition élocutoire du poète, qui cède l'initiative aux mots, par le heurt de leur inégalité mobilisés; ils s'allument de reflets réciproques comme une virtuelle trainée de feux sur des pierreries, remplaçant la respiration perceptible en l'ancien souffle lyrique ou la direction personnelle enthousiaste de la phrase."*

("The pure work of art implies the elocutionary disappearance of the poet who surrenders the initiative to the words set in motion by the collision of their disparities; they kindle each other through reciprocal reflexes, like a streak of fire which seems to blaze over precious jewels; and they replace the discernible respiration in the old lyrical surge, or the personal enthusiastic control of the sentence.")

Crise de Vers in *Variations sur un sujet, Oeuvres Complètes de Stéphane Mallarmé*, (Paris, Bibliothèque de la Pléiade, 1945), p. 366.

Rimbaud, in his verse as well as in the prose of *Illuminations*, indeed, in his whole artistic approach, represents an intermediary stage between Baudelaire and Mallarmé.

[18] *Sonnets to Orpheus*, translated by M. D. Herter Norton (New York, Norton, 1942), Second Part, I, p. 71.

[19] André Maurois, *À la Recherche de Marcel Proust* (Paris, Hachette, 1949), p. 270 ff.

[20] Virginia Woolf, *Orlando* (New York, Harcourt, Brace, 1943).

[21] In his "Essay in Experimental Psychology," *Repetition*, written in 1843 (Transl. by Walter Lowrie, Princeton, Princeton University Press, 1941), p. 114, Kierkegaard poses the existentialist questions: "One sticks one's finger into the soil to tell by the smell in what land one is: I stick my finger into existence—it smells of nothing. Where am I? Who am I? How came I here? What is this thing called the world? Who is it that has lured me into the thing, and now leaves me there? . . . How did I obtain an interest in this big enterprise they call reality? . . . And if I am to be compelled to take part in it, where is the director? I should like to make a remark to him. Is there no director? Whither shall I turn with my complaint?"

[22] Translated by John Linton (New York, Norton, 1930), p. 6 ff.

[23] *Op. cit.*, p. 49 ff.

[24] *Selected Prose of Hugo von Hofmannsthal*, translated by Mary Hottinger and Tania and James Stern (New York, Bollingen Series XXXIII, Pantheon Books, 1952), p. 133 ff.

[25] Compare the amazing similarity of this Hofmannsthal passage to the following one from the story *Tonka* by Robert Musil: "When he looked up nothing was missing. The wallpaper was green and grey. The doors were of a reddish brown and full of quietly reflecting lights. The hinges of the door were dark and of copper. A dark red velvet chair with a dark mahogany frame stood in the room. But all these things had something warped, bent over, almost tumbling over, in all their erectness; they appeared to him boundless and meaningless. He pressed his eyelids, looked around, but it was not the eyes, it was the objects. One had to believe in their existence before they could exist; if one does not look at the world with the eyes of the world, if it is not already part of one's sight, it decomposes into senseless fragments, which live as sadly apart as the stars in the night. He only had to look out of the window and suddenly there flowed over into the world of a waiting cabman that of a passing office clerk, and on the

street there arose something raw and sliced, a disgusting confusion, an intertwining coexistence, a crisscross of gravitational centers trailing their own tracks, each of which had its own orbit of world-relish and self-trust; and all these were supports in order to make it possible to walk upright through a world which has no up and no down."

[26] Corresponding concepts of reality can be observed in the visual arts, e.g., the Picasso of the nineteen thirties and forties. (*Woman in the Chair,* also called *The Dream, Woman Before the Mirror,* and others.) In Sartre (and Rilke) as in Picasso we may notice the same breaking up of the old unit of the organic body structure, the same reaching down to new and deeper strata of phenomenal reality, and the establishment of new connections, combinations, "existences" across the border, as it were, of those body-structures, sub-organic or supra-organic connections.

[27] It can hardly be considered an accident that so much attention has been given recently, not only as before by psychiatrists but by modern authors, to mescaline which could in very truth be called the existentialist drug. William James who took it did not experience much beyond sickness. Now, however, we have very significant reports on its effects by Aldous Huxley (*The Doors of Perception,* New York, Harper, 1954, *Heaven and Hell,* New York, Harper, 1956) and by Henri Michaux (*Misérable miracle,* Monaco, Éditions du Rocher, 1956). In distinct contrast with other drugs, as for instance opium or hashish which intensify vision and create visions of various kinds, but at the same time transport the visionary into a condition of felicity and benevolence, and thus have psychological and humanizing effects—in contrast with these, mescaline seems to isolate observation of visual and acoustic phenomena which it heightens in an overrealizing and finally decomposing degree, thereby estranging the observer from his psychic identity and human environment. Objects lose spatial and temporal perspective and stand out most fulminantly in their "suchness," in colors and structure of their sheer existence. They convey, as Aldous Huxley relates, "the infinite value and meaningfulness of naked existence, of the given, unconceptualized event. In the final stage of egolessness, there is an 'obscure knowledge' that All is in all—that All is actually each," an experience reminiscent of the mystical union in Sartre's *Nausée.* Effects of the drug, however, seem to vary according to the disposition of the person who takes it and the duration of its use. Aldous Huxley seems to have derived from it unnameable enlightenment and mystical delight. Henri Michaux, on the other hand, who ventured much deeper into the test, experienced more extreme and rather torturing sensations, a disruption of the texture of reality: "exorbitant speed of appearance, multiplicity, pullulation . . . a kind of brownian movement . . . in all vision, . . . outburst of perception, . . . a shudder without flesh, without skin, an abstract shudder, . . . a being lost . . . in utmost ubiquity, . . . disjunction, . . . a perfect *nausée* . . ." And the attempt to verbally catch experiences which savagely defy verbalization pushed both, Huxley and Michaux, to the most subtle, the most

rapturously precise, the most beautiful ventures of expression, which again means new analysis, new developments of reality.

Chapter Six

[1] H. A. Giles, *Chuang Tzu, Mystic, Moralist and Social Reformer* (2nd ed.; Shanghai, Kelly and Walsh, Ltd., 1926), pp. 259-260.

[2] Oscar Cullmann, *Christ and Time*, The Primitive Christian Conception of Time and History (Philadelphia, The Westminster Press, MCML), pp. 227-229.

[3] Martin Buber, *Tales of the Hasidim, The Early Masters* (New York, Schocken Books, 1947), pp. 225-226.

[4] Martin Buber, *Tales of the Hasidim, The Later Masters* (New York, Schocken, 1948), p. 212.

[5] Translated from the German text in Richard Wilhelm, *Mong Dsi* (Mong Ko); (Jena, 1921, Book VII A 25), p. 163.

[6] *Discorso di Sua Santità Pio XII alla Pontifica Accademia delle Scienze*, 22 Novembre, 1951: *Le prove della esistenza di Dio alla luce della scienza naturale moderna. Ex aedibus academicis in Civitate Vaticana, MCMLII.*

[7] In a statement issued from Castel Gandolfo on September 8, 1953, Pope Pius XII gave biology, and particularly genetics, high praise for the dynamic quality of its studies. Evolution, however, he admitted only as an unverified hypothesis. This is understandable enough since here not only the Biblical history of creation is involved, but implicitly the crucial Catholic doctrine of original sin, "which proceeds from sin actually committed by an individual Adam and which through generations passed on to all." In the encyclical *Humani Generis* (1950) the Pope strictly enjoined the faithful not to deviate from this doctrine. The biological views as issued by the Pope have, however, been refuted as incompatible with established facts by Professor Theodosius Dobzhansky in his "Comment on the Discussion of Genetics by His Holiness, Pius XII," *Science*, November 6, 1953, Vol. 118, No. 3071, pp. 561-563.

[8] Albert Camus, *L'Étranger*. The quoted passages have been translated from the French edition by E. K.

[9] Style has also dissolved retrospectively inasmuch as the artist's reaction to tradition and inspiration through tradition is concerned. As Kenneth Clark remarks in his book *Landscape into Art* (London, John Murray, 1949, p. 134): ". . . artists have been drawing inspiration from museums ever since the Renaissance, but the works which inspired the great tradition of classicism were all in a single, consistent style. They were part of an acknowledged order, and it was often their consistency rather than the beauty of the individual objects which had led artists to refer to them. But towards the end of the nineteenth century museums began to admit works of all ages and countries; and artists, instead of finding in them a consistent language, began to look for those works in each style that could give the shock of pleasure which had come to be called aesthetic."

[10] The harangue in which the Spanish Dominican, Francisco Vitoria, exposed the atrocities of the Spaniards in America bore the title: *De jure belli Hispanorum in Barbaros.*

[11] Translated by Richard Aldington (New York: William Morrow and Co., 1928, p. 110 ff.

[12] Report of *The New York Times* correspondent, Emanuel Perlmutter, on the findings of the Kefauver crime-investigating committee. *New York Times,* April 1, 1951.

[13] David W. Maurer, *The Big Con, The Story of the Confidence Man and the Confidence Game* (Indianapolis, Bobbs-Merrill Company, 1940).

[14] "The graph of delinquency shows an undeniable correlation between war and threat of war and the incidence of delinquency. . . . We are living under the threat of total annihilation . . . we are living in years of open warfare, although at the moment in an uneasy truce. . . . Our whole economy and social life is geared to war and threat of war. Obviously, it is difficult to instill in young people inner controls on aggressive behavior in a world marked by aggression. . . . We have the draft into military service . . . the threat of involvement in warfare. This makes it impossible for youngsters—both boys and girls—to plan realistically for peaceful, productive lives. It encourages a devil-may-care attitude and heightens anti-social feelings." (Bertram M. Beck, director of the Children's Bureau Special Juvenile Delinquency Project in Washington, quoted by Margaret Parton in her series of articles *Our Lawless Youth, New York Herald Tribune,* June 9, 1955.) Cf. also a heart-rending statement by a seventeen-year-old high-school boy, quoted in the same article by Margaret Parton: "The apathy of the American public toward graft and corruption which runs so rampant is passed on to my generation, which notes the success of illegality, and sees approbation for this method of easy money; the resentment which we feel when we are castigated for doing the very things our elders do . . . most of all, the feeling of complete worthlessness which comes over us when we realize that our life span may be determined by the over-all picture as seen by one or the other of the two major parties, that the value of our life is counted in so many votes—all these are responsible for the ever more prevalent devil-may-care attitude which results in the increase in delinquency . . . I believe you should wage a campaign . . . to instill within my generation a sense of community responsibility, coupled with the feeling that we are wanted by the community. We would like to be able to feel that we are not tolerated as pesky nuisances—abided only because in a few years we can be sent off to war—but that as a group we are wanted and can be of use, not only to the nation by bearing arms, but to our states and hometowns and cities."

[15] *PM,* May 30, 1947.

[16] The attitude toward crime and criminals of the Division of Corrections in the Department of Public Welfare of the State of Wisconsin may very well serve as a shining example. Its guiding principle as stated in one of its bulletins is the view that "the juvenile delinquent and the adult offender

are as sick as the man suffering from a mortal disease. . . . The criminal is a socially sick person who can and should be helped."

[17] Such functional responsibilities correspond to what may be called functional values, which have also displaced and replaced human values. These functional—scientific, administrative, professional—values are mere standards but not real values because they do not admit of an actual choice. They are determined by objective, practical necessities and are collectively enforced. He who wants to be efficient and successful in his field or profession has to comply with these standards. Otherwise he is thrown out of his work and his job.

[18] "Let us pledge not to use the H-Bomb first!" *Bulletin of the Atomic Scientists* (Vol. VI, No. 3, March, 1950, p. 75). Signed by S. K. Allison, K. T. Bainbridge, H. A. Bethe, R. B. Brode, C. C. Lauritzen, F. W. Loomis, G. B. Pegram, B. Rossi, F. Seitz, M. A. Tuve, V. F. Weisskopf, M. G. White.

[19] *New York Herald Tribune,* January 30, 1950.

[20] In the case against Dr. J. Robert Oppenheimer, the Chairman of the Personnel Security Board read the text of "certain information" which formed the substratum of the official questioning of Dr. Oppenheimer's loyalty. This text contained the following passage: "It was further reported that in the autumn of 1949, and subsequently, you strongly opposed the development of the hydrogen bomb 1.) on moral grounds . . ." (*In the Matter of J. Robert Oppenheimer.* Transcript of the Hearing before Personnel Security Board, Washington, 1954, p. 6) This appears like an official legitimization of Mr. Lilienthal's stand. It seems to imply that moral scruples, even concerning such an extreme abomination as the hydrogen bomb, are incompatible with the standard of loyalty required of a person in an influential government position.

[21] Louis Ridenour, "How Effective Are Radioactive Weapons in Warfare?" *Bulletin of the Atomic Scientists,* Vol. VI, No. 7, July, 1950.

[22] A. Mitscherlich and F. Mielke, *Wissenschaft ohne Menschlichkeit,* (Heidelberg, Lambert Schneider, 1949), p. 299 ff.

[23] *Ibid.,* p. 38.

[24] *Ibid.,* p. 307.

[25] *Ibid.,* p. 298.

[26] P. W. Bridgman, "Scientists and Social Responsibility," *The Scientific Monthly,* Vol. LXV, No. 2, August, 1947, pp. 148-154.

Chapter Seven

[1] Gardner Murphy, *Personality, A Biosocial Approach to Origins and Structure* (New York and London, Harper, 1947), p. 912.

[2] David Riesman, *The Lonely Crowd* (New York, Doubleday, Anchor Books, 1953), p. 349.

[3] Erich Neumann, *Tiefenpsychologie und neue Ethik* (Zürich, Rascher, 1949).

[4] T. H. Huxley and Julian Huxley, *Touchstone for Ethics, 1893-1943* (New York and London, Harper, 1947).

[5] Erich Neumann, *op. cit.*, p. 120 f.

[6] Julian Huxley, *op. cit.*, p. 199.

[7] *Op. cit.*, p. 238.

[8] *Op. cit.*, p. 231.

[9] *Op. cit.*, p. 235.

[10] *Op. cit.*, p. 231.

[11] *Op. cit.*, p. 133.

[12] *Op. cit.*, pp. 135 f.

[13] *Op. cit.*, p. 146.

[14] *Op. cit.*, p. 197.

[15] Erich Fromm, *Man for Himself* (New York and Toronto, Rinehart, 1947).

[16] *Op. cit.*, p. 224.

[17] *Op. cit.*, p. 214.

[18] *Op. cit.*, pp. 216, 218.

[19] *Op. cit.*, p. 230.

[20] *Op. cit.*, p. 229.

[21] *Op. cit.*, p. 243.

[22] *Op. cit.*, p. 249.

[23] Jean-Paul Sartre, *L'existentialisme est un humanisme* (Paris, Éd. Nagel, 1946); English ed., *Existentialism* (New York, Philosophical Library, 1947). The translation of the quotations is my own.

[24] *Op. cit.*, p. 21 of the French edition.

[25] *Op. cit.*, p. 23.

[26] Sartre goes so far as to assert that, "A man is nothing else than a series of enterprises . . . he is the sum, the organization, the totality of relationships that constitute these enterprises." *Op. cit.*, p. 58.

[27] *Op. cit.*, p. 25.

[28] *Op. cit.*, p. 27.

[29] *Op. cit.*, p. 29.

[30] *Op. cit.*, p. 79.

[31] *Op. cit.*, p. 64.

[32] *Op. cit.*, p. 66 f.

[33] *Op. cit.*, p. 68.

[34] *Op. cit.*, pp. 82 f.

[35] Albert Camus, *Le mythe de Sisyphe* (*nouvelle édition augmentée*, Paris, Gallimard, 1942). English ed.: *Sisyphus* (New York, Knopf, 1955). Translations are my own.

[36] Albert Camus, *L'homme révolté* (Paris, Gallimard, 1951). English ed.: *The Rebel* (New York, Knopf, 1954). Translations are my own.

[37] Albert Camus, *Le mythe de Sisyphe*, p. 18.

[38] *Op. cit.*, p. 27, 30.

[39] *Op. cit.*, p. 28.

[40] *Op. cit.*, p. 28 f.

[41] *Op. cit.*, p. 18.

[42] *Op. cit.*, p. 20 f.

[43] *Op. cit.*, p. 21.

[44] *Op. cit.*, p. 34.

[45] *Op. cit.*, p. 74 f.

[46] *Op. cit.*, p. 80 f.

[47] *Op. cit.*, p. 86 f.

[48] Albert Camus, *L'homme révolté*, p. 15 f.

[49] *Op. cit.*, p. 16 f.

[50] *Op. cit.*, p. 17.

[51] *Op. cit.*, p. 364.

[52] "The Human Crisis," *Twice a Year*, Fall-Winter 1946-1947 pp. 24, 26 ff.

[53] "Our grandfathers quarreled with corporations because, as the phrase went, they were 'soulless.' But out of the common denominator of the decision-making machinery, some sort of concensus of mind is emerging, by compulsion as it were, which for good or ill is acting surprisingly like a collective soul." Adolf A. Berle, Jr., *The 20th Century Capitalist Revolution* (New York, Harcourt, Brace, 1954), p. 183.

[54] Julian Huxley, *op. cit.*, p. 199.

[55] Professor George Gaylord Simpson introduces his study on *Tempo and Mode in Evolution* (New York, Columbia University Press, 1944) as follows: "The basic problems of evolution are so broad that they cannot hopefully be attacked from the point of view of a single scientific discipline. Synthesis has become both more necessary and more difficult as evolutionary studies have become more diffuse and more specialized. Knowing more and more about less and less may mean that relationships are lost and that the grand pattern and great processes of life are overlooked. The topics treated in the present study . . . are among the basic evolutionary phenomena that have tended to be obscured by increasing specialization and that overlap many different fields of research. Data and theories from paleontology, genetics, neozoology, zoogeography, ecology, and several other specialties are all pertinent to these themes. The complete impossibility of attaining equal competence and authority in all these fields entails unavoidable shortcomings, but the effort to achieve such a synthesis is so manifestly desirable that no apology is in order."

[56] "One of the most striking things about the present state of the theory of learning and of phychological theory in general is the wide disagreement among . . . psychologists. Perhaps the most impressive single manifestation of the extent of this disagreement is contained in 'Psychologies of 1925' and 'Psychologies of 1930.' In these works we find earnestly defending themselves against a world of enemies, a hormic psychology, an act psychology, a functional psychology, a structural psychology, a Gestalt psychology, a reflexology psychology, a behavioristic psychology, a response psychology, a dynamic psychology, a factor psychology, a psychoanalytical psychology, and a psychology of dialectical materialism. . . ." Clark L.

Hull, "The Conflicting Psychologies of Learning," *The Psychological Review,* Vol. 42, No. 6.

[57] Professor Henry A. Murray, Harvard University, formerly Director of the Harvard Psychological Clinic, *Proceedings of an Interdisciplinary Conference on Culture and Personality,* pub. by the Viking Fund, ed. by Gardner Murphy, 1949.

[58] The issues discussed here have been treated more elaborately in my article, "Foreign Policy Today," *Bulletin of the Atomic Scientists,* December, 1950.

[59] Cf. *Preliminary Draft of a World Constitution,* by the Committee to Frame a World Constitution at the University of Chicago, University of Chicago Press, 1948.

[60] Adolf A. Berle, Jr., *op. cit.,* p. 39.

[61] *Op. cit.,* p. 30 f.

[62] *Op. cit.,* p. 31.

[63] *Op. cit.,* p. 28.

[64] *Op. cit.,* p. 40.

[65] *Op. cit.,* p. 45 f.

[66] *Op. cit.,* p. 52.

[67] Cf. J. Kenneth Galbraith, *American Capitalism: The Concept of Countervailing Powers* (Boston, Houghton Mifflin, 1952).

[68] Adolf A. Berle, Jr., *op. cit.,* p. 53 f.

[69] Norbert Wiener, *Cybernetics, or Control and Communication in the Animal and the Machine* (New York, John Wiley and Sons, 1948) pp. 37 f.

[70] Norbert Wiener, *The Human Use of Human Beings* (Boston, Houghton, Mifflin, 1954).

[71] *Op. cit.,* p. 162.

[72] Claire Huchet Bishop, *All Things Common* (New York, Harper, 1950).

[73] *Op. cit.,* p. 38.

[74] *Op. cit.,* p. 5.

[75] *Op. cit.,* p. 5.

[76] *Op. cit.,* p. 53 ff.

[77] *Op. cit.,* p. 6 ff.

[78] *Op. cit.,* p. 7.

[79] *Op. cit.,* p. 14 f.

[80] *Op. cit.,* p. 14 ff.

[81] *Op. cit.,* p. 51.

[82] *Op. cit.,* p. 22.

[83] *Op. cit.,* p. 12.

[84] *Op. cit.,* p. 31.

[85] *Op. cit.,* p. 102.

[86] *Op. cit.,* p. 25.

[87] The difficulties of modern democracy and the suggestions presented in the following have been dealt with in more detail in my essay "Das Schicksal der Demokratie," published in *Synopsis, Festschrift für Alfred Weber* (Heidelberg, Lambert Schneider, 1948).

Index